FLOOR BURNS

Inside the Life of a Kansas Jayhawk

JEROD HAASE & MARK HORVATH

Foreword by Roy Williams

Printed in the United States of America by Mennonite Press, Inc.

ISBN 0-9658392-1-4

Cover photo by KU Sports Information

DEDICATION

To my father, my biggest fan, who

always said to play hard and play smart.

I love you Dad.

ACKNOWLEDGMENTS

I'd like to thank the following people for all they have done for me, whether it be during the course of this year or any other time during my life.

To the people who have enjoyed watching me play. I offer you my thoughts, feelings, emotions, and actions of my senior year. I hope you enjoy them.

To my family, who stands by me and has molded me into what I am today.

To Mark. This "project" would have never materialized successfully without your trust and dedication. I can't thank you enough.

To my friends who know Jerod, the person.

To my teammates who made the journey so enjoyable I did not want to find the end.

To all my coaches who are my great mentors, but better friends. GR, RL, RA, MG, LR, TO, JW, LC, SR, JH, MD, ND, RW.

To the following people: Max Faulkenstein and Bob Davis, Doug Vance, Dean Buchan, Mike Tharp, Wayne Walden, Richard Konsem, The Managers, Rich Clarkson, Bill Maxwell, Father Vince.

You never leave a place you love. Part of it you take with you, and leave a part of yourself behind.

Jerod Haase -1997

ACKNOWLEDGMENTS

There are many people I want to thank at this time. People who have assisted me in some way in the writing of this book. Thanks to...

My wife, Nancy, and my children, Alison and Andy, who supported me through this project, good days and bad. I love you.

To my parents, Louis and Agnes Horvath, who always told me to do things as well as I could.

To Tom Hadt, who never let me slip into self-doubt about the prospects for the book, always encouraging me to believe.

To Kerry Zajicek, who listened and understood my ramblings those many Saturday mornings over breakfast.

To Bob Laude, who was truly sympathetic when KU lost. I needed the support that day more than you'll ever know.

To Jim Klora, Scott Staley, Teresa Proctor, Clint Swan—fellow comrades in arms on the front lines of education who helped me through the rough days at school.

To Doug Vance, who gave me the final shot of confidence and helped during the final stages.

To Mike Tharp, who helped in editing the book. Your professionalism and your friendship are things I will never forget.

To Kim Redeker, who rode to the rescue and saved this book.

To the Class of 1997, Andrean High School, Merillville, Indiana. You were the perfect class for this project. Smart, respectful and enjoyable.

To my Freshman basketball B-team of 1996. You guys were the inspiration for this. You are the best.

To John Downing. Without your help, I never would have met Jerod. The book itself is here because of you.

To the Haase family. Thanks for everything. Jerod is right: you are really special.

To so many others: Scott Gilliland, Rich Clarkson, John Steere of John's KU Basketball Homepage; Donna Bombassaro—computer expert; Bryan Babinec; CB McGrath; Donna Girolami; Nick Neal; and anyone else I may have forgotten. If you aren't listed here, you still are thanked in my heart.

Above all, to Jerod Haase. There have been many people I've known in my life, but none I have admired more.

Mark Horvath -1997

INTRODUCTION

Jerod Haase sat in front of his locker, exhausted and dejected. He had just endured one of the worst days of his life. In an NCAA tournament game which would determine who would go to the Final Four, he had not connected on a field goal. He went 0 for 9. To make matters worse, he was the team's three point specialist, the go-to guy when an outside threat was needed. Why today?, he thought. What a reversal from Friday night.

The previous game against Arizona on Friday was more a typical Haase outing. 16 points, 5 assists, 3 rebounds and the final field goal of the game, a 3-point shot from the left corner with 20 seconds remaining. It was the winning shot in an 83-81 Kansas victory. Early in the game, Haase had landed hard on his right elbow while driving over a defender to score on a layup. The elbow had swollen to golf ball size, and the Kansas trainer had spent two days treating it to get Jerod ready for this game. With the anticipation and concentration for the game against Syracuse weighing on his mind, Haase had not felt anything in the elbow. Now the pain was beginning to return.

It was over. A season that had begun with such high hopes, a Number One ranking from Sports Illustrated and part of the season spent atop the AP poll had ended in frustration. A team that had sped past most of its opponents and outshot them from the field had lost due to one of its worst shooting performances of the season. As a team, Kansas had only shot 4 for 25 from three point range. For the game they were held to 34 percent from the field. It all spelled defeat.

Jerod couldn't shake the loss from his mind for the next week. The Syracuse game was used as a motivator for the next season, his senior season. He worked hard to make sure that he never had this feeling again. He balanced his time that summer, got himself into the best playing shape of his life. It was the last chance for Jerod Haase as a Kansas Jayhawk. He would give it his best effort.

Jerod has had a fairly typical life. There have been moments of intense disappointment, followed by hard earned success. There has been sadness balanced with joy. There have been unexpected tragedies, and unlikely triumphs. Most people can say that their lives are similar.

What makes Jerod Haase unique is the way he uses his misfortunes to push himself to greater heights. Hard work and self discipline are admirable traits in anyone. The length to which Jerod has utilized these qualities is remarkable. He is an example of what college athletics is supposed to be.

His courageous side is obvious. He risked his personal career to help his team try to win a national title. The team came first. That's the way it has always been for him.

Kids need role models. They need to see that being a good guy has its rewards. I think that's what Jerod brings to everyone he touches. A good example of what they should strive to become. Someone who will work to the best of his ability, yet care about others.

It is not necessary to adopt a survival of the fittest mentality. Jerod Haase competed with a ferocity seldom seen on the court. Yet off the court, he was kind and considerate, the nice guy who finished first. We could use a few more like him in the world.

This is the story of a year in his life, a year in the life of a college basketball player, a year inside the mind of a Kansas Jayhawk.

—Mark Horvath

FOREWORD

When Jerod asked me to write the foreword to this book, it made me feel very good. I was extremely flattered that he would ask, and yet he did it in typical Jerod style. He said, "Coach, I would like to ask you to do something, but if you have a problem with it I understand completely and it won't hurt my feelings or anything." Again, just that simple explanation of a very simple request describes Jerod. He never wants to put anybody into a bad situation. If he is asking someone for a favor, he doesn't want it to cause that person a problem.

In thinking about what I wanted to say in this foreword, I saw the title "Floor Burns." My first reaction was a humorous one. My second reaction, though, was that it does describe how Jerod played. It describes such a small part of him as an individual that I decided not to make my decision of what to say until I read through the entire manuscript. Now that I have done that, I am still somewhat confused as to what would be the best thing to say, so I will just give a few of my thoughts.

Reading this book brought back a *lot* of *great* memories and a *few bad* ones. As I was reading it, I was picturing Jerod making every statement and feeling every emotion he was trying to describe. Yes, this book is about a college basketball player and his year's experience, but it goes much deeper than that. It is about a young man and his dreams, the very high "highs" and the unbelievably low "lows" as that young man is trying to reach those dreams. It also tells a story about a youngster who makes up for some deficiency or adds to his game because of his desire. I think that also describes Jerod.

Jerod Haase was a young man who did have big dreams and I will never forget that. Even more so, he was a young man who had a few deficiencies and made up for them. He became a tremendous strength of our program because of his desire and the work ethic, dedication and intensity which he brought to the game. His will to win and his love for his teammates only added to these qualities to make him the *perfect* player for a college coach to enjoy.

I have said many times that our players make me look awfully good. Jerod did that, but what he did even more is made me *enjoy* coaching. I have never wanted to do anything else but coach. After reading this book and being able to coach Jerod, I guess my next dream is to be able to coach someone else like Jerod. I believe it is okay to have dreams and to work as hard as you can toward them, as long as you accept the fact that they may not come true. I am going to have dreams of coaching youngsters like Jerod and I truly hope they will come true, but if not I will still feel very blessed. I did coach Jerod!

There is no doubt that every Kansas fan will enjoy reading this book. It's a story of a season, but also of effort, discipline, dedication and yes, "floor burns." I look at it as a story of a dream! Every college basketball fan and every youngster who *truly cares* will also enjoy reading this. I know I did.

—Roy Williams

CONTENTS

Getting Started: *Preparing for the Final Season*
1

Beginning the Journey: *The Preseason*
9

On the Road: *Non-Conference Play*
73

A New Era: *The Big 12 Season*
123

Last Dance, Last Chance:
The NCAA Tournament
193

GETTING STARTED

PREPARING FOR THE FINAL SEASON

JUNE 1996

I first came into contact with Jerod Haase in mid-June. I had written to him after the Syracuse game and offered words of encouragement. I never expected a reply, and when a handwritten letter arrived on Kansas basketball stationery, I was stunned. Pleased, but stunned. It then occurred to me to propose to Jerod the concept for this book.

Many people have wondered what it must be like to play for a program like Kansas. Others speculate as to the nature of the life of a college athlete. What is it actually like? If one could follow a player through their daily existence, what would one find? That's what I wanted to know.

Jerod Haase seemed to be a logical choice. He had played at two major universities, achieved an extremely high grade point average while taking a difficult course load, and was considered one of the premier players in America. His life had its share of peaks and valleys, moments of joy and moments of intense sorrow. He was said to be friendly and down to earth.

That final point was what made me decide. Someone down to earth would already be an aberration from what most people believed.

After a series of phone calls and talking to his friends and mother, Jerod finally was home when I called in late June. He had been working basketball camps at South Tahoe High alongside his old coach, Tom Orlich. He was spending his summer with kids, tutoring and mentoring young people.

We talked on three different occasions and eventually decided to meet in person and discuss the concept of doing a book. No money would be involved. NCAA regulations prevent a player from doing a project such as this for money. (Perhaps that's why it has not been done before.) There would be no contract. It was simply a matter of mutual trust. I wanted to write a book. Jerod was honored to be the subject of anyone's book. We would operate as a team, he being the subject and I being the recorder of events. His diary, my narration.

AUGUST 8

Jerod trained that summer back in Lake Tahoe as he had never trained before. He followed a regimen that he felt would put him in the best possible shape for the coming season. I got a chance to see this first hand upon my arrival in Tahoe tonight.

The door was open when I drove up to the tan, cedar sided house surrounded by trees. I knew I had the right place. It was the only house with a huge basketball court in front of the house. A two and a half car garage with a basket in the center of the wall between the doors. I rang the doorbell and a voice from inside said "Come in, it's open"

Entering the house, I walked a few feet into the hallway and turned into a room with a fireplace. A smiling figure playing with two small children said, "Hi, I'm Mara Andrus, Jerod's sister. You must be Mark." Feeling a bit puzzled, I acknowledged her greeting and introduced myself. She smiled again and said, "Jerod's not home yet, but he said to tell you to wait. He should be here soon."

I was a bit ill at ease. Here I was, two thousand miles from home, sitting in the room of someone I had never met, talking with his sister, of whose existence I was unaware only moments before. It was strange. I began to think, "What have I gotten myself into?"

Carol Haase, Jerod's mother, appeared at this time. She had a friendly demeanor, smiling, offering me some iced tea to drink. She wasted no time asking me about my background and the most obvious question. "Why did you choose Jerod to write about?"

I had expected this. I realized that this entire scenario was most implausible and decided to waste no time setting the tone for the entire year. I told them the honest truth. "I've followed Jerod since his days at Cal, admired the way he plays, and wanted to make him the subject of a book. He has an interesting story to tell, and this coming year could be the best part of all."

As I was completing my answer to questions about my wife and children, a knock on the door was followed by three young men in their early 20's coming into the house. "Hi, Mrs. Haase," said the tallest one, Brett. "Is Jerod home? We're going to have a farewell party for one of the guys who's leaving for school tomorrow."

"He's not here Brett, but I don't think he'll be free tonight."

"Well, tell him we'll be at Harvey's, if he wants to meet us later. Nice to meet you," Brett said, looking in my direction. He waved and left.

"I don't want to keep Jerod from anything," I said to Carol.

"Don't worry," she assured me. "Jerod doesn't go to the bars in town. That's just not him."

I was not reassured, and felt as if I had intruded. Just then, a tall, well built figure came into the room and I recognized the face instantly. "Hi," he said with a smile and an outstretched hand, "I'm Jerod. Sorry I'm late. It's been like this all summer."

He was tanned, wearing an oversized T-shirt and shorts, and had obviously been outdoors much of the summer. The smile was continual and genuine, and he seemed happy to be the host of a total stranger. He wanted to talk but suggested we go somewhere outside of the house.

"I've got to get in my workout for today. Mind if we go to the gym?" he asked. "I'd enjoy that," I said. He said we'd have to pick up a friend of his first, and then we'd go up to the high school.

It was 10:00 at night. I was struck by the dedication he possessed. Anyone who says they "have" to shoot baskets at that time of night, to keep a schedule on track, is dedicated. I thought this must be something that Kansas had mandated. I was wrong.

"I drew up my own schedule and my own workout," he said in response to my question. "It's pretty good, I think. It makes me work on the things I really think I need to improve upon."

We picked up his closest friend, Scott Gilliland, drove through the dark streets of Tahoe, made a series of turns and suddenly arrived at the high school gym. He had his own key to the place and unlocked the doors. We entered and went through the weight room and out to the main floor.

A janitor came out and told Jerod there would be no shooting tonight. He seemed surprised and asked why. The janitor informed us that the floor was going to be resurfaced and had to be completely cleaned that night. It would be unavailable for about a week.

Haase seemed completely surprised. He muttered a few words to himself and then turned and asked me if I'd mind going with him to the weight room. He'd at least get that workout completed. He lifted weights three times a week, for 45 minutes, following a series of exercises that had been given to him by people from Kansas along with some he had designed himself.

By the time the workout was over, it was almost 11:30 and all three of us were tired. Tomorrow would be the day for the main interview session, the time to see if this project would work. We headed home.

AUGUST 9

The weather can be spectacular in the Lake Tahoe region, and today was one of those days. Clear sky, temperature in the low 80's, low humidity, all combined to make it a great setting. Jerod wanted to sit outside and talk. It made perfect sense. The yard is long and rectangular shaped, with a rock garden in one corner, a small pool of water surrounded by sculpted rocks in another, and huge trees every ten or fifteen feet. If it isn't a national forest, it's the next best thing.

Jerod talked for three hours and answered every conceivable question I asked. Then, feeling as though he was running behind, he decided to go to the junior high gym and shoot. Haase said that he shot every day for almost 90 minutes. And for that amount of time, I played rebounder for the three point specialist from KU.

To make the shooting more interesting, Jerod designed games where he would compete against himself. He would take up positions behind the three point arc and play a game to 10. The catch was that he would give himself one point for a made basket and minus two for a missed shot. When he reached either a plus or minus ten, the game was over. Another game called for playing to 25, with a shot from behind the arc counting for two points, and inside the arc as one point. These and other games would be interspersed with 15 free throws, so that the shooting was continuous in nature, and the workout would go at a full, steady pace for the entire 90 minutes. He never stopped moving.

The sun was going down as the workout came to a conclusion. The gym was more humid than the air outside, and Haase had worked up the full sweat he feels necessary to justify a good session. "I don't want to ever have to look back and wonder what would have happened if I had only worked a little harder, if I had only trained more," Jerod told me. "I'd rather do too much than too little."

After a dinner at his home with family and friends, we concluded the second day of interviews by a fire in a barbecue pit in the backyard. It was a crystal clear mountain evening, and the stars in the sky were an awesome sight. It put Jerod in a reflective mood, and I asked him about how he viewed basketball.

As he looked back and evaluated his life, Jerod realized that basketball had changed for him. It was no longer the passion for playing that motivated him, but now things took on a different meaning. "At this point in my life, things are a bit more serious," Jerod said. "I know that this could be the last time I ever get a chance to play basketball at this level, and I do not want to go out with any regrets."

AUGUST 10

Another beautiful day and a more spectacular summer night. The clear mountain air was a vibrant blue and only a few high think clouds, like frosting accenting a cake, were breaking the sky. It was the perfect setting to conclude the trip.

Jerod had taken me to a spot in the mountains to have another session of interview and getting acquainted. It brought an openness I found refreshing and we made the decision to go ahead with the book at this point.

Since I could not live with him at KU, we decided to use e-mail and phone calls to get much of the material transferred. I would write a series of questions I wanted answered and Jerod would write back a response. This would take place on an almost daily basis. There would be phone calls at least twice a week, more if needed. We set up a time when I could generally reach him in his apartment. The logistics seemed simple, but it required dedication to the project on his part. He had to keep a diary of his thoughts and actions. It was not something he had ever done before, and I was not sure if he could do it. I had my doubts if many other people, let alone athletes, could have done it. But it was the only feasible way.

The NCAA has its regulations about athletes for a good reason. Money is such a corrupting influence in society and sports that to allow athletes to do a project such as this would take away from their studies and potentially open them up to playing a certain way for the sake of selling a book. This is possibly why a book from the athlete's point of view is so rare. We have received the coach's insight through various other books. We know how they planned and dealt with the seasons of their dreams. What about the players who play the real game? How have they lived?

Jerod and I decided to make this a project that would be conducted without anything other than a handshake. There never was a contract. There never was a publisher. There was never any talk of money. We would wait until the end of the season and see what we had. If it was good, it would hopefully be in print shortly after the season ended. If it didn't work out, then all we lost was the time.

From the start, there was just a trust factor at work. I would keep my work to myself, writing but not making the fact known to anyone. He would send the diary. When I had written a section, I would send him a rough draft, to double check the facts. This we felt was keeping it all open and above board.

That evening, Jerod's close friends were gathering on the beachfront of Lake Tahoe to have a going away party for two more of his friends. About 20 people were there, swimming, taking kayaks out onto the lake, cooking hot dogs and just sitting around a fire, talking, laughing and enjoying their final time together. It was an idyllic setting, and it gave me a chance to see Jerod with the people who had helped shape him into the kind of person he had become.

If this was the group he hung around with most of his life, it was easy to see why Haase was so easy going. They were happy, full of energy, and some of the most positive people I have ever met. Everyone was looking forward to the coming year with anticipation, not a sense of dreading the work required. Christi Hosman, a long-time friend, was anxious to get back and begin student teaching.

Scott Gilliland was going to Sacramento and moving into an apartment while attending school. These two were Jerod's closest friends, and along with Christi's twin sister Heidi, gave me help with gaining some insight into Haase's personality. All agreed that if anyone would keep up with the diary concept and be committed to it, Jerod would be that person. It was reassuring.

The time came to leave and I was standing on a beach, looking out at the sunset, realizing what could happen this year.

"Thanks for the opportunity," I said to Jerod, as I started to head to my car.

"You know, I've always dreamed that someone would come along and write a book about me. This is like fulfilling a dream," he said, as sincerely as I've ever heard anyone speak.

"We're going to make this work," I replied. "I won't let you down."

"I hope I give you something interesting. Like a national championship."

"Just keep up the diary. And win a few games," I said jokingly.

He chuckled and extended a hand. "Thanks for coming out. I trust you. I think this is really going to be something good. At least I know my family will want to read it," he said laughing.

BEGINNING THE JOURNEY

THE PRESEASON

APRIL 1996

At the end of the season, Coach Roy Williams spoke at our team banquet about the character of his 1995-96 team. He talked about the disappointing loss which had ended the season. In mentioning the team, Coach Williams stated that he "would rather have this bunch of young men going to battle for him than any other." He felt we were what best exemplifies college sports.

I sat at the banquet and felt a rush of emotion and determination. I listened to the words of my coach, a man whom I deeply respected, and felt as if I had let him down. I glanced at my teammates and felt the same way. I would not let that happen again. There would never be a time when I would feel as though I had not worked hard enough, had not prepared fully for a season or even a game.

The banquet was a time of sadness and yet hopeful expectation. Although the previous season had ended with a heart breaking loss, virtually all of this team would be returning. The character that Coach Williams had spoken about would be the force that would bind this group together and create a unity among teammates that is seldom seen in college sports today. We would be there for each other. We would work together for a common goal.

Hanging over all this was the spectre of professional sports. The most publicized member of our team, point guard Jacque Vaughn, was expected to turn professional now that the season had ended. Would he break up the unit? Would he take the money and run? That was the only dark cloud on what was otherwise a sunny horizon.

The banquet usually premiers a video compilation of the season, a montage of memorable moments, fantastic plays and incredible shots that highlights the past year. It will always bring a smile and a tear to the eyes of those who are there, as they recall with fondness those magic times of competition. The success will always be highlighted, and the losses will be endured, but the point of the video is clear: this is a proud and successful program. It has tradition.

As I left the banquet, I felt as if I could take the court that moment. I wanted to play the next game, to start anew. The only place I could think of going at that moment was Allen Fieldhouse, the venerable old structure that is home to the legend that is Kansas basketball. I drove home, parked the car in the lot at the side of the apartments, and walked over to the Fieldhouse.

I went around to the front of the gray and sandstone building. I gazed at it's exterior, shining in the moonlight, and felt the tradition and history oozing from every brick. This is a basketball shrine, a place where legends played, a place that was home to teams that have left an indelible mark on college basketball. It would be the place where the 1997 Jayhawks would prepare for the opportunity to leave our imprint and make our legend. I grew determined. I knew that I was going to have to work as I had never worked before. I looked forward to the challenge.

MAY 1996
I decided to keep a diary of my activities. It would be something I'd look at and use for motivation. I had visited a sports psychologist in February and this was one of the things he'd suggested. I worked on it for three days and then stopped. I lost interest.

I was completing my final exams, answering fan mail and getting ready to go home for the summer. Jacque Vaughn had announced he was staying at Kansas for his senior year. Everyone on the team was happy, and it meant the team would remain intact for next year. I had so many things on my mind this month there wasn't any time to write a diary. It was a nice idea, but I simply couldn't do it.

As I flew home that summer, I thought about the similarities between my college and high school basketball careers. As a junior at South Tahoe High School, I had high hopes for a state title. The team was playing well, and the season had been tremendously successful. However, things were not to be, and we were defeated in the title game of the Nevada State AAA title game by Western High School of Las Vegas, 84-74.

We set ourselves the goal of winning the state the following year. We had the entire starting five returning. "It's our turn" became the team motto, and we worked hard to achieve our goal. We played pickup games, we conditioned and worked on our shooting. Most importantly, we made ourselves mentally ready to deal with any adverse situation.

We worked so hard for that season. We knew it was our last time to be playing together. We had been focusing on this for years, and we wanted revenge for the junior year loss. Our coach, Tom Orlich, believed that this team was capable of going all the way.

South Tahoe High School is a small school, located in northern California. Due to its location, we played many athletic contests in the Nevada athletic system. Our school has an outstanding basketball record, due in no small part to the efforts of Coach Tom Orlich. He has built an exceptional program, and I have the utmost respect for him.

As my senior year began, I sensed we were destined to win the title. I believe that hard work pays off. I felt that with all the work

Playing for South Tahoe. We won the Nevada State Championship in 1992.
Photo by Tahoe Daily Tribune.

we had put into this season, we had to win. We breezed through the regular season, defeating most opponents easily (including the team that Jacque Vaughn played upon). Our only loss came in a holiday tournament in San Diego.

The title game is still talked about in Nevada high school basketball circles. Western of Las Vegas was the two time defending state champion. They were from the largest city in the state, with an enrollment 4 times the size of South Tahoe.

I don't know if I've ever played another game this well. I've seen the tape and I seemed to be everywhere, diving for loose balls, leading fast breaks, hitting three point shots and rebounding anything I could reach. In one 90 second stretch during the third quarter, I blocked a shot, absorbed a charging foul, nailed a three pointer and then rebounded a miss of my own shot with one hand and laid it in while in a crowd of defenders.

The game came down to an overtime session. Western took the early lead, but I hit a three point shot with 1:10 left to put South Tahoe on top. Then, with 35 seconds left, I was called for my fifth foul. I screamed "No" at the referee, sat on the court for a moment, and then gathered everyone for one last talk. I just told them that they could win it without me. We had worked as a team all year. They could win it as a team. Austin Price hit three free throws, the final one coming with 8 seconds left, and the championship belonged to South Tahoe.

We learned that it was through the efforts of everyone, not just one player, that success was achieved. We set a goal, worked towards it, and never lost sight of what we wanted. It was an infectious spirit, and it led to the state title.

I thought about how my dreams and goals had seemed so distant in grade school, but had been reached by the end of high school. If I give my best effort, if I put forth all that I can, I believe good things will happen. Now the goal was the National Championship of college basketball. Kansas had come close in 1996. 1997 was going to be another story. A story with a happy ending.

JUNE - AUGUST 1996

I came home from one of the basketball camps today and found a letter from someone who was a high school teacher in Indiana. Opening it, I read his proposal to write a book on my life as a college player. It made me think.

I talked over the idea with my mother. I'd often thought about keeping a diary and had never followed through it. I also had always dreamed about someone writing a book about me someday. It always seemed like a fantasy.

Now it was real.

I decided to check with the compliance officer at Kansas. I didn't want to get into any trouble, and certainly didn't want to jeopardize the season for my teammates and Coach Williams. I learned that as long as there was no money involved, there would be no problem.

Would anyone actually want to do this for free? I decided to talk with the teacher when he called, to see if he'd agree to this. Much of the dialogue had gone through John Downing, a longtime friend of my family. John had written an article about me for a website that dealt with Kansas basketball. Apparently they had been in contact through e-mail, and now John was the intermediary. He gave my phone number to the teacher and I received a call one night in June.

The man's name was Mark Horvath. He had already mailed his biography to me and I knew his background. After talking to him, I hung up the phone and discussed the matter again with my mother. We both decided that if Mark was willing to come out and meet with me in Tahoe, I could judge for myself if I wanted to go ahead with the book. I had nothing to lose.

I went with the Tahoe team and Coach Orlich on a basketball trip to Hawaii in late July. A week after I returned, Mark arrived. We spent three days together, talking and getting to know one another. Mark proposed the concept for the book. I'd send him my thoughts and he'd write them into book form. I'd proofread everything beforehand. If we both couldn't agree on something, it would be dropped. It was as honest a proposal as I could have wanted. He never mentioned money. He just wanted to write a book.

I am not an open person, not the type who tells his inner thoughts to people. Yet, I felt this was a chance to do something unique. For some reason, I trusted Mark and felt I could reveal my thoughts without fear. I decided to go ahead. It would be fun. It was time to leave the summer behind. As I packed for the flight back to Kansas, it was with mixed feelings. On the one hand, it was hard to leave family and friends behind again. Each year, the coming home was much more necessary, and much more therapeutic. I drew my inner strength from these times at home, and felt that I was a much better person because of my time here in Tahoe. On the other hand, Kansas was where I now needed to go if I was to fulfill my life's dreams. In a way, I was living the theme from the movie "Wizard of Oz" with a slight variation. Kansas was the land of Oz, and I had to go there to see if my dreams could come true. But as in the movie, I'd always know "there is no place like home."

THURSDAY, AUGUST 15

I evaluated my summer as I flew back to Kansas. I had accomplished much of what I set out to do and it was not all basketball-related. My primary goal was to spend time with my family. I did this , but it never seems to be as much as I would like. My second goal of the summer was to shoot often, with intensity. I am a tough grader, but I feel that I would give myself an A- to B+. As far as lifting, quickness and explosion, I was limited because of my back problems (I had injured my back during the NCAA tournament that spring and visited a chiropractor on a regular basis) but am happy with what I did. All things considered, I am satisfied that I did all I could do to prepare for this season.

I thought about what lay ahead. I felt eager and ready to get started. Not nervous or scared. To some, the possibility of playing your final college season can bring about a bittersweet feeling. It is the future and also the end. Memories of past successes and failures swirl together and form clouds of uncertainty. But to me none of those things were daunting.

I thought about the summer preparation some more. Did I do all I could? Had I forgotten any point of emphasis? I took a drink from the can of soda handed me by the flight attendant. I looked around at the passengers on the plane. They seemed to be relaxed and in various stages of thought. Would these people be the same types who will be screaming cries of support or yelling distractions as I get ready to shoot a free throw to clinch a game? I started to day-

My roommate, CB McGrath, a true team player. Photo by Earl Richardson.

dream about playing in Indianapolis in March of next year. Taking another drink, I also relaxed.

There is nothing left to do but play. I'm confident. I worked harder than I ever have, and can look in the mirror with no regrets. If I believe in hard work and know that I did just that, then what else can I do?" I stretched out as much as possible in the tight airline seat. Feeling calm and reassured, I closed my eyes and tried to get some sleep.

FRIDAY, AUGUST 16
It's time for me to move back to the Jayhawker Towers. That's the place where I've lived since I transferred to Kansas. My original roommate was Mike Sykes, a manager on the team, who has since graduated. Mike is currently working on the staff of the University of Colorado and I know I'll see him a few times this season. Being in our conference, we have a home and away series with them this year, and it should be pretty challenging.

Once again, my roommate this year will be CB McGrath. He is the perfect complement to my relaxed yet serious personality. CB (which stands for Colin Bryan) is treated as if he were everyone's little brother. He is the guy who makes the little comments that get everyone loosened up. He is the joker on the team. At 5'11", McGrath is one of our smallest players, but fills an important role as back-up point guard to Jacque Vaughn. To me, one of the most impressive things about him is the fact that CB was a walk-on to the Jayhawk roster, yet he was offered a full scholarship and increased his playing time as his freshman season wore on. He has been backup guard ever since. He is a determined individual, a pre-med student and another of the many Kansas players with a GPA of over 3.5. In addition to playing basketball, McGrath was an excellent cross country runner and golf standout in high school at Topeka West High School, about 20 miles from KU.

CB chose to come to Kansas after getting recruited by many small to mid-sized schools. CB will tell you that he always loved

Kansas basketball, and felt that he should come here and prove to himself and Coach Williams that he could make and help this team. He certainly has done that, and I expect that he'll contribute to our success again this year.

When I arrived and walked up to the room, I was greeted by CB, who demanded to know, in mock anger, "Where were you? I've had to move everything down two flights of stairs."

I tried to apologize, but then, seeing the expression on his face, pushed past him and walked into the living room. Nothing was there. I turned to face him, and saw that he was laughing to himself. One minute into the year and already he had gotten me. I couldn't help but shake my head at my trusting nature. I should have remembered that CB can be very convincing, especially when he is playing a practical joke.

We began moving furniture and boxes down from the fourth floor to our second floor apartment. Jayhawker Towers is a residence hall set up as an apartment building. These are two bedroom apartments. You enter from the outside into the living room, turn into the kitchen, and head down a hallway to the bedrooms and bath. They have quite a bit of room, and the closets in the bedroom take up one entire wall. It is not strictly for basketball players and is not even an athletic dorm. Instead, in keeping with the philosophy of Coach Roy Williams, the players live on separate floors, no more than two to a floor. Average college students intermingle with us, giving the team more of a sense of what student life is like instead of the sheltered existence many athletes lead at other universities. The Towers are not new luxury apartments, and again this is a departure from the stereotype many people have about how all college athletes live. But to be fair, the living area is not nearly as cramped as the average dormitory room.

Cramped was the operative word today, however. As box after box started to fill the rooms, both of us looked for a way out of the dreary task of moving in. Relief came in the form of Ryan Robertson, another KU guard who lives two flights up. "Welcome back boys," he beamed. Robertson was one of last season's top recruits, an all-state player from St. Charles, Missouri who is being primed to play either guard spot after the tandem of Haase and Vaughn graduates. He is a gifted three-point shooter and another of the excellent students KU possesses, garnering a 3.9 GPA during the spring semester. Robertson is laconic, with a slow, Southern speaking style and a dry sense of humor. He can erupt into a wild spurt of laughter, and has the ability to joke with others easily. He is more typical of 90's athletes, will at times poke fun at authority, but he has respect for those who are trying to help him improve. He is curious and inquisitive about his role on the Jayhawks but also tries to really learn the intricacies of running an offense.

After escaping for a short meal, CB and I resumed getting our apartment in shape. We had to buy a new bean bag chair, and other items like cleaning supplies. In the end, the process of moving in took three days, mostly spent cleaning, arranging and purchasing additional items to make the place seem like home. It's good to be back.

SUNDAY, AUGUST 18
Every year since I've been here, about six or seven of the guys go down to the Lake of the Ozarks, a resort area in southwest Missouri, for a getaway weekend, usually just before the start of classes. We do it before there is any talk of basketball, practice or school. It's pure relaxation and team bonding, time just to get away and have fun.

This year, much of our time was spent water skiing, playing on jet skis and Sea Doos, or swimming and soaking up sun. There were also some traditional moments of craziness. One annual event is cliff diving. The guys go for a hike to the top of a 40 foot cliff and, in the true spirit of youth, jump off into the lake below. It's a little bit nuts, but it does help create the feeling that we are all a part of something special. Everyone on the team who has come here has done it. I've done it every year. I don't know why, but I like the thrill. When I went to Hawaii with the South Tahoe team this summer I convinced many of them to do it as well. Here it was the same thing. I talked about the feeling and the thrill and most of the other guys also enthusiastically jumped. It would no doubt have shocked Coach Williams to see his two big men, Raef LaFrentz and Scot Pollard, jumping off a cliff, but to the rest of the team, it was one of many moments to remember as we started to think about what lie ahead.

The weekend was far too short. I think we all would enjoy staying here for at least a month. It's so much fun. This is one of the things that makes Kansas unique. I don't think too many other teams get ready for the school year, let alone the basketball season, like this.

THURSDAY, AUGUST 22
It's time to get the school year underway. Registration for classes is something all students dread. The endless waiting in line, the uncertainty whether a class is going to be available, the time at which the desired course is offered, all combine to create a stressful day. For members of the Kansas basketball team, some of that worry is relieved.

There is an assumption that athletes get preferential treatment in all areas of college life. While this is not true in all situations, it does apply to registration. I have managed to get a schedule that allows me to take all of my courses in morning time slots, so that I will be free for the practices at 3 p.m.

It's not as if the players go to the head of the line. We are pre-registered into the courses earlier than the average student. It is called priority registration, and there is an understanding that every effort will be made to get an early class time for the basketball team. Regular students are not bumped from their spots in a course. Instead, the players would most likely be entered first, then others would be added to fill up the class.

During my three years at Kansas, I have generally received the class time I requested. We don't get special treatment once the class begins. In class, we are like any other student. We need to get in the sections that take place before 3 o'clock.

If priority registration could not be done or if a class was only offered at a later time, we'd go to class first. Coach Williams would accept that. It's not like it would interfere every single day, but the class would come first. Coach would not be very happy about it, but he'd always tell a player that school comes first.

My courses this semester are not as demanding as in past years. I took a heavy load the past three years, and now I can reap the rewards for all those efforts. I will have only three courses, and may add a fourth in something I enjoy and want to try. I might add a piano class.

FRIDAY, AUGUST 23

I felt like playing golf today so I called up someone who has been challenging me for a while to a game: Assistant Coach Joe Holladay. Coach Holladay is someone I find easy to talk with, and he's a good guy. He has been at Kansas since I arrived, now starting his fourth year on the staff. Coach played at Oklahoma, and was known for his hard defensive style, something that we have in common. He found out how much I like golf and has been telling me he would find it a lot of fun to beat me at this. I decided to take him up on the offer.

Coach Holladay had an interesting idea. He wanted to make this a true test of youth vs. experience, so he would get another assistant coach, Matt Doherty, to join him. I had to get someone from the team to be my partner. I couldn't find CB anywhere so I called up Ryan. The four of us hit the links.

The game was contested right from the start. Ryan and I played horribly. While the coaches were not playing outstanding, one of them would always have a great hole, where their score would be excellent. With the format they constructed, this meant their score was much better than ours. We were getting our butts kicked.

Coach Holladay started to tease us. "Hey Jerod, you know what they call me and Matt?"

"No, what?" I replied, hesitantly.

"They call us ham and eggs, because we go so well together," he laughed, his voice rising at the end of the sentence.

I had to agree that today, they did make a pretty good team. It was a lot of fun, and it made me realize how much things have changed through my years here.

I think I've matured a lot and my relationship with the coaches has reflected this. I've always talked with my coaches, and have respected them as mentors. But now I sense that they are looking at me differently, as if I were closer to them than before. It's something I'll watch this season, but I like the feeling.

SUNDAY, AUGUST 25

I walked down the flight of stairs and headed down the hallway to the main door of the building. As I stopped to check my mailbox, I felt a large hand thump on my shoulder. Turning around, I looked straight up.

"How's it goin' J?" said Scot Pollard. At 6'11", Scot is definitely someone I look up to, and he is without a doubt, the most unique individual on the team. Maybe on any team I've played upon.

Scot is what I would call a typical Californian. The press makes a big deal out of the fact that five of us are from California, but Scot is the guy who best fits the stereotype. He is the guy who changes his hair style, from surfer blonde a few years ago to currently shaving most of it off. He has worn a goatee at times, and long, lamb chop sideburns other times. He loves music from the mid-60's and drives a 1969 Cadillac, rusty and in need of more work that anyone would attempt. The car even has a name. Scot calls it Marvin, after a character from an old cartoon dealing with a Martian.

Scot is blessed with a great sense of humor. He's the guy who can tell a joke with that big smile, seeming to enjoy the look on your face as much as the joke itself. He has a self-deprecating sense of humor, making fun of himself as often as he pokes fun at the rest of us. I think he gets some of that from his family. I remember last year at the Big 8 tourney in Kansas City, when the Pollards arrived, everyone in Kemper Arena knew where they were seated. The entire family had painted goatees on their faces to match Scot's. It was hilarious.

Things don't get Scot down very often, and it's not common to find him in a depressed mood. He seems to be able to pick himself

Scot Pollard. *Photo by Earl Richardson.*

up after any misfortune and many times his attitude helps the rest of us see the positive side.

Many people comment that Scot seems too laid back to be a college basketball player, but that's not the case at all. Once he gets out on the court, Scot is one of the most aggressive workers you'll find. I'm glad he's on my side when we are in a tough game.

We talked for a few minutes about things that each of us had been doing, both wishing we could be back in the Ozarks instead of starting classes.

TUESDAY, AUGUST 27

A few of us got together tonight. As the year goes on we will be eating, studying and living together because we have to as a team that travels around the country. Right now it's something we feel like doing. Sort of another way of catching up on what each has been doing in their own lives the past few months.

Raef LaFrentz is the other half of our big tandem underneath, a 7-footer who is one of the most likable people anyone could ever meet. Raef is one of those people who laughs easily, is very sociable and will talk to just about anyone he meets. We share similar qualities, especially when it comes to family. Raef is close to his family, and the fact that his parents are going to rent a place in Lawrence this year (so that they can attend every home game) will mean that they are close to him as well.

Raef grew up in Monona, Iowa, a small town in the northeastern corner of the state. With a population of less than 2,000, Monona is much smaller than Tahoe, and both of us reflect that background. Raef is a small town boy at heart, a phrase that people apply to me from time to time. I'm not quite sure they mean but I take it as a compliment. I'd like to think it as something positive.

Besides Ryan and CB, Billy Thomas is with us tonight. Billy is someone I really respect, especially because of what he has had to overcome. Of all the guys, he comes from the poorest background. He's from a rural part of Louisiana and has had to make adjustments to the lifestyle and concept of basketball at Kansas. I really think his first year was the hardest, although it's that way for most of us. Billy also had to deal with the social changes that are part of a major university, besides coping with the academic and athletic pressures.

Billy is an assertive person who initiates contact with people. He's very easy to like and will make an effort to talk with anyone in a room. When he enters the locker room before a practice, he always says, "What's up?" and gets everyone talking. At 6'5", Billy is a shooting guard, someone who will be pushing me to better myself this season. He's a junior and will get a lot of playing time this year as the coaches groom him to take over some of the leadership roles expected of seniors in our program.

The five of us spent the time talking about the usual things: girls, sports, and school. We all have fun together, and it seems to me that this is one of the secrets to our success as a basketball team. We get along as friends. We aren't just a bunch of jocks, thrown together at practice and then going our separate ways when it's over. We do things with each other not because we have to but because we want to. We enjoy being with one another.

It's a lot easier knowing that the guys on the bench are supporting you rather than hoping for their chance at your expense. This is a team where everyone knows his time will come during the season, and his role is defined as a member of the team. We know we'll win as a group and we want to push each other to succeed. Isn't that what friends do?

LABOR DAY, SEPTEMBER 2

I can't believe what is happening in college basketball today. I was looking at a report on SportsCenter, the ESPN nightly news show, which announced that the University of California at Berkeley was being investigated by the NCAA for possible rules violations. In

Jason Kidd and I were the freshmen backcourt for the University of California in 1993. Photo by Tahoe Daily Tribune.

addition, the basketball coach, Todd Bozeman, was being asked to step down in the wake of the investigation of his program.

I was surprised. I had begun my college basketball career at California. I had spent the most traumatic year of my life playing ball for the Golden Bears, and the memories came rushing back as I thought about that year.

As a high school junior, I had begun to get some attention as the year came to a close. In spite of my all state status and the success of the South Tahoe Vikings, I still was somewhat of an unknown to most college scouts. Partly because of its isolated location, the Tahoe program was not one of the regular stops most college coaches made while recruiting in California, and my reputation, while excellent, was still just word of mouth.

I attended a few camps after my junior year, and it was at the Stanford High Potential camp that I first gained some notice. I was chosen the camps' MVP, and spent a lot of time with Stanford guard Kenny Ammon, who took me under his wing and spent a great deal of time helping me with my shooting game. A short time later, Stanford was one of the first schools to express an interest in recruiting me, especially when I later was chosen Nevada's AAA Player of the Year for 1992.

As my senior year began, I received offers from many schools, but it was California that made the biggest push. The Bears were recruiting another highly touted high school star, Jason Kidd, and the buzz was that Cal was going to try to gather the best freshmen class it could get. The combination of that determined approach by the university, the desire to play in a major conference (PAC-10), and the closeness to home all combined to lure me to Berkeley. I signed a letter of intent to California before my senior season began, and Cal's backcourt of the future was complete.

The season at Cal began like a fairy tale for me. I moved into the starting lineup, and the coaches said it was due to my outhustling the incumbent, K.J.Roberts. I was so excited my play improved, and I averaged 12 points and 3 assists through the first ten games. Kidd received the attention, but I was quietly making a name for myself as the "other guard". Reporters had questioned whether I could play at this level, since I came from the small town atmosphere of Lake Tahoe, but California coach Lou Campanelli never wavered. "Jerod's come along faster than we thought," he told the media, "but he's got the ability to go along with his heart and desire. Good players come from anywhere in this country."

The season was progressing better than I could have dreamed, and Jerod was gaining confidence in his game and notoriety in the media. ESPN announcer Dick Vitale screamed "I love the way this kid gets on the floor! What a competitor! What a scrapper!" CBS commentator Al McGuire added "He gives up his body without hesitation." They all seemed to like my intensity. My dives for loose balls and the floor burns which resulted, became a statistic tracked by California fans. They seemed to really appreciate the effort. I have always played this way, it's my nature. I don't think anyone can fake something like throwing your body after a loose ball. The team was gaining success and I was part of that effort. It seemed like a dream come true.

Then, tragedy struck. Mom has told me the account of the evening, since I was unaware of events until they had already taken place. Our family was scattered around the state. I was playing a game at Southern Cal, and (my older brother) Steven was playing for the Air Force Academy against Fresno State. My Dad was having trouble with his ankle and was going to decide if he would make the trip with Mom, Karin & Chris (my sister and her husband) to Fresno. Before Mom could leave school, she received a phone call from my Aunt Kay, telling her that she had to call 911 to take Dad to the hospital. She wasn't sure what the problem was. It turned out to be an infection near the ankle that had turned serious.

When Mom and Karin arrived at the hospital, things had gotten worse. Dad was on oxygen and antibiotic I.V's. The doctors said it would be okay to leave and go see Steven play in Fresno, since all Dad needed was rest and if the family were there he wouldn't get that. He could listen to the game on the radio, so the family left for the game.

Family friends in Fresno went to get Steven for a visit at their home. When the rest of the group arrived at that home, they called the hospital to say goodnight to Dad. Instead, they were informed that he was now on a respirator. Apparently he had gone into shock. The family, along with Steven, decided to drive back to the hospital in Woodland. Our friends would try to find out where I was staying, since I was in Los Angeles, getting ready to play UCLA the following day.

It was 2 AM when Mom and the others arrived back in Woodland. They got there just in time to hear Dad take his last breath and see the heart monitor go into a straight line...They knew he was aware of their presence, because Mom said she saw a tear fall from his eye before the vital signs stopped. She felt he had held on until they returned.

Mom called David and Mara first and then finally found out where the team and I were staying. The others had been informed that my father was in the hospital, but nobody could find me to let me know about any of this. I was not told of his death until the team had already left for our next game at UCLA. The news stunned me. Mom called Assistant Coach Jeff Wilbrun and told him, so he could be there when she told me and help me get through the next day. The entire period was a blur of tears and total confusion.

That afternoon, January 24, 1993, I played a game not just for California, but also for my Dad. I scored 16 points, dished out 5 assists, grabbed 4 rebounds and helped lead Cal's 104-82 lopsided win over the Bruins. The effort earned me USA Today's Most Courageous Performance Award for the season. It didn't mean a thing. He was my father, he was only 55, and he was gone. The team flew home immediately after the game, and I left to be with my family.

The whole period seemed unreal. Scott Gilliland, my closest friend, remembers that, "Jerod and the whole family were shocked by the sudden nature of Mr. Haase's death. Jerod remained strong for his family, but there were times when he would break down before a game, thinking of how his dad could not be there anymore to see him play." (Today, to send a silent but personal signal, I still put my father's initials on my shoes, in locations that are not visible to the public.

It's a way to say that I am playing for and thinking about my dad. My father and I were close and I know my dad is proud of my accomplishments. I want him to know that I still think of him. I'm sure he does.)

Returning to Cal, I tried to get back into the routine of basketball, but then another shock occurred. On February 8th, Coach Lou Campanelli was fired in the middle of the most successful season California had enjoyed in years. The controversial firing was broadcast across the country, and the team lapsed into chaos. A few days later, Jeff Wilbrun also resigned, and Todd Bozeman, another assistant, became interim head coach. The program would never be the same.

Neither would my career at Cal. Two weeks after Bozeman took over, I was benched in favor of the guard whom I had beaten out at the start of the year, K.J.Roberts. I had started all 23 of our games at that point. At the time, I was still averaging 11 points per game. By the time the NCAA tourney rolled around , I was down to being the last man off the bench. But I had one more memorable moment left that season.

Cal had made it into the NCAA tournament that season, our first trip in many years. We won our first round game, and were playing Duke, the defending two-time national champions in the second round. Late in the first half, Coach Bozeman surprised me by putting me into the game, and I played as hard as I could. I felt hot and scored 13 points, including three, three-point shots, to help secure California's stunning upset of Duke. I also gained the notice of Kansas coach Roy Williams because of my defensive work on Duke guard and future NBA #4 pick Bobby Hurley. It was this game that provoked Coach Williams to inquire about who I was, and it was this game that motivated me to consider leaving Cal and transferring to Kansas. I liked the way their players acted, the way their coaching staff seemed to conduct themselves, and after the game, I talked briefly with Rex Walters, their starting guard who also was from California. He said he had enjoyed his time at KU. Since he had also transferred from another school (Northwestern) to Kansas, I felt his comments were worth considering.

When the season ended, I called my high school coach, Tom Orlich, and asked him to contact Kansas and see if they would have any interest in me as a player. Three years later, starting my senior year at KU, I knew the answer.

All of this flashed through my mind today as I listened to the story about Bozeman on ESPN. I recalled how I felt at Cal, especially during the rough period after my father's death. I'm not the smartest person, but I listen and observe and I believe I have a keen sense of how the future will unfold. I never knew when or how, but

I had the feeling that things were not going to always be good at Cal. Knowing this, I decided I did not want to be part of the program, if the day ever came when the situation turned negative. Also, I did not fit in as well as I would have liked with the other players, and the disorder after both coaches Campanelli and Wilbrun left was not something I was used to.

I felt relieved to be out of there and glad to be at Kansas. I don't have contact with anybody at Cal, and don't know anyone on the team. It's a part of my life that will always be remembered, but I feel fortunate to be where I am today. Kansas has never looked so good.

THURSDAY, SEPTEMBER 5
I was thinking about the start of basketball today and Coach Williams came into my mind. After reading about the situation at Cal, I was reflecting about how the coaches I've had affected my life. Each has taught me about the game and some, like Coach Orlich from Tahoe, have taught me about life. But there aren't many other people I respect as much as Roy Williams.

When I was contemplating the move from Cal to Kansas, it was the coaching staff that I was most concerned about. I wanted to play at a school with this level of competition, since I have always believed that to be the best you have to play the best. The schedule at Kansas has always reflected the program's desire to challenge the top schools, so that was a plus. However, there was no way I could really tell what the coaches would be like.

Coach Roy Williams. Photo by KU Sports Information.

Rex Walters had told me about the program and he was very positive towards Coach Williams and his staff. Since Rex had transferred from Northwestern to KU, he underwent the same things I would have to experience. His insights were very helpful, but I still wanted to allay my fears and see for myself what things would be like.

I had gone on the one allowable recruiting trip and was impressed with what I had seen. Kansas was a great place to go to school, live and play ball. And Coach Williams seemed to want me to attend. When he came out to visit in Tahoe, my mother decided to make him pizza for dinner. He ate a few pieces and stayed for a nice visit. It wasn't until much later that we found out he hates pizza. Doesn't touch the stuff. Yet he ate it at my house. I'd say I was a pretty desirable recruit, or he was a pretty considerate person, not wanting to make my mother feel bad after she had gone to the trouble of making dinner for him. Maybe both.

After I arrived at Kansas, I learned that the team does many things as a group, and often we will gather at Coach's house for these occasions. It may be dessert or an informal team meeting, but we feel comfortable going there and he enjoys having us around. Mrs. Williams is a fantastic person, who makes us feel right at home. Together, they help create an atmosphere in which I feel at ease. It is as close to home as I think anyone can find.

Coach has always made it clear that he will treat his players with respect and dignity. He recruits players who are not only talented but hold values he considers important. After that, he will go to the wall for us, as we will for him. I remember an incident that occurred my first year at Kansas. We were playing Oklahoma on the road, and their crowd was really noisy. They were into the game and were yelling things at me the entire game. We were down big at the half, and Coach gave us a stern talk at the half. We came out so fired up it was unbelievable. I really got into the game, but as sometimes happens, my emotions got the better of me and I lost control of the ball on a dribble. I dove for the ball and slid a good twenty feet out of bounds, right to the feet of the rowdy Oklahoma student section.

Within seconds Coach Williams was off the bench and at my side. I am still amazed at how fast he moved getting to my side. The fans were pointing at me and he must have thought the fans were hitting me. He rarely receives a technical, but for this incident he did. The fact that he would go to this length to protect a player made me realize that I was going to be appreciated for my efforts here at Kansas. The coach was going to care about his players. That's something I think is important. It makes it easier to play hard for someone like that.

Coach also has a fun side that the press sometimes misses. When we have a mosh pit after a game, he is the first one in the center. Especially if it's a big win. About the only thing that he doesn't like is for someone to mess up his hair. But if it's a big occasion, we'd do it and he'd enjoy it. He helps us enjoy the ride and make us aware of the fact that this is still a game.

FRIDAY, SEPTEMBER 6
Social issues are something that I rarely comment upon. I'm not one for giving my opinions on political topics to the media, and I don't follow those issues as much as I should. I know they are important, and I think I should be a better informed person, but right now I am not as current on some things as I'd like to be.

One issue that I can comment upon is race relations. The public sometimes wants to make a big deal of the fact that basketball is a sport primarily played by black athletes. The "White Men Can't Jump" stereotype is out there, and some folks wonder what it's like to play in a sport where whites are a minority.

I have always been the kind of person who does not judge people. I prefer to take them as they are. I grew up in a town that was primarily white, and attended schools that were not very integrated. The Lake Tahoe region is not a melting pot compared to a major metropolitan area. But playing basketball in many camps and traveling around the state as my high school team did, I was exposed to all racial and ethnic types by the end of my second year of high school.

The adjustment to being on an integrated team in college was not a problem for me. In my time at Kansas I've never regarded my teammates as anything but my teammates. We do not live by any racial grouping and in fact have bi-racial rooming situations on the team. Raef and Billy live together, and Scot and Jacque also are roommates. When we travel on the road, we always switch who we are bunked with, so that by the end of January or so, we have all been roommates at one time or another. It helps break down any possible barriers that may exist and is another example of how well we mesh together as friends.

One guy who comes from a totally different background from me is Paul Pierce. Paul is from Los Angeles and the best way to describe his home is that he's from "the hood". One of the roughest areas of L.A. It could best be described as "dangerous" and is definitely a total contrast to where I was raised. Our backgrounds could not be more dissimilar.

In spite of all that, Paul and I get along well. He's going into his sophomore year, and the difference between us in age is about 4 years. In that sense I feel a difference. But that would be the only way. There certainly is no change in my attitude towards Paul because he's an African-American from the rough side of Los Angeles. He's just Paul, a soft-spoken guy who adjusting to college pretty well. Which brings up another issue concerning Paul.

A certain shyness is evident in Paul's demeanor, and it comes across on television. He really is a quiet guy, not arrogant or loud but actually reserved. He's this way with the press and the public , but when he's with the team he comes out of his shell a lot more. As a freshman, and being younger than most of the guys, he was naturally reluctant to assert himself at first. That is another positive side to Paul. He wanted to be part of the team, to be accepted as everyone else, and he discovered that we automatically do that. I think it helped him adjust quickly and now he's relaxed, showing a side of himself that everyone appreciates and enjoys.

As far as how other schools handle their team situations and racial balance, I don't know and won't speculate. When we play other teams, the type of ball they play depends on the personnel and the coach, not the racial background of the team. I hope they don't get along as well as we do. That would make beating them that much easier.

I'm sure there are people who will think that I'm being naive about race relations, that I'm looking at the world through "rose-colored glasses." But I don't care. I think that we'd all be better off if we learned to accept each other as we are, not as we want someone to be. At any rate, that's how I intend to continue to live my life.

Most of my life, basketball was the only sport that mattered to me. I followed football a bit, since the 49ers have done so well. Baseball was okay, and I played when I was young. But the only real passion I ever found in sports was for basketball.

There was always something special about the change in seasons this time of year. Summer is great, and living in the Tahoe region meant being outdoors year round. I enjoyed the summers, but when the weather changed and got cooler it meant that my favorite time of year had arrived. Basketball was starting.

Autumn at Kansas has been the same. There is an old saying that basketball players are made in the off season. If that's true, then teams are made in the pre-season. The next two and a half months will be when we find out what kind of team we are going to be this year. The coaching staff will work us hard, and hopefully we will respond. We have to get our bodies in condition and our minds focused. There is only one goal for us: the National Championship.

The following sections deal with my life in these important

months. As you will see, there is a certain routine that I fall into where my daily life is concerned.

MONDAY, SEPTEMBER 9

It was the first day the temperature dropped below 60 for the day-time high. Unusually cool for early September, but warm compared to the winters back in Lake Tahoe. I have always connected the change in temperature with the start of basketball. When the fall arrives, I begin to get those feelings that I associate with the smell of empty gyms...conditioning...lifting..pickup games...anticipation. And when the first snow arrives, or when the temperatures get even a little cold, then it is all-out basketball season. I just noticed it today. I felt the old urge to get on the court. It's understandable, considering where I call home.

The snow measures six feet deep most winters in South Lake Tahoe, California. It is a mecca for skiers, and my family has plenty of those. My sisters Mara and Karin and my brother David were strong skiers and most people in the area have hit the slopes at one time or another. To me, however, all snow has ever meant was that it was time to get out the shovels and clean off the basketball court.

My brothers and I were lucky enough to have an asphalt court in our backyard. It was about 15 feet wide and 35 feet long, and became the site of many hard fought games among me, my brothers and their friends. Being the youngest, I would have to dive for the loose balls if I wanted to get the ball at all. My dad once told the local newspaper "There were many times Jerod would come in crying because his brothers and their friends would not let him play. But he would sit in his room for a few minutes, get himself together, and head right back to the court, determined to play." The court was painted with a three-point arc and was well-lit so all of us could play at night. It became almost a tourist attraction when a Sacramento newspaper ran a story on me and the family court, complete with a picture of my brothers and me shooting layups. When our family moved to a new house a few blocks away, it also featured a big outdoor court.

Now it was getting close to that time of the year once again. I looked out at the campus from the front entrance of Allen Field-house. The leaves were starting to change colors, there was woodsmoke in the air, and this year autumn meant only one thing : time to work harder to reach the goal of a National Championship.

TUESDAY, SEPTEMBER 10

"Hold still," CB complained. "If you don't want this to look like hell, you better let me do it right." CB was becoming adept as a barber, at least when it came to shaving the heads of his few customers. The team had decided to adopt a new look this season, and most of the guys had shaved or cut their hair as short as possible. Ryan and I had been the lone holdouts, and now we had decided to get with the program.

Today, Ryan had first taken the plunge. He came down to my room and told me he wanted to go ahead and change his hair. At first, I was reluctant to join him. I wore my hair naturally short, so this would not be a big step. But the thought of a total shave, as Scot Pollard had achieved, was making me hesitate. CB egged me on. "Seniors should be team leaders, J. How can you be a role model for the underclassmen if you look like that?" Ryan jumped on board. "You are my idol," he kidded. "I won't do this unless you do it too."

It didn't take much more. I went into the bathroom, C.B. followed, making hatchet movements with his hands. In a few seconds it was over. What was left of my hair lay on the floor, and Ryan and I had joined the rest of the team. I was a little excited to play a game without much hair. It would be a new experience, something different to start out my senior year. But there was one point I had not thought about. "Wait until your mom sees it," CB reminded me.

WEDNESDAY, SEPTEMBER 11

An important part of the preseason activities were the daily pickup games, played either at Allen Fieldhouse or at the Recreation Center located across Naismith Drive. At these sessions, games could get pretty intense, as the guys on the team tried to have fun, but at the same time simulate game or practice conditions. Players just chose sides and began to play but it was with a purpose.

Today, as usual, Jacque Vaughn was driving to the basket. He took off and went in for a layup. Leaving his feet, he laid the ball off the glass and then landed hard on his right side. When he hit the ground, he did not immediately get up. "We just thought it was the usual Jacque move. taking a few minutes to lay on the floor before coming back to the game," recalled CB. "Instead, he got up and told us he thought his wrist was broken." Jacque went to the hospital and soon discovered that he had torn ligaments in his wrist. Surgery would be required and our point guard would be out of action for three months, which would mean he would not be returning to the lineup until January.

Many of us were surprised at first. It didn't seem real, since we always played hard and there were many times guys would fall. Injuries were usually minor, and this was not expected. The team would react with a sense of determination, and would draw close together. We went to see Jacque after his surgery. He was pretty down, and it helped him to see all of us there for him.

I was trying to imagine what must be going through JV's mind after this happened. I'm sure the fear of losing his entire season had to be the most frightening, since this is the year he has dreamed about. Of course, this happened after the choice he made last spring. Turning down the NBA.

Many people have asked me about Jacque's decision, and I always give the same answer: ask Jacque. It was totally his call. He didn't talk about it with the team, and it was sort of an unspoken offer that if he wanted to do so, any one of us would listen. But we never asked, because we felt that when the time came, JV would tell us what he'd decided. I know that Coach never pressured him, because that's not his style. Roy Williams encourages us to talk with him, but he will never tell anyone what to do. He wants the person involved to make his own decision. He's more like a sounding board and counselor, and in this case, Coach never wanted to be the one to tell Jacque what to do. It was solely up to Jacque.

The story JV tells is that he made his decision, then thought about it for a few more days. During that time, he was playing with myself, Ryan and CB in some daily softball games. The four of us enjoyed last spring, mainly because we felt so carefree, as though we were just regular college guys and not intercollegiate athletes. I still recall one game when Jacque chased after a fly ball and made a diving catch, going right up to the curb of a busy street. It showed his real determination and was a spectacular play. He got up and grinned that special smile of his. You could tell he really was having a great time. We all were.

Shortly after that day, he announced at a press conference that he was staying for his senior year. He said that the NBA would be there another year, and he just wanted to complete the college experience. He wanted to help Kansas win the National Championship. I went to the press conference and remember feeling happy and relieved. We had all worked so hard and had become so close that none of us wanted to see the team broken up before we had one more chance to prove ourselves. Jacque had just guaranteed that we would stay together, all of us, to make that final push.

Today, I think he knew again that he had made the right decision. Visiting him made him feel better and let him know we were there for support. We would have done it no matter which guy on the team it was. That's the kind of team we have. I have had injuries in the past, and I know how frustrating it is not to play. I could really sympathize with him. Jacque would have to remain in the hospital for a few more days.

On the way out of the hospital, a few of us stopped off in the children's ward. Kids in hospitals always like to see someone who is famous, and in Kansas, we are certainly that. This time, however, the person we visited was not really a kid. An 18-year-old young man with a fatal disease had asked the nurses if we could come by for a few minutes. He must have heard about Jacque being injured and figured we would come to visit, so he told the nurses to let us know he'd appreciate a few minutes of our time. He was 18, but was smaller than my 7-year-old nephew Zac. It was pretty sobering.

The team talked with the patient for a few minutes, said hello to other children and left. I thought about it on the way home. Here I am, worrying about a few missed shots, and this kid is going through something I can't even imagine. The mental picture of this boy stayed with me, especially after I found out he had only four months to live.

THURSDAY, SEPTEMBER 12

St. Anne's Grade School in Kansas City had called a few days ago. They wanted a guest speaker to come to talk to the fourth grade class, and I was the requested player. I gladly accepted the invitation.

I had spoken at this school the previous year and always felt good about these trips. Sure, the drive to Kansas City was 45 minutes one way, and it meant getting up three hours earlier than a normal Thursday morning, but I could not say no. Some of my friends are puzzled by this. "He never says no," CB tells people. "I can't always understand why he does it, but Jerod really can't say no to these people when they call. At times, it becomes a joke around the locker room. Anyone need a guest speaker? Any group, anywhere in the U.S.? Call 1-800-G-E-T-J-R-O-D."

Scott Gilliland, my oldest friend from Tahoe, says "Jerod has always liked talking to and working with little kids. He gets a kick out of their energy, and feels he is helping them just by being with them. That's why he does the speaking trips. He feels as if he is giving something special to the kids."

This is not something that began once I arrived at KU. Back in Lake Tahoe, I was sent to talk to local elementary schools about sports, drugs and alcohol. My message was simple: this trio doesn't mix. Stay off drugs and away from alcohol. Parents loved the talks. I received thank-you notes from people I had never met, stating how much my appearance had affected their child. Local organizations asked me to speak for a few moments at their functions. This trend continues at Kansas.

At the end of the 1996 season, the team met and signed hundreds of basketballs, pictures, programs and other gear, to be mailed to kids who had written in, asking for these momentos. It took us about three hours and it's not easy. On my own, I sign photos of myself and mail them to children who write me letters of support or just ask for my autograph. That's something I have always done. I know that if I were a kid and wrote to someone who I saw on TV, I'd be really hurt if I never got an answer. I don't want to be the one who lets a kid down like that. That's just not right.

The trip to St. Anne's seemed to go well. I usually open any talk with a few comments about the need to study in school, the success anyone can have if they put in hard work and effort, and the importance of being a good person. Then the kids get their chance to ask questions. Sometimes, the questions are predictable, dealing with the team and our opponents. Other times, they get personal, ranging from my family background to whether I have a girlfriend. If the session is in a classroom, I may sit in a chair in front of the room. If it's for the whole school, then the setting is probably a lectern on stage or in the school gym. Either way, I generally get a lot of questions from the students I talk to.

I know that the guys wonder why I do this. But they should see the looks in those kids' eyes. I never cease to be amazed at how much I affect them. What the kids don't know is how much they affect me. I can't get their looks out of my mind.

I've talked about this with people and my friend Scott probably says it best. "Jerod takes his position seriously," he says. "He feels that he can be a positive role model, and wants to do this to help other people. There is no ulterior motive. That's just the way he has always been. He cares about other people."

MONDAY, SEPTEMBER 16

Some days it's better to stay in bed. There are days you wish you could just forget and today was one of those times for me. It was a comedy of errors, collisions and events I would rather not remember.

The misadventures began with a trip to the weight room. The preseason conditioning included lifting for 90 minutes, every other day. The team doesn't gather as a group, but rather whoever is free would agree to meet at Allen and lift at regular times. My time to lift was usually in the early afternoon, and I'd go over there, confident someone would be there to assist me. Today the weights seemed to have their own sense of aggression. I went to lift some free weights and hit my chin with the bar. Instant tongue bite!

Next, the pickup game was as brutal as ever. In spite of the injury to Jacque, the guys continued to play with the usual intensity. Driving to the hoop, I caught an elbow to the temple from a defender. I saw stars for a few seconds and was almost knocked out. I thought I had a concussion. But I continued to keep playing. This proved to be an unwise decision.

As soon as I returned to the game, I caught another elbow in the mouth. Had I not been wearing a mouthpiece (something I recently started) I would have lost three teeth. As it was, my teeth were sore, one felt loose, and I was now sporting a fat lip. All in all, not my day.

I know that people think I'm aggressive, and I am, but I'm certainly not alone. One of the guys who can mix it up with the best of them is TJ Pugh. He is a quiet guy most of the time, studious with one of the higher GPA's on the team, the kind of person who picks his spots to open up and be vocal or funny. He spent a lot of time this summer working out and gaining weight, so he would be more effective under the boards. As a sophomore, TJ is expected to be a big help in those games when Raef or Scot get in foul trouble. He was a strong scorer in high school and was Mr. Basketball in the state of Nebraska his senior year. Last year, TJ progressed well and we are counting on him for some important minutes this year. But in games like today, TJ's desire to show his intensity can turn downright dangerous, especially to someone like me who seems to be accident-prone. I was glad to avoid have any collisions with him.

By the time evening arrived, I still had a headache and Ryan had a solution. "Go to bed and dream that this never happened," he joked. For once he's right.

WEDNESDAY, SEPTEMBER 18

One of my courses this semester is titled "Managing a Small Business." What it entails is assisting a local Lawrence business in all aspects of its operations. This could include advertising, promotion, marketing, accounting procedures, personnel decisions and the like. It is part of the business major I'm pursuing, and involves working with a team of students to improve the fortunes of the cooperating business.

An architect will become the focus of my efforts this semester. My group will design a marketing analysis, attempting to devise a plan which will increase the firm's clientele and boost consumer awareness of its existence. This means conducting interviews and gathering data relating to this business, its competitors and similar firms in the area.

The convenient part of this course is that there is not a lot of in-class time required. I will have to meet with the entire class at first, but then as the project proceeds, we have to do much of the work on our own, meeting from time to time with our groups to complete our projects. We meet with the professor periodically to monitor our progress, but actual daily class time is minimal.

This is the semester schedule I've wanted for a long time. During my first three years at Kansas I have taken fairly heavy course loads, averaging 17 credit hours per semester. My freshman year at Cal was also a full load. The stress of practicing, studying and traveling would, at times, get me down. The result was no time for simple relaxation. This year I wanted some time of my own.

I have always maintained an excellent academic record throughout my years in school. I believe the key to good grades is listening in class, being organized and getting the work done. Studying is not a matter of not having enough time as much as it is using the time in the right way. I try to use the dead time when we are traveling to get a lot of my work done. If you're sitting in a terminal or on a plane, you might as well be reading. It has worked for me, as well as for some of the other guys on the team.

My group decides to meet on a semi-weekly basis to get the project underway. We will coordinate all our efforts and share the information each has gathered as we design this presentation for the architect. It means that there will be some weekends where I'll be working most of the time, but at least I can sleep in a couple of mornings.

FRIDAY, SEPTEMBER 20
Kansas has produced a few professional players in recent years. Danny Manning, Greg Ostertag and others are still active in the NBA. Rex Walters fits into that category. Walters maintains an off-season home in the Lawrence area, and likes to keep in shape by shooting and working out at KU. Currently playing for the Philadelphia 76ers, Walters occasionally will call me to come over and try to give him some competition.

I always look forward to these sessions. There is some irony to the two of us getting together at Allen Fieldhouse to shoot. In my season at California, when the Golden Bears made it to the NCAA Sweet 16, it was Kansas who ousted us from the tourney. And the guard who led the Jayhawks in that victory? Rex Walters. And the Cal guard who came off the bench and shadowed him for a time? Jerod Haase. Now the two of us were soon to be alumni of the same school. It was as if one had followed in the footsteps of the other.

Mark was making his first trip to Kansas to see firsthand what life at KU as a basketball player was like. I had taken him on a tour of the campus, and then I told him about having to meet Rex for a shooting session. I wanted him to come along and watch.

We walked across the lawn from Allen Fieldhouse and headed towards the Robinson Natatorium across Naismith Drive. There are many open courts in this building, which serves as a rec center for intramurals. Mark asked me to compare myself to Walters.

"I'm not Rex and he's not me," I said. "There are some things that he does that I probably can't do, but there are things I can do which I feel I'm better at than he is. We're different players with different styles. It's a compliment to me to be compared to him because he's a great player."

This day, we both followed a shooting workout that Rex has designed. It included spot shooting for about 30 minutes, interspersed with free throws, always stressing movement without the ball. One of us would pass to the other, the emphasis on constant movement. In no time at all, we both worked up a sweat and were concentrating on our shots. Eventually, there's a game of one on one, one point per basket, first to seven wins. Rex sprinted out to a 4-0 lead. But I got hot, and after tying the score at 6-6, hit a soft jumper from the left corner to win.

I was pleased with my performance. As we walked out of the gym I let myself enjoy the workout. It's always nice to beat someone like Rex. That's when you know you've improved.

FRIDAY, SEPTEMBER 21
It is a beautiful fall afternoon. The sky is sunny, the weather is warm and I was thinking about playing golf. This is not unusual, since I have become an avid fan of the sport, trying to get in a game at every opportunity. During the summer, I became especially addicted to playing a round with anyone I could find. In fact, on the final day before I had returned to school in August, I had played one of Tahoe's most exclusive courses, Edgewood, with my brother-in-law Chris Holmes, another golf fanatic.

Today, Mark, CB and I head to a local course for a round of 18. It is a challenging course, and we engage in a friendly competition as the game wears on. CB was a member of the golf team in high school and loves to provoke my competitive side. He would state the number of strokes it would take to reach the green, or the number of putts he'd use to sink a shot. I tried to beat him, and succeeded about half the time. The afternoon is relaxing and the atmosphere is perfect. It is a beautiful autumn day.

But that night would be different.

Ryan Robertson was in a weird mood. He wanted to do something, but couldn't make up his mind what it should be. I'm used to this. Ryan and CB are both wired at times, and one tries to outdo the other in zany antics. At first the conversation dwelt on girls, then football, and finally got back to the topic at hand.

"I just can't sit here all night," CB said.

"Well, YOU decide what to do, because I can't," Ryan complained.

"I know, let's go bowling"

"Bowling? Are you nuts?"

"Shut up. I really want to go bowling." And with that, CB sprinted from the room and began to change clothes. He returned a few minutes later with a baseball hat, tilted to one side, a T-Shirt over a long-sleeved T-shirt, and jeans.

"Oh my God!" exclaimed Ryan. "You look like a dork who just lost his skateboard. I'm not going bowling with someone who looks like that."

"What's wrong with this outfit?" CB asked.

"Jerod, tell him how fricking stupid he looks," Ryan pleaded

I couldn't answer. I was laughing at the way CB looked and at the two of them arguing over how to dress to go bowling. Ryan got an idea.

"I'll be right back", he said, and he ran from the room. "Wait for me."

"What do you think he's gonna do?" asked CB.

"Who knows?" I replied. "Let's call somebody else and see if they want to go with us."

I was on the phone in the other room when wild shouts erupted and crazed laughter hooted from the living room. I ran out to see what happened. There I was greeted by Ryan, dressed in the ultimate skater outfit.

Ryan had changed from Kansas basketball player to the ultimate alternative wannabe. He had a flannel shirt, two T-shirts, baggy khaki pants, baseball hat turned backwards and a wallet with a chain. The sight provoked a round of hysterical laughter.

"Let's do some bowling, dudes!" Ryan shouted. "Party time!"

SUNDAY, SEPTEMBER 22, 1996

"Where are you going?" asked CB It was 5 o'clock and he wanted to go out to dinner.

"Coach wants to have the seniors over for dinner tonight," I replied.

"OOOH. Big senior meeting," Ryan teased. "What is this, we

lowly underclassmen are excluded from your little fraternity?"

"He just wants to talk to us about the start of the season," I patiently explained. "No big deal."

"If it's no big deal, why can't we go?" Ryan persisted.

"Yeah, please take us, Big Jerod, please?" CB added, piling on.

"Watch it," I threatened, jokingly.

"OOOH, the big senior is getting tough," they mocked in unison. "Why can't we go to your special meeting? Is coach excluding us from team dinners? What are we supposed to do—starve?" Each was taking turns throwing out questions.

"He's not excluding you," I explained.

"Wait 'til next year, he'll never have any of us over," Ryan continued, trying to sound like a whiner. "When you guys leave, we're really going to have to work our butts off, and we still won't get a free meal. It's not fair."

I ignored their remarks. "I should be back soon," I said, opening the door.

"WHO CARES? WE"RE ONLY UNDERCLASSMEN" was the last thing I heard as I got the heck outta there.

MONDAY, SEPTEMBER 23

The first day of conditioning goes well. Our team is basically a group of veterans, with most of us having gone through this program from two to four years. With only one newcomer this season, freshman Nick Bradford, getting in shape takes on a different dimension.

The biggest change has come in the attitude of Coach Williams. He knows he can trust us to work hard, and he's showing that trust in his approach to conditioning. The conditioning program has been revised this season to reflect that trust. Gone are the old fashioned running-to-get-in-shape workouts. We all were supposed to report to school in shape, and Coach had us perform a 12-minute run the first week of September. All the guys made it easily.

The new workout designed to sharpen basketball skills by Al Vermeil, strength and conditioning coach of the Chicago Bulls. It's considered cutting-edge material in the sports world.

Some of the highlights:

> Jumping over cones quickly
> Jumping with a medicine ball
> Medicine ball passing and passing against the wall
> Slides in the lane and other agility drills

The team moved through the various stations quickly, exhaustion and excitement present in equal proportion. I gathered the team around for a huddle at center court.

"Look, guys, it's our responsibility to stay in shape. This is our year! Let's do it!"

"Yeah, let's do it," they responded. The team broke the huddle and the first workout was over.

This was a great workout. It is day one of the journey, and I'm eager. Tonight I went to dinner with Raef LaFrentz, the 7-foot junior center from Monona, Iowa. Raef has been blessed with a ton of talent, and this is the year he will surprise many people by demonstrating just how good he can be. I honestly believe he will emerge this season as one of the premier players in America.

He is confident in his ability, but not to the point of being cocky.

Raef is one of the most straightforward people I know, and will tell you exactly what he thinks. He is outgoing, good natured and loves to have fun. He also has a tendency at times to be too open, and I've been telling him to use a little more judgement before he speaks to people.

Tonight we talked about the coming season, and our plans and dreams for the future. Raef is expected to play a major role in the success of the team this year. He has spent the summer training extremely hard and is ready.

I thought about how I seemed to be an adviser to some of the younger guys. It was not difficult with Raef, because in some ways he and I are the same. We have the same beliefs about many issues regarding basketball, we both hold Coach Williams in high regard as a hard-working and honest individual, and we are both "small town boys". I believe that he is as tied to Monona as I am to Tahoe. We both come from large families and are close to them. And we both have the same dreams for the future, an NCAA title and then the NBA. It was one of those times when I felt the heavy responsibility of being a senior and helping lead this team. I felt honored to be in that position.

TUESDAY, SEPTEMBER 24

I've been doing some more thinking about Coach Williams and the changes I notice in him this season. Actually, there aren't that many, and maybe the differences are more in my perception rather than in Coach himself.

Coach once told me that there are times when he wishes he were still an assistant instead of the head man. This feeling isn't from the pressure of the job, rather from the desire to be at home with his family a bit more. He'd also like to be with the guys in a more relaxed state than he is as the top coach. Coach Williams doesn't like all the traveling he has to do, and he's not a fan of interviews. He'll do them and he'll be cordial, but if he had his choice, they are one part of the job he could do without.

I think I know Coach about as well as anyone. We respect one another and if there's a line drawn in our relationship, it's been drawn by me and not by him. I know how busy he is and I don't want to impose upon his time. But I think he cares about me and how I'm doing, not just in basketball but in school and my personal life.

I remember when I first came to Kansas on the recruiting trip. I was preparing to sign the letter of intent and Coach noticed that someone had misspelled my name (not an unusual thing, believe me). He was irritated by the fact that my first name had been misspelled. He told me, "I'm sorry, we'll correct that right away." Then he noticed that on the second page of the document, my LAST name was spelled incorrectly. This really upset him and he told me, "Don't sign anything. We'll mail you the correct form. I don't want you to have to sign something that isn't right for you." He then went into another room and talked to the secretary who had typed the forms. To put it mildly, she was chewed out by Coach right then. I felt terrible and thought she would hate me forever. To me, this was something I had gotten used to, as I have a somewhat unusual name. But to Coach Williams, this was an inexcusable insult and he wanted me to feel as though I was wanted as an individual and not someone added to a program to fill a vacancy.

Coach has a saying that he tells all new recruits: He doesn't intend to treat everyone equally, but he will treat each person fairly. This is something I learned my first year at Kansas. Someone might be taking it easy at practice and Coach would come down on him hard for not putting out enough effort. However, in my case, Coach would just give me a look and I'd start to go harder.

On the surface, this might seem to be preferential treatment for me. But we all understand that Coach tailors his methods to our personalities. I respond to things differently from Scot Pollard, and he is different from Raef. Each of us is unique and Coach treats us as individuals. He will not single out one person, and he won't expect us all to follow rules in the same manner. He knows we all have our own methods of responding to his criticism and his leadership. I think that where he excels is in his ability to reach each of us and motivate us, yet not follow some rote blueprint that is never altered. He adjusts to the situation. That is an asset as a leader as well as a coach.

This year Coach is adjusting again. He knows that the seniors on this team are capable of assuming responsibility and he is willing to give us more flexibility. There is a structure and there are rules, but we are allowed room to move within that framework. We know he expects us to do certain things his way, and we accept that. He is the coach. We are the players. There is never a time when we think differently.

I am happy to be in this situation. I like the fact that I'm treated as an adult and not as a high school kid. I think that only a person secure in himself would allow their players to have this kind of freedom, knowing all the while they will never go too far. We have a unique arrangement at KU. It's a tribute to Coach Williams that it works so successfully.

THURSDAY, SEPTEMBER 26

The seniors on the team have responsibilities that are not known to the general public. It's always assumed that the seniors are leaders in terms of court savvy and game experience. But there are other areas in which we can lead, and at Kansas it is in the area of discipline.

Team rules are set by the seniors. The coaching staff will review the choices, but in general they abide by what the players want. Considering the fact that the seniors are not high school kids but rather 22 and 23-year-old men, the rules we choose to implement will be those that govern our conduct all year long.

I am one of the four seniors who will decide on the rules for the season, and I feel there isn't a need for a long list of regulations. After all, most of us have been together a while, we know each other, and we know what's at stake this season. With that in mind, we set the following rules:

1) No public drinking will be allowed during the season.
2) Curfew will be at 1 a.m. two nights before a game, and at midnight the night before a game.
3) We will wear a sports coat and slacks when we travel commercially. The same attire holds for all pregame meals and when we go to a game. Coach has added a few points to this. Sports coat and tie are to be worn to dinner. If we are in a private room we can take the coat off. Otherwise the coat remains on. We travel to and from games dressed for success.

There is a simple philosophy that Coach follows and I agree with: If you act first class, you will be first class. It carries over to all we do, on and off the floor. We are expected to be courteous and respectful to everyone, although that has never been a problem since I've been here. We represent the university and we are a reflection upon one another. I think everyone realizes that the team is judged by what we do in public and one bad incident will give everyone a bad image.

That's the extent of the rules. All are expected to comply and are monitored by fellow players Coaches may occasionally check with a phone call, but that seldom happens.

I have been at Kansas for three seasons and have yet to see anyone disciplined for violating the rules. I've never even seen or heard of anyone violating the rules. We usually don't test them because we all agreed on these things before they were submitted. If anyone did violate the rules, they would be dealt with fairly by the coaches, but it's not a concern with this team. We have too much to accomplish.

WEDNESDAY, OCTOBER 2

Today I felt like being analytical. It's not a mood I often get into, but every once in awhile I just sit and think about things. Today, it started with someone's comment about the schedule and being a senior. The season is drawing closer and there is a sense of finality to it all. It has struck me that this is the year all of my goals regarding basketball may be realized. At the same time, there will be no more games for me as an amateur after next April.

At this time of year, some people tend to become reflective. Introspection and nostalgia in autumn are not uncommon phenomena. There are many songs in which the singer is looking back at his life in the autumn, the later stages of the year or metaphorically, of life itself. I've reached this point in my basketball career. I hope it will continue to prosper in the "golden years". For now, however, I have reached that point as an amateur. The curtain is about to rise on Jerod Haase as a Kansas Jayhawk for a final time.

I started to think about the nature of the sport of basketball. Why have I spent hours, years, shooting that round ball into a hoop? Practicing dribbling, playing in the snow, rain and in any gym that was open? Why do I like it so much? Maybe because the game is continuous, a team game that requires every element inherent in the word "athletics". It involves fine motor skills and athletic ability, stamina and conditioning, knowledge and intelligence. It provides the ultimate competition in sports.

I like basketball because I can be creative. I know that every coach hates to hear this, but I like making the great play, the spectacular play, diving for the ball and saving it. I like making the incredible pass or the impossible shot. The floor is where I can express myself. Some people express themselves by rebelling, some by artistic talent, but my expression is done with a basketball.

Allen Fieldhouse, the best place to play or watch college basketball.
Photo by KU Sports Information.

Some people are rebellious with haircuts, drinking, driving like maniacs or alcohol. The rebellious side of my nature comes out on the court. I can be wild and loud, rough and aggressive, an unusual basketball player, and I like that sense of uniqueness.

It's a cool but sunny autumn day, and I took a walk around the campus. Looking over the rolling hills, the changing leaves and the comfortable setting of the University, I felt a sense of warmth and serenity. In its own way, Lawrence has become a second home, not the formative place that South Lake Tahoe had been, but a place where I've been allowed the freedom and support to grow and mature. I stopped at the entrance to Allen Fieldhouse.

A few months earlier, there had been another walk and another time to gaze at the venerable structure. Then, it was to gain motivation to work for the coming year. Now, the work was completed and the building was sending off other signals. Flashbacks......

I remembered the first time I saw this fieldhouse. I was on a recruiting trip. I went to the second level and was in awe. I remember the banners for national championships, final fours, and retired numbers. The ancient look of the interior, with bleachers and not chairs. The sign that sits atop the bleachers, near the fieldhouse windows, which says "Beware of the Phog"....it still gives me chills.

There is a word for this place: tradition.

Scot Pollard once said that Allen Fieldhouse has "original air. We breathe what Wilt breathed." It's so true. This is the kind of place where basketball should be played. I know that today, players want expensive new arenas, huge, clean, modern. But I'm old-fashioned. This is where the game was meant to be played. This is the place that reaches to the roots of basketball. This is the real game.

I kept on walking, looking around and appreciating it all. The sun cast the glowing look of October upon the landscape. It's autumn. It's great.

SATURDAY, OCTOBER 5

The final few weekends without basketball are here. People wonder what members of the University of Kansas team do at this time of year. Many would think that we attend the football games, parties, drive to Kansas City and go to the hot spots. Of course, some of the guys do, but not nearly as much as you would think. It's rare to find us at big parties. A few of the guys are pledging fraternities, but the rest of us don't get into that.

On this day, most of the team got together in my apartment for an evening of....not much. There were card games, dominos, football on TV, music blaring from the CD player, pizza and other food. That's it. Just a bunch of guys in their early twenties, sitting around and talking like friends do. One of the last times we will gather and discuss everything but basketball. No talk of coaches, no worries about what went wrong or what worked well, no anticipation of the next game. Just hanging out.

It's unique but not extraordinary. Many schools may have this camaraderie among their teams. But in an age where people are constantly told about scandals involving money, drugs and athletes battering their girlfriends, an evening like this is a refreshing reminder that good clean fun still exists on college campuses. It's not the sport that brings out the bad side of young men. The environment we are in can have a lot to do with it. Kansas is a great place to play and to go to school.

When players are recruited to KU, the coaches allow team members to evaluate the character of the individual. Recruits spend their time eating, visiting and touring the campus and town with the guys with whom they eventually will be playing. After a weekend of seeing the new recruit in action, seniors are asked their impressions. If the new prospect passes muster, he is moved up the ladder to a position where he is more than likely going to be offered a scholarship. The talent is evaluated by the coaches. The personality and character are seriously evaluated and the players will be allowed to state any objections. For the most part, any recruit has already been deemed a positive addition, or the coaches would not waste their time bringing him to Kansas.

This system seems to guarantee that those who become members of the Jayhawk basketball program are more or less joining an extended family. The fact that graduated players come back in the summer, as Rex Walters and Kevin Pritchard have done this past year, demonstrates the bond that unites past and present Kansas players. We realize that the guys who make the team are people with whom we will live for most of the next four years. We are aware that what occurs with one will be a reflection upon all. The reputation of the entire program and those who have been a part of it can be ruined by one careless individual.

WEDNESDAY, OCTOBER 9
It's the last day for conditioning without the coaches. Coach Williams and his staff have gone to South Carolina on business and the team has been going through our workouts without any supervision from the staff. To be sure, the weight coach is present, but no basketball personnel are present. This is a sign of trust on the part of Coach, trust in the leadership of his seniors, and the rest of his team.

Workouts have continued as if the coaches were there. The length and difficulty of the conditioning program has increased as the days have passed, and our work ethic has been tested. But in spite of the temptation to slack off, the team has continued to work hard. I was pleasantly surprised at this development. I know how much the guys are dedicated to this season, but things are happening that I have never seen since I have been here. We played games today after an hour of conditioning. I have never seen a team do this. The games were great, and it shows how much the team really cares and is willing to make sacrifices. Nobody took the easy way out. We played as intensely as we always do, and I think a large part of that is the leadership we seniors have demonstrated. The young guys would feel pretty dumb leaving while everyone is working and doing such a great job.

The seniors, as in most programs, are the key to success. With myself, Jacque Vaughn, Scot Pollard and B.J. Williams, Coach Williams has four stable, solid building blocks. All of us have been with Coach for four years, and we know what is expected of us. We realize what it takes to get to the Final Four, having been so close twice in our careers.

I feel that my job is to lead by example. If I works hard, and the other guys notice this, then they will know what it takes to achieve the team goals. This is nothing new. Three years earlier, Scot Pollard told a Lawrence newspaper that "Jerod is the hardest working person I have ever been with on a team. If you want to see the definition of effort and what it takes to make yourself a good player, look at him." That's good to hear, but Scot is no slouch himself when it comes to practice. I'm glad he is on my side whenever we take the floor.

Jacque is still out with the injury, but he attends the workouts as an observer and joins in the social activities we've had the past few weeks. The team does not dwell on his situation, but includes him as if he were healthy. It is not something we want to get hung up on, although everyone is anxious to see how it will be playing without such an integral part of the team. He is another senior who leads by example. Considering the fact that he turned down a chance to enter the NBA, and is now enduring this injury, he is in relatively good spirits. Again, it is a sign to the younger players of how much he wants to end his career at the top of college basketball.

It's become clear that JV and I are the leaders of this team. Many sports magazines have written that we are considered the top guard tandem in the country. Both of us do well in the classroom, as well as on the court. I honestly believe the Kansas Jayhawks are a team that works together. We both try to make sure it stays that way.

I was pleased with today's events. This team really cares. We're headed in the right direction. At this point, there is definitely a reason to feel optimistic. The year is following the same course as my senior year in high school. Another title could be down the road. All it will take is a lot of hard work.

SATURDAY, OCTOBER 12

The phone rang, and when I answered, it was someone from Sports Illustrated calling. Generally, magazine and newspaper writers will meet with team members on media day, which is scheduled in about a week. But this was the premier sports magazine, and they wanted to ask a few questions concerning the outlook for KU, especially in light of the injury to Jacque. The questions concerned my shooting, comparing last season with the prospects for this one, and how we were adjusting to life without Jacque. Nothing really penetrating, and now the only question was how would it appear in print.

When a request comes for an interview, it usually is done through the Sports Information Director, an office that is present on most, if not all, college campuses. At Kansas, the SID will contact the desired player and inform them about the interview. The player then has the option of giving the interview or declining. All time with the media is handled in this fashion.

The media has always been friendly to me. Back home in Tahoe, the local papers helped promote my career, from the nickname "J-Man" to the updates from KU, to the special coverage of Kansas games on the local cable channel. I really don't mind talking to reporters or media people. I'll sit and answer anything they want to ask, within reason, and know that it is part of the territory. Even after heartbreaking games such as last year's Syracuse debacle, I still knew I had to talk with reporters. People want to know things about us, and it's their job to find out.. Besides, as I have said before, the day will come when nobody wants to talk with me, so I might as well enjoy this now.

I don't think there will be anything to worry about in this story. When it 's written, I'll deal with it. For now, my time was going to be occupied with a new recruit. I'll spend the rest of the day showing the new prospect around the campus, taking him to lunch and playing tour guide. I remember when I first came here, how I must have looked. I try to see it in their eyes as well.

SUNDAY, OCTOBER 13

People ask me how I can accomplish the requirements of school, practice and the other things I do (like speaking before groups or having any kind of social life) within the normal hours of a day. Some may think think we get special privileges as athletes, such as skipping class without penalty. That's not at all true. The secret is good time management.

I'm a big believer that you can accomplish anything you desire. You simply have to be willing to put in the hard work and the time required to become successful. Nothing comes easily, especially if it has value. I have always had to work at the things I do, whether it was basketball or school, but I knew that if I worked hard and kept at it, good things would happen.

I didn't spend as many hours at homework as you might think, considering my grades. I don't like to talk about my personal grades, but without trying to sound conceited, I only received one B grade in school. (That was from my mother!) Otherwise, I was a straight-A student in grade and high school.

That didn't mean I was some kind of study freak, spending hour after hour reading book upon book. I learned that if you listen in class and pay attention, you only need to review material at home after class. I'm not saying you can omit homework as unnecessary. I'm saying that homework is much easier and less time is involved if you have already heard the information. You understand what you are doing and can complete the tasks in less time. Teachers explain things in class. If you listen, you will comprehend.

It's not always easy paying attention in class. Any student will tell you that. It requires self-discipline and a desire to improve yourself. That means work. It was the same in basketball. I would spend hours shooting, working on my ballhandling, just trying to understand the game. Of course, it was easier since I was good at it, but I would have remained merely average if I had not been willing to put in the extra time.

Setting goals is another thing in which I believe. I was thinking today about goals for the coming season. I have always been a methodical person, writing the next day's schedule the night before, checking it as I get up the following morning, and adding details as the day goes on. Setting goals for a season is just one more task.

This year the job is more difficult. I am determined to have my season end just as the final year of high school had ended: with a title. I also want to be a leader, by example and later (hopefully) by words. Of course, I want to have fun this season, and not having any specific numeric goals will help because that means I won't concentrate on reaching mere targets. Relax, play hard, be aggressive, and have fun.

The only specific goal is the ultimate one. Winning the national championship. Anything less than that will not be good enough. I am determined to be the best. The team is determined. Will our focus be enough?

MONDAY, OCTOBER 14
The final conditioning test has been posted. It's going to be brutal. Check this out:

> A free-throw line sprint, then back pedal
> Free-throw line sideways run
> Cone jumps
> Backboard touch, then slide and repeat
> Suicide run (in 26 seconds)
> 500-yard run in 90 seconds

The entire drill is repeated once, with a one-minute break between each segment. In addition, there are 12 stations where each activity is performed, and players spent 30 seconds at each. There is a designated score that must be achieved by each player. One score would be called the "tough" time, and another would simply be noted as the "assigned "time. In the end, three players completed the program in the "tough" time: Myself, BJ Williams, and CB. Everyone else made the assigned time. Conditioning seemed to be on track.

That evening, the team gathered for dinner and some serious talk. To stress the seriousness, Coach Williams had everyone wear coat and tie. Then he told us some of his views. Coach stressed the fact that nobody should look back at this year and say, "What if?" He read motivational material and talked about things we had all heard before..hard work, perseverance, goals. This is a veteran team, and we know what we are doing. Coach knows this. It's his way of reminding us.

Coach Williams is someone the guys respect immensely. I know that players always say nice things about their coach when asked by the media, but if you bring up the subject with any of the guys, at any time, the answer will be the same. The man is held in high regard by all his players.

There are two reasons for this. Roy Williams is hard-working and honest. He has taken a program that was on probation nine years ago and turned it into a first-class operation. His office door is always open, and that's not a cliche. He will sit down with any of us and listen to our problems. Not only as a basketball player, but as a person. Not because he has a scholarship invested in us, but because he cares about us as people. We all know this and I think that helps make the team spirit such a positive thing. We get our unity and our strength from what we see emanating from the top. We defend one another because we know that Coach is behind all of us. We believe in ourselves because he believes in us.

I know he has faith in me. He gambled on me when I wanted to transfer here from Cal. He gave me the chance to prove myself and made me believe in my ability, even when I was beginning to have doubts about myself. After the Syracuse game last year, he made me realize that in spite of my poor shooting performance I was still someone he knew would bounce back. He never made me feel that I could not achieve my goals, and has supported all my efforts. I think we are both the same type of people: hard-working, with a passion for competition and, of course, for winning.

He is as honest as anyone I have ever met. He will not tolerate tampering from anyone outside the program. Agents are forbidden from contacting any of us, and if they ever somehow make it through Coach's barriers, that person is barred from anything associated with Kansas basketball. He has told all of us that if this person would try to skirt the rules now, what do we think will happen in a major situation? He makes sure we go to class, that we do our own work, that we are aware of all the NCAA regulations and that we know to come to him if there are any questions about any issue. He won't put up with people who are less than forthright. He wants a clean program and believes that success will follow if you do things the right way. I'm a believer in the same things.

The dinner ended and the team headed over to practice for our LateNight performance. We had one final chance to learn the dialogue and the dances we will be performing. Tomorrow is the day the real season begins, the first official day of practice. It's time. I'm ready.

TUESDAY, OCTOBER 15

The alarm didn't even go off and I was already out of bed. Something hummed in the air, a sense that this was a special day. I could feel it and it made me excited. I jumped in the shower, got dressed, ate a quick bowl of cereal and rushed out the door. Getting to class seemed something that had to be done, but also gotten over with.

Sitting in the class, I could feel my mind wandering. All my thoughts were centered on the same place, the floor of Allen Fieldhouse. Normally, I have no trouble concentrating on class, but today was different. It was the next step in the journey, and it was almost too much pressure to wait for 3 o'clock to arrive.

Finally, the time had come. Crossing the campus, I entered the side door of the fieldhouse. I walked across the indoor track, and stopped to gaze at the ancient walls. Heading down the hallway, I stopped at the door, put in the correct code and the security lock opened. I walked inside and just stood still for a second. Here it is, I thought. The room was filled with memories, and many of them came flooding back to me. I remembered sitting here as a redshirt player, listening for the first time to the pregame talk, mentally comparing it to what I'd heard at Cal. I recalled the nervous anticipation before my first game at Kansas, getting ready to run out on the floor for the home opener in 1995. That feeling never left. Every game was, and is, a special occasion.

I gazed around the room, at the chairs, white vinyl cushioned, painted blue with the name of that particular player stenciled on the back. I noticed the lockers, wood-grained with a gold nameplate on the front. In one corner of the room, built into a wood-grained wall cabinet which curved out into the room, was a television and VCR, which would be used to show film demonstrating how to dissect an opponent's defense. Also in this athletic version of an entertainment center, was a receiver/CD player, for those times when we simply wanted music in the background. I looked at the Jayhawk painted on the center of the floor. It was as if the past season had never ended.

I walked through into the next room, which contains a whirlpool and tables for getting taped or a massage. Off to the right are the showers, which have the look of the original fieldhouse, with yellow tile that has been here since the 1950's. One unique feature about the shower room is the height of the shower head. It's 9 feet from the floor, not the standard height. It sure makes it easier for Raef and Scot to take a shower here than in their apartments, where the bathroom ceiling is only 7 feet high.

Moving to my locker, I opened it and started to dress for practice. Others arrived, and soon the place was alive with the sounds of the guys talking, laughing and reassuming our positions as the select few who represent the University and the state of Kansas in college basketball.

We moved to the floor and began dynamic stretching drills. They consist of working on running form, jogging, balance beam simulations, quick-feet drills and medicine ball timed throws. It lasts about 20 minutes and really gets a player loosened up and ready to play. I was feeling great.

Drills followed, but they were shorter than in past years. I realized that Coach Williams was aware of the veteran nature of this team and so had readjusted his practices to reflect that fact. Practices were going to be shorter, but harder. We would be pushed to accomplish the basics in less time, since most of us already knew what those were. By the end of practice, which concluded with more stretching, I felt as if my life were back to normal. It was good to be playing basketball for real again.

WEDNESDAY, OCTOBER 16

It's never easy to assess those with whom you work. Nonetheless, I thought that this would be a good time to privately evaluate the rest of the team as the season is about to begin. What follows are my candid thoughts regarding Kansas basketball, pre-1997 season.

On the whole, this is a good team that could be a great team. Jacque is a great player, Paul is the best athlete, and Raef could be the most talented basketball player of all. Scot is tough and talented, more than anyone in the media thinks. Ryan has matured physically and is ready to play. BJ Williams and TJ Pugh are question marks, with lots of potential. Billy Thomas seems to have a new, more aggressive attitude. And CB will give us quality minutes backing up either Ryan or Jacque. At this point, I can't evaluate Nick, since he is the lone new freshman, but I'm sure he'll contribute much to the team.

I'm doing this evaluation with the idea that there will be changes down the road. But it will be interesting to see how this team evolves, and what the final outcome will be. I'm also curious about the sports magazines assessments. Which will be the most accurate?

FRIDAY, OCTOBER 18

LateNight at Kansas University. A season-opening tradition that has become an entertainment extravaganza. Many schools have taken the original idea of practicing at midnight on the first day basketball is allowed by the NCAA and altered it to fit their current student body. High schools have also adopted the concept and held practices at this strange time as a way to build team unity and school spirit. At Kansas, we have turned it into a show.

The theme this year is "Star Search '96". All sports are represented during the festivities, but at this school, at this time, basketball is center stage. I'm not trying to sound conceited, but I really think that's appropriate this year. The players are involved in skits, other students act as supporting players, directors, writers and choreographers. It is a major event, and Allen Fieldhouse is filled to capacity.

The night opens with a volleyball game, followed by cheers and an all-sports rally. Every sport is given its moment. Then the stage is turned over to the basketball program. The team runs out to a thunderous ovation and a banner is dropped signifying the conference championship we won last season. It is all the more poignant because it will be the final Big 8 title, since the conference has now expanded and will be called the Big 12.

The show begins. First there is a commercial. Jacque and I play roles as customers for an insurance agency. (No surprise here, they had me dive for a loose piece of paper.) There were other mock commercials and all of these were hilarious. Next, the senior players did a dance, followed by the entire team forming a circle, with each player taking turns in the center of the circle. I am not a dancer, but I decided to do a break-dance in the center of the gym, to the amazement and (I felt) delight of the fans. It might have been the highlight of the night, but then comes the showstopper.

Just before we were going to leave the floor, Scot Pollard proposes marriage to his girlfriend, Mindy Camp. The crowd goes wild again. It is a complete surprise to everyone on the team.

Following this, we go back to the locker room, change into game uniforms, and play two halves of basketball games, with a nonstop running clock. The fans got their first look at the Jayhawks of 1997, and the evening concludes.

I love this night. Friends from back home in Tahoe have come to see me in this final LateNight event, and this buoys my spirits even more. Along with the excitement of the night, the fact that there is someone from home seeing all this makes it even more special. It makes me realize that this has been the best season- opening practice of all.

MONDAY, OCTOBER 21
We've had several days of serious work. Now that the season has begun in earnest, Coach Williams is running us through some hard practices. There has been a rash of minor injuries, from Nick Bradford, who suffered a broken nose, to CB McGrath, who has the most serious, a knee injury that will require his knee to be scoped. He will be out of action for about two weeks.

We all go as hard as we can in practice. Coach is the type of person who gets annoyed at players who try to avoid doing the little things. For example, he will be far more upset if we don't touch the end-lines during sprints up and down the court than if we miss four shots in a row during a scrimmage. You can have an off-day shooting but you better not try to get off easy during the drills. There is no place for slackers at Kansas.

Coach will vary the routine of practice as the season progresses. He doesn't want us to dread workouts, so he'll switch from running defense-oriented drills to simple run-and-shoot sessions, where the atmosphere is not quite as serious. It helps break the monotony that could set in during the long season, and it keeps us from being able to predict what we'll be doing on any given day. I know that many players reach a point where practice is something they try not to think about, but I think most of the guys here don't feel that way.

Another thing we don't do compared to other programs is watch film. There are teams that spend a lot of time looking at films of their opponents' tendencies, offensive scheme and defensive strategies. We don't. Coach Williams believes that if we play our game well, it's the job of our opponents to stop us. Our style will take care of us, on both ends of the court. We don't need to know what they might do. Our defense will be fine if we do our job correctly.

The assistant coaches have a great deal of input at practice. Each of these people is unique in his own way. Coach Matt Doherty is the

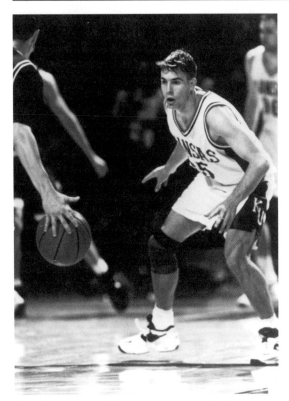

Playing tough defense is one of the key components to our success at Kansas. Photo by KU Sports Information.

one who has made us repeat a play as many as 17 times because he feels that if we can master it to perfection, and anticipate anything our opponents may try against us, we will be successful. He's right, and we need that focused approach as one part of our practice structure.

Coach Neil Daugherty is a more technical member of the staff. I don't think I've ever met anyone with his intricate knowledge of the game. If I need work on a fine point of defense or my ball-handling skills, he's the one I ask for advice. He's been a big help to everyone who plays the guard position as well as other positions. While not as vocal at practice as the others, Coach Daugherty is always watching, trying to spot areas where improvement is needed and offering suggestions.

Coach Joe Holloday is the free thinker of the group. He is more likely to offer ideas that deviate from what we are currently trying, looking for a new way of doing things. He has the attitude that if something isn't working correctly, try a different approach.

Among the three assistants there is a balance that I believe Coach Williams desires. He can coordinate activities, combine the attributes of his staff, pick their brains for ideas and produce a successful team. This has been the case during his entire time at Kansas.

I like coaches that have set basketball principles and a solid philosophy. I think that our program is founded with a belief that playing good fundamental basketball, doing the little things the right way and working hard will achieve success. We take pride in our defense and help one another. We play unselfishly on offense which produces balanced scoring. In turn, that makes it hard for other teams to defend against us. They won't know who to try to contain, because it won't be one person. It will be all of us. We will be tough to beat this year if we can all stay healthy.

Injuries are a part of sports, but they can still be discouraging. At no time have we had 10 players for scrimmage. Tryouts for the walk-on players (those without scholarships) are still continuing, so the team must simply go through individual drills, 3-on-3 and half-court practices until the rest of the guys heal.

I notice that my right knee is also beginning to swell up after practices. While it doesn't hurt during the workouts, near the end of each session, it begins to bother me. After any period of extended sitting during the practice, it is harder to get flexible. The knee is building up fluid, and I think it may have to be drained.

I'm a little worried. This is not what I need or want so early in the season. It's too important a season to be ruined by an injury. The thought of sitting out most of the year is almost too much to bear. I don't even want to think about it because all it would do is depress me. I think I'd rather concentrate on how to heal quickly.

Another way the visits to the sports shrink have helped me.

WEDNESDAY, OCTOBER 23

Some of the sports magazines have arrived on the newsstands with their college basketball preseason issues. They have the Jayhawks ranked anywhere from number one to number four. The main thrust of their articles is that we are a team that has veterans, talent and depth but our shooting is suspect. The focus of the doubts about outside scoring seems to be me.

After my sophomore season, people wrote that I was considered one of the premier three-point shooters in the nation. I had two fairly successful seasons behind me. However, last year had been "nightmarish" (in the words of one magazine, Street & Smith, and also in my own mind) and my stock has slipped among the sportswriters. In some magazines I was considered a questionable starter, in others I became someone who was listed as a "former dependable shooter" who needed to come back if this team is to reach the Final Four.

The magazines are sometimes harsh on our team. Most dwell on the fact that last year we were defeated by a team that played zone defense, and they repeat the conventional wisdom that, although we run the floor well, our outside shooting is "weak". This is particularly surprising since they still rank Kansas in the Top Five. I think it may also be a symptom of what I believe generally happens in the press, the "pack" mentality. If it becomes fashionable to promote a certain team and bash another, then that is what will happen until the record proves this to be unwise. Until we beat a highly ranked team with an outside shooting barrage, the harping about our three-point shooting is going to continue.

This stuff motivates me. It is much easier to prove people wrong than to live up to their expectations. The only expectations that matter are my own. I think that I am going to have a great time showing these people that they are wrong. They don't realize all the work I have done this past year to get ready for this season. I love the fact that these people think I have lost it, because I know that I haven't.

THURSDAY, OCTOBER 24
Sometimes, I need a diversion in my routine. One thing that people don't realize is how much of a regimented life-style we lead as basketball players. I know that to some, it must seem as if we have all this time to run around and party, especially now, before the actual games have begun. The reality is different.

We have to go to class, we have to be ready for practice, we have to eat with the team at certain times, and Coach can call a meeting at any moment. It means that we must put school, basketball and then free time in that order.

Some of the guys are television junkies. I think most of us watch sports on the tube, but guys also have favorite shows. (You'd be surprised how many watch the soaps.) Some of us are movie fanatics. I have been known to spend an entire day vegging out, watching movies. I have gone through phases and currently enjoy dramas. (Someday, I'll build a movie library with my favorite titles, but for now I'm just a renter. I only own three videos.)

Tonight, I felt like going out and JV suggested the riverboats. Some people may immediately conclude that we are a couple of compulsive gamblers. That's not the case. I grew up within two miles of three large, popular casinos back in Tahoe, and the lure of those places has never been strong for me. I will go and play blackjack, but that's about the extent of my experience in the casinos. Some of the games don't interest me, and others I feel are either too complicated or depend too much on sheer luck. Either way, I don't have the money a person needs to be a regular at the casinos. People who always go there need to learn how to lose. I hate to lose at anything.

Jacque likes the boats. He enjoys the games, but mostly is a blackjack player. There are other games he'll try, but he also can't stand to lose. We both go more because it's a night away from the routine than for the gambling. We spend time watching the people, enjoying the atmosphere and forgetting about things for a while. We are the only two seniors who are free. BJ is married and now Scot is engaged. In a way, this is a senior thing. I think I've gotten to know JV better this year through doing things like this. He's a unique individual.

MONDAY, OCTOBER 28
Anyone who thinks playing college sports is easy should have attended our practice sessions today. Intensity was everywhere, and it started at the top. Coach Williams put us through the toughest practice of the season so far.

The day began with our usual practice warm-up, but then things became anything but typical. There was a defensive shell drill, followed by a scrimmage which lasted nearly two hours. This included three 30-minute scrimmages, followed by a 20-minute session. Lineups were switched each time, and we were encouraged to play as if this were the real thing. Big 12 Conference referees were present to add even more reality to the proceedings. Coach Williams was not especially pleased with how we executed our offense, but was satisfied with our overall effort.

When it was over, I was exhausted. I felt that I had left it all out on the floor. It was drained and went over to the scales to check my weight. Looking at the dial, I couldn't believe my eyes. I had lost 10 pounds! I decided that I 'd better get something to eat quick. Going back to the apartment, I fixed a snack and then thought about the days' events.

I felt that I played under control at all times and made some good plays, some solid "basketball" plays. I was running the offense well, being more selective in my choice of shots, and working the ball inside to our big men, Raef and Scot, as Coach wants. Looking at the whole picture, I felt satisfied that I had laid a good foundation upon which to build for the year. If I play like this and improve upon today's performance, I should be in top shape by the time December rolls around. I added this to my list of goals.

There is an exam in two days, and I needed the study time. But I couldn't concentrate or focus enough to read anything, so I decided that studying would have to wait until tomorrow. There was only one thing I felt like doing. Sleep.

WEDNESDAY, OCTOBER 30

From time to time, a moment arrives when a person feels as if "life is good" to paraphrase a currently popular commercial. For me, one of those moments arrived today. Here's how it happened:

I had been cleaning the apartment and put on some music to help make the work more enjoyable. My musical taste runs the gamut from hard rock (AC/DC and Guns N' Roses) to pop (Mellencamp/ Chicago) to New Age (George Winston). It was Winston today. Last year, I bought four of his CD's. It relaxes me, and I get a comfortable feeling listening to him. His music is what inspired me to try to learn piano. Listening and continuing to work, I felt my mind start to wander and I let myself follow those thoughts.

I sat and gazed around the apartment, looking at the furniture and pictures on the wall. There was a special favorite of mine on the wall farthest from the door that caught my eye. It is a wonderful painting of a young man sitting on the lawn,looking with reverence at Allen Fieldhouse.The boy in the picture can't be more than 10, but the thoughts running through his head are something I am feeling right now.

I feel a wave of emotion running through my body. I am carried by the feeling back home to Tahoe, to people I have known all my life. Scott, Coach Orlich, Christi, my Mom and Dad, my brothers and sisters, all are present in this daydream. The faces of the people I have shared my life with, the times that were the best of all. I want to reach out and thank all of them, tell them how much they have meant to me. I have become the little boy in the photo, dreaming of the opportunities that await, but wishing to take those who mean so much to me along for the trip as I chase my dreams.

The feeling persists, and now it is moving to a gym, not one but two basketball floors, interwoven and yet distinct in their own ways. Now I am thinking of the games at South Tahoe High School, with the cheerleaders decked out in blue and gold, the fans screaming my name, the friends in the stands yelling words of support and encouragement. Then those faces dissolve into a sea of blue, red and white, and instead of a Viking, a funny little bird with a yellow beak is sitting on the sideline. The players on the team are older, taller and stronger. The pace of the game quickens, and the roar from the crowd is louder, almost deafening. The action suddenly stops. I look around to see other people, friends from all over the country. Mike Sykes, my first roommate at Kansas, Coach Wulbrun, CB...all are now here, replacing the folks from home. And now I feel that same feeling again, the desire to let these people know that they too have a special place in my life. I am thinking of all that has taken place and realize how lucky I've been.

I've achieved more than I could ever have imagined. At this point, at a time when others my age would have been worried about going to a war, when others my own age right now are wondering about jobs, kids, and bills, I have the chance to study and play basketball. To continue to do something that has given me enjoyment and has provided me with experiences that I will never forget. To work and improve myself as a person and as an athlete, and yet provide entertainment to thousands of people. How lucky can anyone be? I have reached the end of my journey, the end of my daydream.

The music stops and the daydream ends. Only a few minutes have passed, and yet it seemed as though it were an hour. The memory lingered for the rest of the day. I felt good about my life. I still want more out of it, but every once in a while I think it's good to sit back and appreciate what has been. To live in the past is not a good practice, but to remember it is a source of comfort and at times, of joy. This was one of those times.

MONDAY, NOVEMBER 4

The sky is cloudy, and the atmosphere on the practice floor is half-hearted. The windows at the top of Allen Fieldhouse are letting the gray sky of early November through, and the tone of the day is apathetic. Maybe it's the time change from daylight savings. Maybe it's the routine of practice, the fact that there is always a drill to run or a play to learn, but no real opposition to challenge the offense. Whatever, it was producing some disturbing tendencies in the Jayhawks.

I was frustrated. I was worried about what I was seeing on the floor. Guys were running the floor, but not with the intensity that was here just a few weeks ago. Some were simply trying to get by with the least amount of work required, stopping before crossing the baseline, jogging down to defend the basket, complaining about the length of time spent on a particular point of emphasis. It was not a sign of a team that was hungry for victory.

I am a senior, one of the leaders on the team. I'd like to think an important leader since I am actually a year older than the others. But what does being a leader mean? It was a question that I dwelt upon as I walked home from practice that night.

Whenever I want to think I take a walk. The fresh air, the activity involved, combine to help me clear my mind of distractions and deal with a problem. Last season when my shooting slump emerged, I think I became a familiar figure to anyone who was looking, a solitary soul trudging across the cold landscape of Kansas in February. Hands in my pocket, eyes focused on nothing in particular, a year later, I was walking again, my mind deep in thought. Tonight, the thoughts were about the dilemma facing me as team leader.

Am I doing a good job? Is leading by example good enough? I consider my own abilities. I think I am more encouraging to my teammates than anybody, but maybe I need to take charge more. To do more than encourage, but speak up about our attitude. Right now I question the leadership on the team, which is the same as questioning my ability as a leader.

I think that the biggest problem facing this team is that it could fall into a trap that has snared many other ballclubs.Whenever a team thinks that it can turn on the talent at will, there is a danger that someday that may not work. We can't rely only on talent to get beat tough opponents. There has to be a preparation that comes only from hard work. I was worried that the team was not remembering this equation.

One of the quotes that Coach Williams uses has always stuck in my mind. "Respect is not inherited, it must be regained every day." From my time at Cal and at KU, I have learned to believe in this statement. The problem is getting the rest of the team to buy into the concept.

I looked up and realized that I had arrived at the Towers. I sat outside on the brick planters and continued to brood. Co-eds walked by, looked at me with a smile, and hurried on. People seemed to realize that I wanted to be alone. Nobody came up to me. Good thing, too, because I was getting frustrated with myself. I couldn't figure out if I was getting too worried, or if this was really as bad as I believed.

I went inside, climbed the stairs to my room, and threw myself on the couch. Staring at the wall, still obsessed with this lack of effort, I decided to call the only other senior I felt could relate to the situation. Picking up the phone, I dialed Jacque's room.

JV answered, and I proceeded to spill out all the frustration I felt. We both agreed that we were disappointed with the tone of the last few practices. It was not only one part of practice, it was everything. Breakdown drills, offense, defense, you name it, the team was not trying to get better. What should we do about it?

Jacque felt that it was not time to panic. Not yet. Maybe we should look for a way to get inside the heads of our teammates, a way to motivate without exaggerating it as an issue. I agreed. I thought that maybe I should open up, yell a bit more and stir things up. Since Jacque was not on the floor, I felt that I was the only one who could actually do something at practice. It might be time to be more vocal.

As we hung up the phones, nothing was resolved . I realized that this was something that I had to figure out. I thought about my relationship with Jacque. We had become closer since the end of last season, especially after Jacque had decided to stay for his senior year. At the time, Jacque had told the media that one of the factors that made him remain was a softball game he played with Ryan and me. The closeness JV felt then and his happiness at being a college student was something he couldn't ever regain, especially if he turned pro. Jacque announced he would stay at Kansas.

I've always felt he made the right decision. The pros will be there. College is a one time experience, an opportunity to live in a place where almost everyone is the same age, yet from different backgrounds. It's the chance of a lifetime to meet different people and get a real look at what they are like. Except maybe in the military, there is no other part of our society where this occurs.

This fall, after the accident that tore the ligaments in his wrist, Jacque and I became aware of the common goal we each had set for ourselves: winning the NCAA. That goal might seem obvious, but the desire to help the team win was more intense than either of us had realized in the other. I discovered that we were different people with a lot in common, including a mutual respect and the desire to lead the team to that title.

The approach to being a leader was one of the differences. Jacque was the kind of leader who would pull people aside and give advice. For example, he had become a tutor for Ryan in how to play point guard. On the other hand, I'm more of an on-court leader, at times yelling encouragement. I feel as if I am the director on the floor. We had become an effective tandem. While we weren't extremely close friends, we were getting to know each other better.

Even so, our newfound dynamics still was not producing results that satisfied me. Being a leader is not all it's cracked up to be. At times, it 's no fun at all.

THURSDAY, NOVEMBER 7

I checked the calendar board posted on the wall of my bedroom. There was a long list of little things that I had to get done, and this was as good a day as any. Coach would probably keep me for an hour, and after that, I would get the rest of the list done.

I had to meet with Coach and assess my progress so far. I felt the meeting would be interesting. I put on my jacket, grabbed my books and bounded down the stairs. As I walked across campus to my first class, I thought about my own situation as a senior. I was now the oldest person on the team, and looking at the students I was passing along the way, I suddenly felt much older. It made me think about the other guys on the team.

Am I out of touch with these guys? I'm trying so hard to make everything perfect. I know this is the last time around for me, but in their eyes the end is not in sight. I have a perfectionist's drive, and maybe that's part of the problem. I'm in a different position from theirs. They know that they can do it again.

When I arrived at the classroom door, I wandered in mechanically. Simply taking a seat and trying to concentrate were problems. Sitting wasn't easy. The class was difficult to follow, and it was a relief when the foghorn rang. Usually, I am able to focus on the lecturer and easily retain material. Today, it was a chore and I wasn't very successful.

(One unusual note about classes at Kansas is that there is actually a foghorn that sounds when a class period ends, generally at 90-minute intervals. This loud moan can be heard across the entire campus.)

I arrived a few minutes early for my meeting with Coach Williams. "Come on in Jerod," Coach said smiling, and he motioned me into a chair seated near his desk. I had started to notice since summer how easy my relationship had become with all the coaches. It was as if I were now on a par with them, and some, like Joe Holladay, I was starting to regard as friends. Not that there was any loss of respect, only a very comfortable attitude between us. I sat and waited for Coach to begin.

"Jerod, there are some things that I want to know," he began. "What do you think about practice this year?"

"What do you mean, Coach?"

"I guess I'm talking about my attitude."

"I like the new approach," I answered. "It's more laid-back, and to tell you the truth, it's better for a team like ours with so many veterans. We know what to do, and what you expect, and it's a sign of how much you trust us."

We both continued in this vein for a while, discussing how to ensure the team remained as fresh at the end of the season as it is now. Then the conversation shifted to my individual performance.

Coach Williams pinpointed one area he wanted me to emphasize. He said he thought my goal should be to become the leading rebounder, for a perimeter player, in the Big 12. He told me that he knew I had been passing up shots to help the team. That I had been passing the ball inside, to get higher percentage shots. The inside game was going to be one of our keys this year. With Scot, Raef and Paul, we had one of the strongest inside games in the nation. We intended to exploit that advantage.

"But I'm concerned about your state of mind, Jerod," Coach

Williams said. "Are you happy with this type of game?"

"Coach, you know me. I'll do whatever it takes to help this team," I replied. "I'm just worried about the team in general right now. We need to pick it up and play hard."

Coach seemed to agree with my feelings about the team's progress. He thanked me for giving him such candid statements and ended our meeting.

I left the office, but kept thinking about what we discussed. I was passing up a lot of shots. It wasn't bothering me too much, but there were times when I felt that I could take the shot and hit it. I had worked so hard this summer to improve my shooting. I felt confident in my ability. But were the coaches feeling the same confidence? Was the emphasis on the inside game a signal that they had lost some faith in me? It made sense to feed the big men, but I sensed that there was more emphasis on this than in the past. Was it due to my poor season last year? Could I change their minds without harming the team? Should I?

That night, I went out to dinner with a friend from the women's basketball team, Angie Halblieb. She had just played an exhibition game and scored 24 points. She felt good about her performance, and the conversation eventually turned to my prospects.

"You're going to have to start shooting more, Jerod, "Angie said. "After all, you are a shooting guard."

"But I want to help the team win, and if being more selective with my shots is what it takes, it's what I want to do," I replied.

"Come on, you know that you put in all that work for a reason. You want to redeem yourself for last year."

I knew she was right. I paused for a second, and then said, "I'm not worried about it right now. Coach wants me to do other things. It will all work out."

Angie looked me in the eye. "Everything with you is a mind game," she said forcefully. "You need to just play ball and stop worrying about everything. The team. The past. Just play ball. You are a good basketball player. Go out and do it."

I agreed. "' That was last year. It did turn into a mind game. I was always worried about what was happening. That's why I went to the sports psychologist. But it's different now. I just want to enjoy my senior season. "

"Jerod, you sound like it still is a mind game," she said wearily. "I hope, for your sake, that you have gotten over it."

"Don't worry," I said, "that's all in the past. This year I'm focused. I'm prepared. No mind games this time."

FRIDAY, NOVEMBER 8
Another sign the season is about to begin took place today. We held the annual session on how to deal with the media. As I've already mentioned, reporters will call to try to arrange interviews directly with players. However, there are always moments after games when reporters converge on the locker room or even as we come off the floor. It's those situations that we are dealing with today.

Coach Williams has always felt that we should conduct our interviews with respect and courtesy for everyone. He holds mock interviews between us and representatives from the media in order for us to learn how to deal with press questions. Everything is videotaped and we are shown replays of how we handled the interview. This is especially important for the freshmen, since it's probably the first time they have dealt with such media scrutiny. If they are too open with what they say, it could cause problems. We don't want bulletin board material for our opponents to come out of our mouths. The new guys need help with how to respond to and handle the press. The rest of us need to be reminded.

After every game, some of us are chosen to do the interviews. Coach will usually select someone and he rotates the process so that all of us have an opportunity for an interview. Most of the guys don't really enjoy it, but I think it's fun. It's another of those things I realize I should do now, because this time is never coming back.

There are ways to make the media session fun. After all the games I've played in two years at Kansas, I have gotten to know most of the reporters on sight. That makes the interview easier, since it can be on a first-name basis. And it allows me the chance to relax and get the other guys to loosen up. One thing I've done in the past is to distract Raef by pulling the hairs on his leg as he's answering a question. He'll try to keep a serious look as long as possible, but eventually he'll lose his composure and start laughing and shoving me.

The other guys are just as bad when I'm up there. They'll make faces or comments to try to shake me from my earnest interview look. Sometimes it works and they love it. Everyone thinks I'm too serious when I'm in the media room.

The reporters seem to like our team. Jacque has always maintained a good rapport with the press, and Ryan is becoming known as "Mr. Glib" for his quick- witted comments. Paul is soft-spoken by nature and has needed more encouragement to go through this, but now handles it well. Of course, Scot is the colorful guy the press loves and Raef has that friendly personality. I'd say we are a pretty easy group to interview, and not all of that comes from the mock interviews we are doing today. It's the way we are.

SATURDAY, NOVEMBER 9

I was shooting before practice and Billy Thomas came by. As soon as I fired up a shot, Billy said, "Donkeyshnure."

"What's that?"

"Nothing. Donkeyshnure."

Billy likes to make up words that have no meaning. He will often put together words to create a new word that no member of the team can figure out right away. Today, he was having fun with my mind.

I was puzzled. "Come on, what's donkeyshnure?" I asked.

"Nothing," Thomas answered. "Just donkeyshnure."

I started to laugh. "Billy, what's donkeyshnure?"

Other guys overheard this and came over to where we were shooting. Ryan thought he'd get involved. "Hey, J-rod, you mean you don't know what donkeyshnure means?" he asked.

"I thought everyone knew what donkeyshnure means," Paul Pierce added.

They all began laughing at me because I'm sure I looked frustrated and puzzled. It was normal for the team to tease me about my lack of a slang vocabulary. I just have never been able to pick up the street language common to so many players, and combined with my notorious lack of dancing ability and rhythm, it made me the perfect target for my teammates' rips.

Billy wasn't finished with me yet. "Jerod, what's the haps on the craps?" he asked.

I started laughing again. I looked at Billy and couldn't figure out what he had said. Finally Jacque came to my aid , sort of. "Jerod, he means ' what's up", Jacque said, sarcastically.

But I still didn't get it. I still looked confused.

Billy and the others were on the floor, doubled up with laughter.

TUESDAY, NOVEMBER 12

I tossed and turned in my sleep. It seemed as if there were someone shaking the pillow all night. Something kept tugging at my mind, and sleep wasn't an option. Then the alarm rang in the semi-darkness of the room. A slit of gray light came through the blinds, reflecting off the walls, announcing the arrival of another day.

I reached over and turned off the radio alarm. Sitting up in my bed, I looked around the room. The rust and brown brick walls that could appear cold and unappealing seemed to cast a shadow from the cloudy light coming in from outside. I looked at my desk, full of papers and unfinished work, and groaned. I fell back into the warm comfort of the bed for a few minutes more and then realized what day it was. The first game of the season was tonight.

Immediately, I had a reason to jump out of bed, turn on the light, and gather up my clothes. It took only a few minutes to get in and out of the shower, get dressed, eat a bagel and head out to class. I crossed the campus with little bounce in my step. I quickly walked the final few yards to the classroom building, bounding up the stairs. People seemed to look curiously at my animated appearance, for I seemed almost too eager for class to begin. I had to get the day completed. The faster the day progressed, the sooner the game would begin.

Although it was only an exhibition, it still was the first test of the year. The coaching staff regarded this game as a chance to have a serious practice against an unfamiliar opponent. The game was not one that counted on any season record, and the stats accumulated would not register in the record book of Jayhawk basketball, but still, it was a game.

The team gathered in the locker room and listened to the usual pregame talk. It was not as serious as those which would be delivered during the course of the season, but coach Williams meant to establish a tone tonight that would carry through the year. As I listened to Coach, my mind wandered for a second to last season. I flashed back to the awful feeling of last March. It was a brief and unpleasant recollection.

I focused back on Coach. When he was finished and the team prepared to leave and hit the court, I found myself thinking about what I had to do. It was time to apply all the practice, to get something from all the hard work of the past summer. As I ran out onto the court for the first time as a senior, a roar went up from the 16,300 fans who had packed Allen Fieldhouse. It was awesome.

I suddenly felt an almost overwhelming emotion in my mind and throughout my body. "It's a fresh start," I thought to myself. "The past is just that....the past." I realized that the energy I felt was due to the fact that the monkey I had been carrying all year had now been lifted from my back. I could start anew. The crowd was letting me know that, and they made me feel totally confident again.

I thought about Angie's words again. "Just play ball," she had said. "You are a good basketball player. Go out and do it."

She's right, I thought. I always knew it. Why did I ever make such a big deal out of it? It's only a game. Right?

FRIDAY, NOVEMBER 15

Now that the season is nearing, my friends and family are planning their visits to watch me play. This means that I've got to sit down and allocate the tickets for home games.

Each season since I've been here I compile a list of those who have said they'd like to see a home game at Kansas. I try to get in touch with everyone about two weeks before the season and confirm the dates. Then I'll make a list so I can let the managers know names and dates. They will let the ticket office know which tickets to set aside for each game.

As players, we get four tickets for each home game. This includes parents and family members. It can get difficult for guys with large families or those who live nearby. What some of the guys do is ask for extras from those of us who may not have people coming for each game.

We never actually see the tickets. They are left at the Will Call window in Allen Fieldhouse under the name of the person receiving the ticket and the player who is responsible. The guest will present a photo ID and state their name and the name of the player. They will be checked against the list prepared for the game.

Alumni never contact us for tickets, contrary to popular belief. Maybe that's due to this system of ticket allocation, because I couldn't get them for anyone even if I wanted to. And I think this is a good thing. It prevents anyone from actually selling the seats, since we never have possession of the actual ticket. There is no way anyone could ever resell the seat and pocket the cash, as has been done at other schools.

I'm going to have quite a few visitors this season. My Mom will be making her visits near the end of the year, for Senior Night, the final home game, and for the Big 12 conference tournament. In fact, my whole family is going to try to come for that tournament, which will be in Kansas City the first week of March. It would be our first time together as a family in four years.

My close friends from home will come out at least one time. Scott, Lon and Brett will show up from home for a game over their Christmas break. Jason Ura plans on making the trip for one game and I'm sure there will be others. Mark will be here for a few games and to do research for this book.

It's more fun than a chore to make up this list. I feel good about having people come here to see me and my teammates perform. Some cynics would say they only want to come because we are one of the top teams in the country, but I know better. These are the people I care about and they feel the same about me. I'm glad I can give them an opportunity to see a team as good as ours in action.

SUNDAY, NOVEMBER 17

As the season nears, I've been thinking about the problems I had near the end of last year. My shooting became erratic and I was desperately trying to solve the problem. Finally, I decided to have a few sessions with the KU sports psychologist.

I had never suffered through a slump such as the one I experienced last year. It seemed as though the harder I worked, the worse things became. Since I have always been a guy who praised the virtues of hard work, finding out that the extra work was not producing results only made things worse. I didn't know what to do or where to turn.

It was driving me crazy. I'd spend a lot of time taking extra shooting practice.

There were nights when I would repeatedly ask Coach Williams to let me shoot around late into the night. Coach would give me the keys to Allen Fieldhouse and trust me to lock up. I'd spend an hour or more shooting from spots, trying to find the solution to my problem.

I followed routines out of superstition. I'd put on the same shoes, wash and wear the same clothes, chew the same brand of gum at the same time of day. I was not sleeping, I was bothering CB with questions about what I should do, and I was taking long walks to try and figure out what was wrong. Nothing worked.

So, I went to the KU sports psychologist. Not because I thought I was losing my mind, but because I felt it would help to talk with someone who was removed from the actual situation, someone who was not right there in the locker room or on the bench.

The sessions were helpful. They didn't produce some magical result, although they did make me relax. I learned to stop worrying about things I couldn't control. This wasn't easy, since I have always been something of a worrier. I realized it did no good to spend time thinking about possible scenarios and theories when the reality of the current situation was all I could deal with.

I tried to calm down. I thought about the games I'd played where things had gone well. It seemed to help when the NCAA tournament began, and I had some good games, especially against Arizona in the Sweet 16 victory. After the Syracuse game, well, that's when the real application of these sessions began.

I learned to put negative things behind me. If I had a bad game in the past, it would eat away at me and I would try to perform the next time out with the intention of erasing the previous performance. Sometimes I would try too hard to do that and it would make things worse. It became a cumulative force, one negative

The 1996-97 Kansas Jayhawk Men's Basketball Team

Front Row (from left) - Neil Dougherty (assistant coach), Joe Holladay (assistant coach), Jerod Haase, Jacque Vaughn, B.J. Williams, Scot Pollard, Roy Williams (head coach), Matt Doherty (assistant coach), Mark Cairns (trainer). Back Row (from left) - Blake Flickner (manager), Jill Johansen (head manager), Stephanie Temple (manager), C.B. McGrath, Billy Thomas, Steve Ransom, Joel Branstrom, Raef LaFrentz, T.J. Pugh, Paul Pierce, Nick Bradford, Ryan Robertson, Terry Nooner, Joel Suniga (manager), Olivia Thompson (manager), Damon Miller (manager). Photo by KU Sports Information.

building upon another.

This year I honestly feel that I've grown past that. I will look at any bad games or flaws in my performance as something I need to correct. They will not be things I intend to erase. The past is the past. I can only deal with the present and the future. If I play as hard as I can, and work to correct weaknessess, I'll succeed. But I can't go back and replay old games because the outcome will always be the same. It's over and I think I have learned to accept that.

My new attitude is already apparent to the coaches and my teammates. I'm more under control than I ever have been. I haven't lost the fire, and I still will be the first to get to any loose ball. But I have a better understanding of myself and what it takes to make a successful basketball player. The lessons of those discussions are something I'll use this season. I think I'm a much better player because of those those sessions and the lessons I learned.

On the Road

Non-Conference Play

The start of the season. I've been dreaming of this day since last March and can't wait to get going. The preseason exhibition games were a good tune-up, but we all knew they didn't count and we couldn't get excited. It's always good to get out on the floor and play against opponents other than your teammates, but I knew they weren't meaningful games.

Now it's different. The first ten games are taking on an important dimension. People who believed in us last year are having their doubts now. Some of that has to do with Jacque's injury. Most of the predictions have us ranked anywhere from No.1 to No. 4, but they all contain a reference to the fact that we will have to play the first half of the season without JV. They expect us to lose at least two games.

It appears that Cincinnati is our chief rival for the top spot in the rankings. The Bearcats have a rugged front line and their power forward, Danny Fortson, was the cover shot on the College basketball issue of Sports Illustrated. Wake Forest will be another contender, and their center Tim Duncan is regarded as the best big man in college basketball. Kentucky is always there, and as defending champions will be difficult to dethrone. Ron Mercer has been getting a lot of attention in the preseason articles.

Other teams that are considered strong are Michigan, Arizona, North Carolina, Iowa State and UCLA. Our schedule will pit us against some of these teams in the early going. We play Cincinnati in the Great Eight tournament at Chicago and UCLA on their home court within the same week in early December.

Iowa State is a conference rival. In fact two other conference teams are also ranked in the top 25, Texas and Texas Tech. We also play George Washington University, also ranked in the preseason poll.

It's a tough schedule, and many of the games against ranked opponents will be played on the road. I really don't care. I came here to play for the best against the best. This is a schedule that any player would look forward to. It's the ultimate test of our talent as a team and of my individual ability against top athletes.

By the end of this stretch, at Christmas break, we will have played ten games. We have two additional non-conference games after Christmas and then the Big 12 season begins at Kansas State. Of course I want to win every game and be 12-0 by then. Do I think that's possible? Yes. We have the talent and we've always felt that our bench can step up and meet a challenge. That's what has to happen now. Ryan has to meet the challenge and take over for Jacque. The rest of us have to play to our ability.

I've got to set a tone as the senior leader on the team. With Jacque out, the burden falls on me and I believe I'm up to it. Coach Williams believes in us and we believe in ourselves. If we keep that mentality, we'll be the No. 1 team in every poll after the Cincinnati game. Then we'll have to maintain that spot until April.

THURSDAY, NOVEMBER 21

College basketball involves a great deal of traveling and getting ready for a road trip involves a lot of preparation. I've spent about an hour getting everything I think I'll need arranged.

I'd say that the first thing any of us would pack is an alarm clock. It's understood by everyone that you will be on time. Nothing gets Coach Williams more upset than someone arriving late for any departure, meeting or practice. Even during the regular season, we would never dream of being late for anything. I have two alarm clocks in my bedroom and will take one of those along on this trip. Even so, I'll have the hotel give me a wake-up call every morning. I know that I have more of a paranoia about this than some of the others, but I don't want to have to deal with the consequences, although I'm not quite sure what they would be.

Actually, packing for a trip is easier than people think. You just pack your personal items. All other basketball related equipment is handled by the mangers. The managers have the most difficult job during a road trip. They have to pack all the equipment and make certain everyone has the right uniform, shoes, socks and other essentials for games and practices. This isn't as easy as it sounds. In effect, they are packing for 10 people and on this trip, planning a 9-day wardrobe. When we get to the airport, they will be responsible for baggage check-in and making sure everything is accounted for when we land. They have to get the luggage to the correct rooms when we arrive at the hotel, and make sure everyone's personal items are in the right rooms. It's a very demanding job.

I've always respected the managers and tried to show them how I felt. It's got to be tough dealing with guys who are as competitive as basketball players. The managers have to get our clothes ready everyday, and have them cleaned and in our lockers by the time we arrive for practice. They get the towels and water in place before we ever set foot on the floor for practice and are continually replacing and refilling things for us. During practice, they are constantly wiping up sweat from the floor, keeping stats and running the clock. If we have things that need to be cleaned or even sewed, they do it for us. I've known of times when they will get fast food for the team so we can eat something after practice.

Managers get paid monthly. I don't know the amount but I'd say it can't be enough. They put in hours and hours of work and never get any credit. The team appreciates them, but not as much as we should. I've heard players say that the managers are one group and we are another. I don't agree with that.

I get closer to the managers than most. Maybe it's their work ethic. They are always busy, they work hard and always try. I respect that. Managers are the real people in sports, the ones who do the hard, behind the scenes work that is never recognized unless something goes wrong. When I think about it I realize that some of my better friends in college have been managers. I roomed with Mike Sykes when I first arrived at Kansas, and he was one of our managers at the time. One of the few people I keep in contact with from Cal is Jason Ura, who was a manager for the basketball team during my freshman season, which was his senior year. Jason now works for the Chicago Bulls in a marketing capacity and I still keep in touch with him.. He'll probably be down for a visit later this year.

Of course, the current group of managers at KU have been supportive and helpful to me. Jill Johansen and Stephanie Temple have spent countless hours rebounding for me when I wanted extra shooting practice, and the time was all voluntary on their part. The rest of the staff would do the same if I asked. I always thank them and get them little things from time to time. I think they are surprised and appreciative and it's something I want to do. We couldn't run the quality program we have if it weren't for their efforts.

FRIDAY, NOVEMBER 22

San Jose, California is about a four-hour drive from Lake Tahoe, crossing the Sierra Nevada Mountains. It had already snowed twice this year, and the snow- packed roads would make the trip that much more hazardous. But a little snow was not going to deter the fans from my hometown.

As we prepared to play our first game of the 1996-97 season against Santa Clara, South Lake Tahoe was preparing to see Jerod Haase. During my two previous seasons at KU, the local papers carried detailed accounts of every game, and the local television station carried all the Kansas games, home and away. It was as if the town had been transplanted during the basketball season, relocated from the mountains to the wheat fields. Members of the Jayhawks were more familiar to residents of the town than members of any college team from California. Strange, but true.

The days' headline of the Tahoe Daily Tribune read: "Tahoe jazzed for Haase's 'home' tilt." A sub-head said that number 35's cheering section would be unrivaled in the San Jose Arena. The headline would prove to be correct. Nearly 500 fans from my home-town would attend this game. They had bought tickets, planned car pools, and were ready for this one chance to see me play close to home. The entire high school basketball program was going. Nick Romangnolo, a senior starter on the Tahoe Viking basketball team, told the Tribune, "I can't wait to see him play. Jerod's a great role model and really fun to be around. We all look up to him" Made me feel honored and humble all at once.

Another resident of the town, Les Wright, said something that reinforced those feelings. "He's probably the biggest big-time athlete we've had around here. He's such a super and real charismatic person. I guess we all live vicariously through him." Fans like Kerry David bought 10 tickets for this game. "I've been watching him since grade school and just appreciate his style of play. It's special," commented David. Reactions from people in my hometown made me proud to represent them.

While Lake Tahoe was getting wound up, so was I. It was my senior season. The last chance. The dreams of my childhood were about to start coming true, and I couldn't wait to get going. "Hopefully, I'll take my game up a step or two from where it's been in the past, "I told the Tribune. "It's just a matter of stepping out there and performing." And there was one other thing I wanted, but didn't mention: to duplicate the senior season from high school and take home the NCAA title.

The trip out west would be a long one. After this game, our team would head for Hawaii and the Maui Classic, a three-day tourney that would mean a five-day stay on the island. All told, the trip would be nine days in length. It was a tough way to start the season, but one that would be memorable.

After the four-hour flight, we had landed in San Francisco and headed straight to the hotel. Most of the flight was spent working on school assignments. Since the players would be missing six days of class, work had to be done on the trip. I worked on my business class project most of the way out, using the laptop computer I was so fond of carrying.

The next day was like a day off. We rode up Highway 101 to San Francisco. The team took a bus tour of the city and stopped at all the landmarks. The Golden Gate Bridge, a view of Alcatraz from the mainland and other tourist sites were all destinations along the way. CB took along a video camera and captured moments of this trip. And there were some good scenes.

If you like to watch people, there is no better place than Pier 39 near Golden Gate Park. It's hard not to be seen when you have 14 rather large men walking together as a group. 6'11" Raef LaFrentz stands out in any crowd, but today, with 6'10" Scot Pollard at his side, he caused many heads to turn. Of course, both big guys feel that it is the other people who look odd. CB spent some time just catching the startled looks passing among residents, tourists and basketball players.

Some guys took turns jumping into a bungee pit, trying to do flips and other acrobatic tricks. Others tried to feed the birds. We went to pier 39, ate and spent time looking at the sea lions and other sights in the area. After dinner at another restaurant, the Elephant Hut, the team headed back to the hotel, and relaxed in a hot tub.

Friday. Game day. The bus trip took an hour, so most guys tried to get some sleep. The team was ready. After all the work, after all the conditioning and practicing, we were ready to play for keeps. As we ran out onto the floor of the Arena, I could sense the support of the crowd. I knew the Tahoe contingent was large, but the noise from that section made it seem almost like a bipartisan gym. They were the loudest people there.

The game began, and we got off to a poor start. For whatever reason, the early moments of the season were "ugly". Santa Clara came out playing with determination and we were thrown off balance. It seemed like we were never able to find ourselves, although we managed to hold on to the lead most of the half, and went into the locker room with a 34-30 advantage.

It was not a pleasant gathering at halftime. All of us were mad at our play and Coach Williams was serious. There were not a lot of words spoken. Coach told us what we needed to do, especially in the area of rebounding. We knew. It was simply a matter of getting the job done.

I sat listening and growing angry with myself. I had also played an ugly half, missing three free throws, a three-point attempt, committing two turnovers and not getting a rebound. It was not at all what I had planned. This was just not my style. But unlike the past season, I did not start worrying about what was wrong. Instead, I decided that all the work of the summer would now be put to the test. It was time to take charge.

All that talk about leadership was only talk. Unless someone has to set the tone by example. The coaches talked. The press had spoken about the wonders of this team. But nobody was executing. If I was going to be the leader I felt I was, and other expected me to be, then it was time for me to step up and produce. I had felt a few weeks earlier that the team thought it could turn on effort whenever the need arose. Well, it was time for me to do just that.

The second half began and I saw the chance. Santa Clara had cut the lead to two, scoring the first basket of the half. We were in trouble. And then I saw my opportunity to take charge. In the next 30 seconds, I felt like I was on fire. I took a fastbreak pass from Ryan, leapt high towards the rim and laid in a basket while crashing into the backboard standard. I drew a foul on the play. I converted the free throw, intercepted a pass at the other end of the floor and raced 70 feet for another layup. The crowd went wild.

The team seemed charged. Suddenly the rest of the guys picked up the tempo. I hit a leaning 12-foot jump shot and converted the free throw when I was fouled on the shot. Paul and Scot scored from the paint and we went on a 17-4 run that ended with the score at 48-34. As Santa Clara called time-out, I was so pumped that I slammed my fist into the palm of my hand. The team was back and I had helped. It was a great feeling.

The crowd from Tahoe was going wild. They started to chant, "Jer-rod Haase, Jer-rod Haase" just like the old times at South Tahoe High. Now, however, it was interspersed with "Jay-hawks, Jay-hawks". The rest of the game would hear the chants repeated as Kansas went on to control the tempo and the game. The final score was 76-64, and we had won our opener playing the second half the way we knew best. Up tempo basketball.

I finished the game with 7-10 from the field, and 4-8 free throws for 19 points. Also, seven rebounds, six steals and four assists. But that didn't make up for the fact that my turnovers were way too high. Six turnovers means I had a new area of obvious improvement, but I did not let that dampen my spirits tonight.

"I can't express how much the support of the people from Tahoe means to me," I told a local writer. "People say it's nice of me to come back home and give my time, but they don't realize what they give me in return. It's tenfold what I give to the community."

After the game, I noticed swelling in my wrist area. When I crashed into the backboard support, I had slammed my wrist hard. It didn't hurt right away, but after the excitement of the game wore off, it started to throb. I tried to through it that night.

I visited briefly with Scott and my other friends from home and all too soon it was time to say goodbye. They had come a long way to see me play, and I regretted that all I had available was a half hour. The bus took us back to the hotel and the next morning we had to get up early for the trip to Maui.

When I awoke, I knew something had happened to my wrist. I couldn't pull up my socks with my right hand because it hurt the wrist area. My mother and sister noticed it right away, and said to get it looked at. I assured them that I would, and after a quick breakfast, it was time to catch the plane. We were leaving for Hawaii and the Maui Invitational. The first leg of the trip was a success.

SATURDAY, NOVEMBER 23
The flight to Hawaii was five-hours long, and I used the time to get some work completed. I slept the rest of the way and when I awoke, the sky was sunny and clear. I looked out the window and saw the beautiful blue of the Pacific Ocean. And to my right lay the island of Maui, looking like an emerald jewel in the midst of the water. It was an incredible sight.

The Maui Invitational had become one of the nation's top preseason tournaments. The entire concept of early tourneys had evolved since 1980 into a must situation for major programs, and attending one of the premier events like this, the Great Alaska Shootout or the NIT was important to the image of a school. Not only that, but the level of competition was a barometer of a team's performance.

The team arrived to a postcard picture of a Hawaiian day. As soon as we were settled into our room assignments, all of us headed for the hotel pool. Some guys stood on their balconies and stared at the magnificent scenery. CB took out his video and panned the landscape, getting images that he would carry in its electronic memory forever. Ryan kept repeating how beautiful everything was.

The team assembled and we went for a walk down the beach. After a few minutes, Paul let out a kamikaze yell and tackled Jacque, throwing him into the ocean. Ryan and TJ Pugh started to try to throw each other into the water. Other guys started to dive in and splash around, acting as most people do when they get near the ocean, getting their companions wet, floating in the water and enjoying life in this paradise.

After walking for about a mile, we decided to go snorkeling. I had done this during my trip in the summer, with the South Tahoe high school team. Feeling more experienced, I encouraged the less eager guys to try it, and eventually about seven players joined in. After a couple of hours, we went back to our hotel for the team dinner. Much of the evening we spent walking around the hotel area, enjoying the warm weather. We knew that this would be our last chance to relax for a few days, and we wanted to take advantage of the time. The hard work of winning the tournament would begin tomorrow.

MONDAY, NOVEMBER 25

The opening game for Kansas was against Louisiana State University. LSU had recently fallen on tough times, but they were still capable of defeating any team that took them lightly. We were not going to make that mistake.

After the Santa Clara victory, Coach had taken us to task. He pointed out the areas in which we had been deficient, and stated very clearly how he expected improvement. Coach also made it clear that he felt we had not put together a complete game at Santa Clara. I wanted to get on the court. The start of the game could not have been scripted better than what happened.

We took the opening possession and scored. I stole the next pass and drove down the floor for a dunk. I like beginning a game by making my first few shots, and a dunk is even more exciting. I can't explain how great it feels, but it sure gets me pumped . It also carries over to other aspects of my game, and it makes me feel that I'm playing to the top of my capabilities.

Our pressure defense forced three more LSU turnovers and quickly the score was 10-0. But the run would continue. A time-out could not change the momentum we had built, and we raced out to an 18-0 lead before the Tigers could manage a score. We were taking control of the game early, and it would make us more confident.

The team continued to play with a defensive intensity that made Coach Williams smile. It made me realize how good we could be if we really worked hard. We were fighting to get rebounds and loose balls. We were trying to create confusion with our defense, and that certainly happened. LSU seemed completely disoriented. And we wanted to put the first game behind us with a much better display this time. We wanted to set a tone for the rest of the tournament.

The one unique factor in this game came from the playing floor itself. High humidity, unusual for the island, had created a dangerous situation on the hardwood surface. The Lahaina Civic Center, site of the invitational, was a nice gymnasium but was lacking in one feature common to the mainland: air conditioning. There was no way to get all that humidity created by the atmosphere, the fans and the sweaty players out of that building without air conditioning. Towel boys were constantly mopping the floor whenever someone fell. At one point in the game, during a temporary break in the action, I hit a wet spot on the floor while walking backwards and fell flat on my backside. During time-outs, the towel boys would mop areas around the free throw lane. But the effort was in vain. The floor remained wet, dangerously so, and many of us were beginning to slip and fall while driving to the basket or guarding someone on defense. I felt like I was playing on an ice-skating rink. I tried to keep my balance and avoid getting seriously hurt.

The final score was 82-53. It was a satisfying win for the team and got us off to a good start. We were a third of the way to the title.

TUESDAY, NOVEMBER 26

It could have been a more emotional game. Certainly a few years earlier, playing against California would have been a highlight on my calendar. After all, this was the school I had left to go to Kansas. This was the coach who had benched me in favor of another player only two weeks after I had been named USA Today's Most Courageous Performer. And it was a team from my home state.

But things were not the same. None of the players or coaches I had known were still at Cal, except for Al Grigsby, and he was injured for this game. The chancellor and others who worked in the department were there, and I talked with them momentarily. They were good people and I wanted to say hello. But there was no revenge factor in my mind and all I wanted was to once again prove I had made the right decision in switching schools. And, of course, to continue the early success the team had achieved.

I thought California was a very talented and well-coached team. Under the new system they were using, the Bears were playing a more aggressive style. Ed Gray, their small forward, was on fire this game. We could never seem to get going for any extended period of time, and Cal stayed close the entire first half. I was being guarded by Randy Duck, a guard who had been recruited to replace me when I left for Kansas. It was a matchup I liked, for it gave me the chance to prove something to myself. When I transferred in 1994, it was announced that the program had found an adequate, possibly superior, replacement for me. This was our first head-to-head meeting and I wanted to perform at my best. Near the end of the half, I drove the lane in traffic and dropped in a shot from the free throw line. And with three seconds left, I broke free again, driving the lane and again hitting a short jumper from the same spot. As the horn sounded, we held a 37-34 lead.

After the half, we again tried to get our game going. I was moved over to guard Ed Gray, and I had some success in holding him down, but only for a while. He was simply in a zone, and we still needed to break this game open soon, or California would gain confidence in its ability to stay with and defeat us. With the score 41-40, Raef hit a turnaround jumper and on the following possession, Ryan led a fastbreak down the floor. Scot Pollard ran the lane, taking two defenders with him. I came barreling down behind, took the shovel pass from Ryan, and dunked it. We were up by five.

Cal held its ground. Sean Marks, their blond center, hit a jump shot from the corner, and after another basket and free throw combination, the game was tied at 45. The Bears took a three-point lead and held it for the next five minutes, until a Robertson jump shot allowed us to reclaim the lead at 53-52 with 11 minutes left.

I had been sitting on the bench during this stretch and growing impatient. Like any player, I wanted to be back in there, helping to make a difference. But I had complete confidence in my teammates. I believed that all the guys were capable of helping the team, and the constant shuffling in and out of players caused confusion in our opponents strategy. It also wore them down. Not many teams have a bench as deep as ours, and that would prove to be true in this game.

Coach put me back in with 10 minutes remaining. Immediately, Ed Gray eluded me and scored a basket driving the lane. I was angry with myself for letting Gray get free so easily. What was I thinking? On the drive, Gray was fouled and after making the shot, California took a 58-56 lead. But we answered with a basket and when Cal missed the next shot, I rebounded and drove the length of the floor and tried to pass to Scot. It was intercepted, but I leapt and deflected the ensuing pass, then dove on the floor to get the ball. It felt like in one motion I picked up the ball and shoveled a pass to Ryan, who buried a 3-point shot from the top of the arc. The crowd went wild as the momentum appeared to be shifting back our way.

With four minutes left in the game, we finally took control for good. Raef, Scot and Paul each hit short jump shots and then I drove the baseline for a reverse layup. I was fouled on the shot and when the free throw was successful, we had opened up a seven point lead. The surge continued until the end of the game, with the team completing a 17-0 run, winning the game 85-67.

It was a satisfying way to win, because Cal had thrown their best at us. I believe that our superior depth won out. Cal Coach Ben Braun said as much after the game, commenting in the papers how "they ran numbers at us. That's a reality. We have to learn how to stay with it when fatigue takes over."

I came off the court to a happy locker room. It had been a struggle out there, but we had won. I was happy with my play. I felt that I had provided a couple of sparks for the team and my defense was a helpful plus in the win. I had finished with 13 points, and other than a minor back injury, caused when I had landed squarely on it during the first half, had come out of the game feeling great. I knew that since Coach Williams had arrived at KU, all his teams had made it to the championship game of every holiday tourney. That streak would be kept alive for another year.

WEDNESDAY, NOVEMBER 27
Another plus from the night before was not known to the us or the coaching staff until the game with California was completed. The top-ranked Cincinnati Bearcats had been upset by crosstown rival Xavier University 71-69, so Kansas was now the consensus number-one team. All we had to do to solidify the ranking was to win the title game tonight.

Our opponent would be Virginia. Getting to the title game, Virginia had played surprisingly good basketball, defeating two opponents convincingly. Their defense had been better than advertised, and they posed a real threat for us. I recalled that it was this team which had knocked Kansas out of the NCAA tourney my sophomore year. There was not a lot of history between our two teams, but what did exist seemed to be in the Cavaliers favor.

This game began with KU taking a quick 7-2 lead, but Virginia bounced back and led by four points with 3 minutes remaining in the half. The entire half was characterized by tight play under the boards, with Virginia's guards, Alexander and Staples, keeping them in the game with clutch outside shooting. I was having an especially tough time keeping up with Staples, who ran off screens continually to free himself for quick jump shots. A Scot Pollard three-foot shot at the horn tied the game at 30.

I went into the locker room grateful for one thing. The conditioning we had done all fall was paying off tonight. After two consecutive nights of tough basketball, I still felt as though I had quite a bit left in my legs for the second half. Most of the team seemed to be in the same great physical shape. Due to that, and the depth of our bench, we believed that we could win this game. We simply had to play our kind of game in the second half. After reminding the team of this at the half, Coach Williams sent us out.

Our run for this game started early in the second half. Each game so far had seen us put together one long, sustained run and this game was no exception. Paul and Raef had quick baskets and I fed Nick Bradford for another score. Suddenly, we were up by 7. The margin grew from that point and Virginia could not catch up. We continued to pull away steadily, and won the game, and the tournament, 80-63.

The all-tournament team was announced at the end of the game. Raef, Scot and I all made it, with Raef getting the honor of being chosen tourney MVP. I felt that being selected to this team was evidence that I am doing some good things. I'm encouraged by the start to the season. As a team, we look tough, and if I personally continue to progress at this pace, I'll be fine.

Sitting in the locker room, I noticed how thrilled my teammates were. This is a time when I feel a sense of completion. These guys really are something special. We are the champions of this tourney. If we keep playing like this, and improving, we could win a lot of games this year. Maybe win it all. I sat back against my locker and smiled at the thought.

THANKSGIVING DAY, 1996

The alarm woke me around 9 a.m. It was a beautiful sunny day, and for once the humidity was not noticeable. This was the day off we had been waiting for. Time to get going and enjoy Hawaii. I called a few of the guys nearby, got JV (my roommate on this trip) out of bed, and headed down to the pool.

For the next three hours, we all turned into typical vacationers. We swam, we sunbathed, and most of us went down the water slide. We sat and talked with one another, exchanging stories about our lives and memories. Later that afternoon, we went for another snorkeling adventure. Spotting some 30-foot cliffs enticing us towards the water, I and some of the others engaged in some distance diving. The island was our playground, and we felt we had earned the time off. After practicing for the past month and conditioning since August, winning this tournament and enjoying this day were sweet rewards. Reality would set in tomorrow. Today was for fantasy.

We came back from our day in the sun and had a Thanksgiving dinner in the hotel dining room with the families of the coaches. That night, I went for one of my solitary walks. Just a time to get alone and think again about how fortunate my life has been and how much the success of this season meant to me. The difference between this and other walks in the past year was not only in the location. It was Thanksgiving but it felt like late July. I also noticed how relaxed I was, how free of stress and worry I was. Sure, the season had just begun, but there was already a feeling of accomplishment. Maybe it was being a senior and having endured it all before, or maybe it was the fact that I had prepared so well for this year. Whatever the case, I just felt good about everything.

The next day we left for home and the cold weather of December in Kansas. A second Thanksgiving dinner was served on the plane and while it would never compare with anyone's family meal, in a way it was a family setting. As much time as we players spend together, we were in effect our own family. Differences and arguments would be set aside and times like these would reinforce the idea of helping each other.

It was certainly a different Thanksgiving than others I had spent. But it was one I know I would always remember.

SUNDAY, DECEMBER 1

It was cold, and the ground was covered with the first serious snow of the year. I woke up early and had a bowl of cereal, thinking about the game against San Diego today. It would be our first home game of the year. The crowd would be wild, I knew, but would the team be ready? It had been a long week, and many of us still hadn't fully recovered from the trip back from Hawaii. Jet lag could be a problem.

Looking ahead could also be a threat. With the game against Cincinnati coming up on Wednesday, the team couldn't be blamed for not concentrating fully on San Diego. After all, the next game was a matchup between No. 1 and No. 2 in the national polls. It was in Chicago, at the United Center, the home of the Bulls. If Allen Fieldhouse had the air that Wilt breathed, then the United Center had the air in which Michael Jordan flew. Wednesday was the big game.

But I knew better than to look ahead. Being a senior had taught me a few things, and one of those was that any team was capable of knocking off another team, especially one that was not fully prepared to play. Sure, we were off to a great start, but this team still had to prove to itself that it could win in all conditions.

I put on a coat and drove over to the Alumni Center, the place where the basketball team meets before each home game, about two miles away from my apartment. It was time for the pregame meal, looking at film and going over the scouting report. This was not as intense as some other games, and part of that was due to the lack of information about our opponent. It bothered me some, because the team seemed to lack some of the intensity of the previous week. But I thought that once the game began, we would change our attitudes, so I put the notion out of my mind. Meanwhile, with the meeting over, I went back to my apartment and took an hour-long nap.

When I awoke, I got ready for the game as I did for most home games. Nap, change into casual dress clothes, put on some music, and sit for a few minutes. This year, I have changed the routine somewhat from past seasons. I don't think I'm as superstitious as I have been before. In the past, I had run through a series of activities before games, adding items to the routine if the previous game had been especially good. It had gotten to the point where I was even chewing the same brand of gum, including the same number of sticks, before every game. The nature of my superstitions increased as my shooting suffered last season. I knew it was ridiculous, but did it anyway. This year, I thought about abandoning it completely, but settled for a little peace of mind and only a few actions.

It was time to head back to Allen for the game. The University of San Diego was not a national power, but they could be tough, and we were a tired team. As the game began, it was clear that we were not playing with the same intensity that we had displayed in Maui. The first few minutes were characterized with offensive spurts and defensive lapses. At the half, Kansas led by 12 but we were playing uninspired basketball.

The second half was not much better. San Diego cut the lead to one midway through the half, and it took that to wake us up. We finally began to play with some desire and managed to get the lead back to 78-65 with three minutes left. San Diego closed the game with a 7-1 spurt. It was a win, but not one the team would want to save for the video library.

One thing that I will remember from this game is of a personal nature. My high school teammate, Brian Bruso, started for San Diego. When we won the state title our senior year in high school, we both were important parts of the team. Brian was the force underneath, a big strong rebounder who could score. He and I have not kept in constant contact through the years, and we haven't been home during the summers at similar times, but it was good to see him today. We only got a chance to talk briefly before the game, but he played very well for them and helped keep the game close. It brought back memories of the games back at South Tahoe.

I guess it's human nature to have a letdown after what we've been through. After winning a big tournament and coming back home, we felt comfortable. When you get THAT comfortable, you sometimes let down in effort. That can be a dangerous trait. We've got to fight that feeling, overcome obstacles like this and still perform.

MONDAY, DECEMBER 2

The San Diego game was now behind us, and I had no time to think about it. One negative aspect about traveling the nation playing college basketball is the time lost in class. It is just not possible for a student-athlete to have time to live a social life similar to other students. If that were the case, then the area that would have to be sacrificed is the classroom. Consider this schedule.

We left to play our first four games of the season on November 19. The first game was in Santa Clara on Friday, the 21st. The day after that game, we left for Hawaii. The Maui tournament continued until Thanksgiving, and the team arrived home November 29. Classes also resumed today. Tomorrow, we leave on another road trip and return home in time for class next Monday, December 9. Out of the last 12 possible class days, the guys on the basketball team would be present for exactly 2! We would have traveled 11,500 miles and sat for almost 30 hours in airports and airplanes. And upon returning home from the next road trip, final exams would be only three days away. With that in mind, the coaching staff takes great pains to ensure that the players get all possible help in maintaining our studies.

Tutors travel with the team. Laptop computers are provided for those who are writing term papers. Textbooks were always visible on the Maui trip, and since many of the guys have trouble sleeping in the uncomfortable airplane seats, homework becomes a more viable option. While in Hawaii, Scot consulted research material and wrote a paper for an anthropology course. I took my laptop to the pool.

Since each course has a syllabus that is handed to all students, we know where we are supposed to be in relation to course work at all times. An academic adviser, Wayne Walden, is there to assist anybody who needs help in fulfilling the work. Wayne makes certain that concepts are explained and that the guys who need help are following a pre-ordained study schedule. Walden will check up on the younger players regularly, since they are new to this kind of regimen. It is up to the individual player to complete his course work, and the needs of each player vary with the material involved, but the fact is that this is a burden for any college student. Dealing with the normal academic load is difficult, but doing it while meeting plane schedules, packing and unpacking, and playing games in between is extremely demanding. It calls for self-discipline, and that is not something all 19-22 year old possess.

Grade point averages (the total value of grades received calculated by the number of courses attempted) are used to determine the top students academically. The GTE academic All-American award, presented each season to the top student athletes in every sport, is a signal that athletics and academics do, and should, mix well together. I was named to the second team, with a 3.60 cumulative GPA, after posting a 4.0 (straight A) average the previous spring. My teammate, Jacque Vaughn, made the first team, with a 3.70 GPA. In addition to the two of us, four other Jayhawks were named to the Academic All-Big Eight team.

I think it is a truly remarkable fact that this team has one of the highest grade point averages (GPA) of any in college basketball. Last years' team averaged 2.87 (a record for Kansas), and most of that team is back. And none of us have the so-called "soft"majors. Pre-Med and Business Administration are not cushy courses.

I spent this day catching up on the project that has been the center of my academic life this semester. It was time to coordinate all the information into a comprehensive report, and my work had been less than what the professor had expected. After a session with my prof that could only be described as "highly critical," I spent the next six hours re-writing and editing my section of the project. Finally satisfied, I contacted the others in the group and received their material. This led to another five hours of compiling data, organizing details and assembling the final copy. It was almost midnight by the time I was done. Welcome to the glamorous life of a Kansas basketball player, I thought, as I feel asleep.

WEDNESDAY, DECEMBER 4 -CINCINNATI
The United Center in Chicago was hosting the Great Eight tournament. We flew in to Chicago the previous day, and practiced at the Bulls facility, the Berto Center. To make it an all-around Bulls trip, the team had eaten at Michael Jordan's restaurant that night, and on this game night, we were given the Bulls locker room. And to top it all off, when getting ready for the game, I discovered that I was sitting in Jordan's chair. I regarded it as an omen.

This was a game that the media had built up early in the season. And why not? After all, had it not been for Xavier's upset of Cincinnati the previous week, the nation's two top teams would be meeting. As it was, we had claimed No. 1, and the Bearcats were dropped to No. 4. It still was a marquee matchup, the perfect way to end the two-day festival.

It struck me that this was a game between two different types of programs. Kansas stands for what is good about college sports. I think that our work ethic and the type of student-athletes we put on the floor are make that point evident.. The previous week, Sports Illustrated had come out with a story on the University of Cincinnati and the conflict within the basketball program. The implication was that this was a program rife with problems, some of which the NCAA might choose to investigate. Whether it was true or false, I would not try to determine. But I felt that it was important for us win this game, to make a statement that our way of basketball is the best way.

The local papers in Chicago had also gotten into the act. Chicago Sun Times columnist Jay Mariotti had written that this was a struggle between "Kansas' Roy Williams, the Dudley Do-Right of college sports, vs. Bob Huggins, the Snidely Whiplash of college basketball." It would be the best thing for college basketball if the good guys win this one, Mariotti declared. The hype was on.

The United Center was filled to capacity as 21,300 packed in to see the game. As the Jayhawks entered to cheers from our fans, the Cincinnati band began to play and the Bearcats came charging onto the floor, greeted by the loud music and much louder cheers from their more numerous followers. It would be a crowd that, while mostly non-partisan, would favor them over us.

I could sense that something was amiss in the huddle. We seemed strangely flat again, and the fears I had put aside a few weeks earlier were returning. I felt it was time to get a spark going early. As we gathered around the center circle for the opening tip, I thought to myself that if I had the chance, I would gamble on an early steal. Sure enough, the opening tip went to Cincinnati, but as they brought the ball up the court, the first pass was thrown softly to the left side of the key. I had been playing inside my man and I reached out and slapped the pass away. Accelerating, I reached the loose ball and drove down the court for an easy layup to start the game! The crowd was barely seated, but our fans rose in a loud cheer and we had drawn first blood. It made me feel much better, and the rush of adrenaline was getting me pumped.

But the next few minutes were not to follow that opening pattern. Cincinnati dominated the boards, took the ball to the hoop, and simply outplayed us. They scored the next 8 points, held leads of up to 10 points, and late in the half were up by 29-14 with about 3 minutes remaining.

Nothing we tried was working. The rugged Cincinnati defense was forcing us to start our offense farther away from the basket, and it caused our patterns to be ineffective. Quite simply, the Bearcats were more intense and aggressive.

After the opening layup, I had not hit a shot from the field. I was struggling and couldn't find the range. It was as if the early season games were a mirage. I noticed that I had begun to catch the ball with the intention of passing rather than looking for an open shot. Knowing my shooting was off, it seemed as though it would be best to set the others up for open shots rather than continue to shoot the ball badly. But this was not working either, since our big men were being pushed out of the lane. I grew more frustrated as the half progressed and felt the anger welling up inside me as I sat for almost six minutes, watching my team get completely outplayed.

Right before the half, Cincinnati forward Damon Flint fired up a 15-foot shot that fell off the rim. Between two of our guys, the Bearcats' Rodrick Monroe went for the ball and tipped it in, bringing the score to 35-23. The crowd roared as Cincinnati jogged off the court, players waving their arms flashing No. 1 signs in response.

In the locker room, Coach Williams was not pleased at all. He had decided not to let out all his feelings, but began to challenge guys to compete, to not act so tentative under the basket. But we all knew the real meaning behind those words, and Scot Pollard opened the door completely. "I'm tired of people saying we play "soft" basketball," he said. "It's time we stepped up and did the things we know how to do."

I had been sitting quietly, listening but growing angrier by the moment. I could see what was happening. Doubt was settling in. The guys were starting to question their ability to come back. This was, after all, the team that had been ranked number one in most polls until this week. This was a big team, a physical team, and a team that played on the edge. There was a lot of extracurricular shoving, grabbing and pushing going on. It was brute force basketball, and we were being physically intimidated. I thought about what this meant, about the toughness of my teammates being questioned, and about how it would be to lose a game this way. This kind of loss would leave a mark on the psyche of the team that would be hard to erase. I grew so angry that I stood up as the team was about to head back for the court. I blocked the doorway.

"What's going on here?" I shouted, looking everyone in the eyes. "We're getting our butts kicked. I don't know about you guys, but I don't want to go out there and take any more of that. It's time we fought back. I am going to war out there. Either join me or don't leave this locker room!"

I could feel myself shaking with anger. My intensity had spilled over and I was speaking with emotion that had been pent up for a long time. Maybe it was the frustration from last spring. After all, I had been ineffective in that game, much as I had been thus far tonight. That was another case of Kansas being pushed around by a physical team. I just couldn't stand the thought of it happening again.

I had never spoken to my teammates with such strong emotion in my voice. It was done without thinking. It just came out. But it had an immediate impact.

Ryan and Raef looked determined. Others line started to yell. Ryan began to yell , "It's war!" And the Jayhawks raced from the locker room back to the floor of the United Center, prepared to give Cincinnati a taste of Kansas basketball.

We came out and took control. Raef and Scot began to work the boards, and Paul started to shoot with the confidence of a seasoned veteran. I could feel the intensity of the locker tirade spilling over into my teammates. They were playing under control, but with an anger that had been absent in the first half.

I started to adjust my own game. Still not clicking from the outside, I took the ball to the basket, driving the baseline for a quick score. I fed both big men with lob passes that they dunked with authority, causing the crowd get back into the game. This was the KU team they had come to see. And it was just the beginning.

We took off on a 15-2 run to open the half. When Paul swished a 3-point shot from the left corner, we had come all the way back, taking the lead with the most impressive six minutes of basketball I thought we had played this season. Angrily, Cincinnati coach Bob Huggins called time-out and began berating his team even before they had reached the bench.

It didn't help. We were in a groove now, and everyone was contributing. I swiped the ball twice in the next three possessions. Once, I drove the lane for a hanging layup, getting fouled and completing a three-point play. Another time, I drove the baseline and three Bearcats converged on me. Shifting the ball to my left hand, I dished off a pass around the defenders to Raef, who jammed the ball home. We were up by seven and Cincinnati called another time-out.

I raced to Raef and gave him a look. "It's war," he yelled. Ryan came up, jumping and screaming over the noise of the crowd, "It's war. Cover my back and I'll get yours." The team had picked up on the theme, and it was driving us to the most impressive win of the young season.

Cincinnati never recovered. Kansas kept the lead between 7 and 12 points the rest of the game, and when the final horn sounded, we felt we had earned our No. 1 ranking with an impressive 72-65 hard-fought victory. Deliriously happy, we raced off the floor, hugging each other and waving our arms to the crowd of fans assembled near the exit ramp.

The locker room was a madhouse. Guys were yelling at one another and the feeling of satisfaction was everywhere. I was right in the middle of it all, enjoying every second. It was vindication, proof that Kansas could play our game and win.

We really did rely on one another tonight. We would have done anything to protect each guy on the team. We played our "soft" Kansas basketball and kicked their butts. It's such a great feeling to know that if we play our game, we don't have to worry about winning. It will happen.

THURSDAY, DECEMBER 5
The team left the Hyatt-Regency O'Hare early the next morning. We headed to Chicago's O'Hare airport, sometimes called "the World's

Busiest Airport." And on this day, we would become well-acquainted with the terminal.

As the team arrived, we were hustled through security only to have to wait to board the plane. After a half hour wait, we walked on board and chose seats. But 45 minutes later, still sitting on the airstrip, we were informed about a mechanical problem which would force us to return to the terminal and wait for another flight. Accommodations had to be made with another booking agent, and two hours later we were finally in the air. The flight to Los Angeles would take four hours, and eventually we arrived at our hotel and ate dinner around 9 p.m. All told, it was a twelve hour experience in endurance.

To try to relax from all this aimless waiting, I decided to go to the hot tub provided by the hotel. I was unable to just sit in my room, having done nothing but sit all day in planes and in terminals. Some of the other guys joined me and eventually there were nine members of the team present.

"Who knows the answer to this?" CB asked the group. He proceeded to tell a riddle. It was typical McGrath and it was not very difficult to solve, but it started a wave of copycat riddles. For the next hour, there we were, most of the nations' No. 1 college basketball team, sitting around in a hot tub telling cheesy riddles to one another at 11 o'clock at night. In Los Angeles.

We would laugh at the ridiculous comments. Almost every time a riddle was too difficult, someone would get splashed in the face. Billy Thomas and I both joined in and told our share of lame jokes. And when it was over, we returned to the room we were sharing on this trip.

"Man, that was sure one strange time," Billy said.

"Yeah, but I enjoyed it," Haase replied.

"You really get into those things, don't you?" Billy asked. "I mean, you like those kind of team things, where everyone is together."

"I guess I do," I answered. "I never really realize it until I'm doing it, but I get a good feeling when we're all doing something. A night like this seems dumb when you think about it. But I think it's something I'll remember for years."

"I know what you mean," Billy said "I guess you gotta think about it."

"I think I realized something else after tonight," I added.

"What's that?"

"It just hit me how much I'm going to miss everybody next year. Things like this couldn't happen unless you're on a college team. I'm going to miss it."

"Kind of like what Jacque said last year?" Billy asked, referring to Jacque's decision to stay at KU for his last year.

"Yeah," I responded, and it made me think. "Now I know exactly what he meant."

FRIDAY, DECEMBER 6
We had an early practice today and had some free time to do some sightseeing. As always, we tried to get in as much as possible. Tonight was going to be something really special, a trip to Niketown and then to the Forum to watch the Los Angeles Lakers play against the Orlando Magic. It's the first time Shaquille O'Neal plays his old team. It would be my first time in this arena and I was looking forward to it.

I was looking forward to seeing some people today. My friend Jay goes to school here and I'm going to connect with him later on. And Scott and Christi are coming to watch the game. In addition to that, my sister Mara and her husband Cameron are coming in from Seattle. Of course, my mother is going to fly in for the game. This will be the last time we play out west, unless we are sent here by the NCAA tournament and even then it won't be in California. So for me, it's the last time I'll be playing college basketball in my home state.

Both Paul and JV are feeling comfortable today. They are the ones who are close to home this time, being from the Los Angeles area. Jacque is a bit down, since he won't be able to perform in front of his family and friends, but he's still pleased that he will get to visit with them rather than just make phone calls. Paul is excited, and I would expect a big game from him tomorrow against UCLA.

Before the game, we went out for dinner. I usually try and order something unique from the menu, something that I can't get back in Lawrence. It's become something of a trademark, but it drives Paul crazy.

"Why are you gonna eat that?" he demanded tonight.

"Because I want to become cultured," I answered in mock seriousness. "You should try this food."

"Hell no, I ain't going to eat some fried seaweed with worm liver or that sauteed dirt with horseradish sauce," Paul declared vehemently. "You've got to be crazy to eat that stuff."

I chuckled because I knew that I'd gotten to him again. But he had one more trick up his sleeve. When the waitress came around to take our drink orders, Paul told her to bring me a V-8. The drinks arrived and everyone had their Cokes and lemonade, but there I was

Paul Pierce. Photo by Earl Richardson.

sitting with a tomato juice cocktail. Paul and some of the other guys laughed at the look on my face, and he was content for the night.

The game at the Forum was fun and we returned to the hotel for a brief team meeting. Soon it was time to get to bed. Tomorrow was going to be an important test for us, playing UCLA at legendary Pauley Pavilion. I'd been there before, and the memories were starting to come back, but I pushed them away and fell asleep quickly.

SATURDAY, DECEMBER 7

Game time was an hour away. Playing UCLA at Pauley Pavilion was another of those experiences kids who are basketball junkies dream about. It's the legendary atmosphere of the place. So many national titles. So many banners hanging from the ceiling. So many greats who have run the length of this court.

I was sitting in front of the locker, looking around the room. It had been a good road trip. The day before, I had gotten in touch with a few of my friends from the area and hung out with them for a while. The team had a morning practice, which left the rest of the day open. After seeing my friends, I had gone with the rest of the team to Niketown in LA and then off to the Forum to watch the Lakers play a home game against the Orlando Magic. The first time Shaq would play against his old team. The first time I had ever been in the Forum. All in all, a heckuva basketball day.

But now my thoughts were going in another direction. A more emotional location. I was thinking about the last time I had been in this place. It was the day after I had learned my father had died. My freshman year. A lifetime ago.

I couldn't help but flash back to that awful day. I was in a state of shock from the news, and recalled that I had sat in exactly the same spot, in front of exactly the same locker, and nearly broke down in front of everyone on the Cal team.

Jeff Wulbrun, the Cal assistant coach who was with me when I was told about my dad that morning, noticed my state and had taken me off to a side of the room where I would be more isolated, where I could deal with the emotions I was feeling, before I returned to the rest of the team. I had gone out and played one of the best games of my freshman year. It was dedicated to the memory of my father.

Now, I could almost feel the presence of my dad again. I knew that I would have a good game today, if for no other reason than the memory. I checked my shoes and made certain the initials were still there. G.E.H. Still emblazoned on the back. I rubbed the letters with my right hand and put the shoes back on.

This was another of the games regarded as critical to the early season success of Kansas. UCLA was ranked No. 17 coming into the game, and had been in the top 10 just one week earlier. The Bruins were always difficult to beat at home, more so than most teams. They had just endured a difficult period of transition, losing their coach, Jim Harrick, in a rules violation incident the university had decided to deal with immediately. Adjusting to a new coach, playing the top- ranked team in the country, both of these things were obstacles UCLA had to overcome.

We had our own problems. My wrist was still giving me problems from the fall I took at Santa Clara. It had been so sore I couldn't shoot the first two days in Maui, and I had been taping it ever since, keeping it tightly wrapped during games. Raef LaFrentz had strained his right foot in the San Diego game and it was still bothering him. On top of this, the team was playing its sixth game on the road. We were getting tired.

The game was receiving national attention. KU was playing its second ranked opponent in four days, and this was going to be another test of our ability to win on the road, and without Jacque. It was going to be tough.

We broke out early, running to an 8-1 lead, but UCLA came back with an 8-0 run of their own. The margin would stay within 4 for the next 10 minutes. They were one of the most athletic teams I can recall playing against. It was a fast-paced game, with both teams committing numerous turnovers. The crowd was roaring much of the way, and the noise level seemed to inspire both teams. I felt that I was inexhaustible today, feeling energy that made me dive, run the length of the floor continually and rebound with abandon. It was as if I were still playing the game from three years ago, driven to accomplish all that I possibly could to help my team win.

With the score 22-18, I found a sudden burst of increased energy. I was able to steal the ball at mid-court and scored off a two-on-

one break with Raef. The next time down the court, I hit a three-point shot from the left corner to give Kansas a nine point lead. After a time-out, I took the lead on a three-on-two break, feeding Raef for an easy score. Billy Thomas came in for me off the bench and went 3-for-3 from the field. The team was off on a 32-8 run, one which would close out the half. The crowd sat in stunned silence, looking at the unbelievable score of 54-30.

It was a happy locker room at halftime. There wasn't much Coach Williams could say to this team. We had really only one flaw at the end of the half, failing to put away UCLA completely. Other than the first few minutes, Kansas had played a close to perfect half of basketball. I thought to myself that it was like a practice, a time when everything we tried was working to perfection. "We're spanking them pretty good," I told Raef. "Just hope we can keep it up," he replied.

We did. UCLA made one attempt at a run, closing the gap to 14 points in the first seven minutes of the second half, but then the balanced attack of Kansas went to work. Paul, Raef, Billy and I all scored in the next two minutes, and the Bruins seemed to lose what little fight they had left.

It was over. The margin never seemed to move much after that, and the final score was 96-83. The first half margin was the largest deficit (28) that any UCLA team had ever encountered in the history of Pauley Pavilion. In my freshman year, the defeat the Cal team put on UCLA was the worst the program had ever suffered. All told, both of my appearances at Pauley had resulted in embarrassing firsts for the Bruin basketball team.

I was very happy when it was over. I had finished with 22 points, second only to Raef, who had 31 for his career high. I also had 6 rebounds, went 7-7 from the free throw line, had 3 steals and 2 assists. It was as good a game as I had played all year, and it was in a building that would always carry memories for me.

"Hope you enjoyed it, Dad," I said silently, looking around the gym one last time. "This one was for you." Somehow I knew that my Dad was smiling.

WEDNESDAY, DECEMBER 11 - GEORGE WASHINGTON
Our third game in seven days against a ranked opponent. At least, that's the way it was supposed to be. George Washington University (GW) was ranked in the top 25 at the start of the season, and rose to a peak of 19 before losing a game last week. At the moment, the Colonials were just below the top 25, but it didn't diminish their potential.

The KU Huddle. We do this to talk over situations, keep our poise and play under control. Photo by KU Sports Information.

ESPN was in town to televise the game. It meant that the tip-off would be delayed until 8:30, and that was not one of my favorite things. Ask any player about late starts. It means that his day is thrown out of kilter. Normal eating times are changed, study patterns are thrown off, and postgame relaxing is basically just crashing into bed, if that's possible after being on such an emotional high an hour earlier. But that's the price of big-time college sports in the 1990s.

I had a busy day leading up to the game. The biggest part of the day involved my course. It was time to present the final report to the architectural firm. I had compiled the work into a binder for every person involved, and also had managed to put together a presentation which involved computer graphics. The semester- length course came down to this presentation, and to my relief, the 90-minute session went well. Our group was pleased with the reception the suggestions elicited from the businessmen. The project was complete.

That afternoon, I squeezed in a short nap and then made it over to the pregame meal, held today at 4:30. I came back to the apartment, but found I couldn't relax and spent the next hour listening to music and pacing around the room. Finally, I left for the fieldhouse around 6:30, to have a larger place to roam.

The gym was packed, as usual, and the anticipation was high. After all, we are the Number 1 team for the second straight week. This hasn't happened since Roy Williams has been head coach. In all previous years when Kansas had reached No. 1 in the polls, we had lost the very first game after achieving that ranking. This year, we beat two ranked opponents in the week following becoming top dog. Fans sensed that this was a different kind of season, and certainly a different kind of team.

To add to the excitement, 15 professional scouts were in the building, all looking at the big men on display tonight. George Washington's center, 7'1", 285- pounder Alexander Koul was the main focus of interest. How would he fare against the twin towers of Kansas, Pollard and LaFrentz? I had been hearing this for two days on television. They were even talking about Paul Pierce and myself, because we were off to excellent starts this year. It always is nice to hear good things about yourself from the media, and it made me feel as though the work of the past months was paying dividends, as I knew it would. Hard work is always rewarded.

I was ready. Some nights, a player knows that it is his night. There is something about the way you warm up, something about how everything feels, that lets an athlete know he is on. I had that feeling tonight.

The game began with both teams trading baskets, but the next time down the floor, I earned a floor burn to get a loose ball under the GW basket. As the teams came back to the KU goal, the ball moved around the perimeter until I found myself open in the left corner. Swish. I'd connected on a three, and the mood of the night was set.

In the next 60 seconds, I grabbed a rebound, came down the floor, received a pass from Ryan and drove between two defenders and around Koul to lay in a basket. Then I dove on the floor to swipe a loose ball and when Scot Pollard was tied up and lost the ball, I was down on the floor again, diving to save the ball from going out of bounds. It was three floor burns in the opening seconds, three "Haase burns," as the KU scorers label them, and the crowd roared its appreciation.

I continued to push myself on defense. I stole a pass the next trip down the floor, deflected a pass inside for Koul and tried to keep in constant motion. We were playing some of our best defense of the year, playing with intensity and emotion. It was just what Coach Williams wanted, and I started feeling like a senior leader.

With 10 minutes to go in the half, the score was only 14-11. Although we had played tenacious defense, we had committed numerous turnovers, a problem still plaguing our otherwise impressive play this year. As the half continued our errors mounted. Although we continued to lead, each time it appeared we would pull away, something minor would occur. By the end of the half, we had 13 turnovers but thanks to a Billy Thomas 3-pointer at the buzzer, left the floor with a 36-29 lead.

Halftime was quiet. We knew we had not handled the ball well and realized that the spark provided at the start of the game had been wasted. I thought about what I could do. It was not a game for another fiery speech, and besides, I didn't feel anything I'd say would mean much. Tonight it was not time to talk. It was time to put it all out on the floor.

The first eight minutes of the second half were about as close to perfect as we have played so far this season, Coach Williams told us later. I opened the half hitting a three-pointer from the top of the key, Ryan drove for a layup, and then Ryan fed me for another driving layup. Suddenly the lead was 14 and we were taking control of the game. Raef and Paul both hit 15-foot jump shots, and then I again took a feed from Ryan and drove to the hoop, leveling my defender on the way. The basket was good, no foul, the crowd was on its feet. Kansas led by 20. We went on a 21-2 run, and were never challenged for the rest of the night.

The final score was 85-56. I had my most complete game of the season tonight. I led the team with 22 points (8-10), 4-4 free throws, 7 rebounds, 2-2 three-point shots, four assists, 3 steals, a blocked shot and zero turnovers. I was the only KU starter to not turn the ball over. That is the statistic I rate the most important. I have tried to improve my decision-making and ball-handling, and this was the game where I felt it all paid off.

Coach Williams told the reporters after this game that, "Jerod's worked so hard and I can't think of anyone who deserves to have things going his way more than him. He's helped us in all areas on the floor, especially with his leadership." Compliments from Coach are the best praise of all.

The team put on an impressive performance which resulted in a very impressive win. We had made believers out of many doubters. We are really coming together and the goals we set for ourselves in September are definitely within reach. We have to keep trying to get better and not get complacent. This is an opportunistic team. We take advantage of a few opportunities in a row, and suddenly we've strung together a quick run. I'm never aware of how it starts, but I notice it when it goes on for a while.

I don't think any of us feels he's at the top of his game yet, and that's the motivation we need, to still try to reach that next level. It's really satisfying to play like we did tonight.

FRIDAY, DECEMBER 13
We were taping a segment for Coach's television show today. Coach Williams does a weekly talk show with Max Falkenstein, the leg-

endary broadcaster of Kansas basketball games. Each week he discusses the games and analyzes what's happened, our progress, and other things that are of interest to our fans. Following this, there is a segment on an individual Jayhawk.

Today the team helped tape the Christmas special, which will be televised next week. We all had to make Christmas wishes, some of which would be selected and used in the show. The guys took turns trying to break each other up in front of the camera and we also gave good-natured shots at one another. Nick Bradford stuck me pretty well, saying that my Christmas present should be a girl, so I'd get away from my computer a little and go out on a date. The camera showed me walking away shaking me head saying," Geez!" There's a lot of laughter in the background. It was funny, especially coming from Nick.

Some may wonder how we meet girls, whether we date, when we find the time, and those types of things. It's never been easy for me to carry on a relationship during the season. I get so focused on basketball that I'm not as attentive to others as I should be. I know I'm that way, and I know it's not fair to any girl to have to put up with this kind of behavior. She'd always be in second place and we'd probably fight about that.

I've had girlfriends. I went with someone I met my freshman year at Cal through the first year I played at Kansas, a period of almost three years. The distance and time changed us and we broke it off. During the off season I've dated quite a bit and started to get serious with a couple girls. It just didn't work out.

I knew what I really wanted this year. I've always been someone who prioritizes his life and I decided last summer that basketball would come first this year. The grades were set and I knew the toughest courses were over. I was not going steadily with anyone and I had worked very hard preparing for this season. I had to decide if I would continue to put my lifetime goal of basketball first, or rearrange things.

I'm looking long-term at things. I know that if I meet the right person, it will all work out the way it's supposed to. She and I will agree on certain things and there will be no arguments about what I'm doing. But she will have realized that basketball in 1997 is the most important thing in my life. Until this season is over.

And that's not easy for most people to accept.

I've gone on a few dates this fall and am going on one tomorrow night. But I can't see myself getting into a serious relationship this year. I'm so focused on basketball. I'll date for fun but I'm not looking for a lifetime partner. At least not till the season is over.

Playing defense, the most important part of basketball. Photo by *Earl Richardson.*

The second home game in a row was against the University of North Carolina-Asheville. This being a Sunday game, the crowd would be filled with a few more families and kids, all of whom want to be a part of Kansas basketball history. And history oozes from this building. There is a lot of basketball lore to gaze at in Allen Fieldhouse.

As the fans enter through the main doors, they are greeted with a series of trophy cases holding photos and awards gathered by the Kansas basketball program. In the center of four glass display cases is a section of the original wooden floor laid in Allen Fieldhouse. A section of momentos is also devoted to Dr. James Naismith, the founder of the game of basketball. Placed on the walls on either side of the indoor track are team photos of the mens' basketball team from the past two seasons. Famous coaches and alumni also have portraits in the hallway.

Spaced at strategic intervals are vendors selling the latest T-shirts, sweatshirts and other articles of KU clothing. Books dealing with Kansas basketball are also available, along with the program for the evening and the Kansas media guide, a treasure trove of KU basketball information.

Today's game was decided early. UNC-Asheville tried to keep pace, but it was simply a case of Kansas having too much talent. I had a particularly good game, hitting 6-8 from the field, including 3-4 from 3-point range, and an assist to turnover ratio of 7-1. I seem to be playing in a zone right now. The entire team was performing well, everyone was clicking, and the final score of 105-73 indicated how lopsided this contest had been.

During this game, there was a moment to remember, something so unusual that it made the highlight portion of the ESPN Sports-Center broadcast the next day. In the final seconds of the game, CB McGrath stole the ball and raced down court for an uncontested layup. Seeing himself all alone, CB decided to go for the dunk. He picked up speed, took off from the center of the lane, leapt into the air, left arm stretched towards the rim.........and bounced the ball of the front of the rim!

The image of CB hanging onto the ball and hitting the front of the iron, then running back downcourt, arms outstretched as if to say "what went wrong?" was replayed numerous times on television. The bench was in hysterics, laughing at the sight, and later on his weekly television show, Coach Williams said it was one of the funniest things he had ever seen in all his years of coaching. We all had fun ripping him about this for days.

WEDNESDAY, DECEMBER 18
"Where's Elmo?" CB was asking. He had purchased the hottest Christmas toy of the year, Tickle Me Elmo, a few months before the hysteria had set in, and loved tormenting me and our friends with the laughing sound made by the doll. CB would carry Elmo around the apartment, talking to it as if it were a real person. He left messages on the answering machine with the sound of Elmo laughing. He put it on the stuffed chair in front of the television and let it watch his favorite shows. He would continually tell me how much he loved his little Elmo. He was driving everyone crazy with Tickle Me Elmo.

But today, he was getting upset. Elmo was nowhere to be found. "Jerod, what did you do with Elmo?" he asked plaintively. I just smiled and answered, "You'll just have to take better care of him, I guess." I winked in the direction of Kris Sell, CB's girlfriend and her roommates, who had come to our apartment to see the hot toy of 1996.

CB was starting to search the living room. He looked behind the couch and under cushions. He searched behind the CD towers and the entertainment center. He scoured the kitchen, opening cabinet after cabinet and even checking the oven and refrigerator. Elmo was nowhere to be found.

"C'mon J, tell me where he is," he begged. As he started to walk down the hallway towards his bedroom, CB let out a shriek of dismay. Kris and I leapt from our chairs and raced to the hallway to see what had happened.

There was Elmo, hanging from the top of the door to CB's bedroom. A tie was wrapped around his neck and CB was hysterically trying to untangle the doll. He started yelling, "Oh my God, what have you done to Elmo?" I couldn't hold my laughter back any longer. The sight at the end of the hall was too much for me to contain.

CB was desperately trying to revive Elmo and get him laughing again. I had finally gotten the practical joker with something he'd remember for a long time. He carried the doll around for the rest of the night.

FRIDAY, DECEMBER 20

Even in the midst of the season, there is still the daily routine of practice. No matter how successful a team may be at the moment, there is always room for improvement. At this point, Kansas is 9-0, but most of the team has the same feeling that I do. We could still get better.

Basketball can be a rough game. *Photo by Earl Richarddson.*

Mark had come out for the weekend to watch the NC State game, and also to observe the growing interest in the Jayhawks. People were starting to suspect that this was an historic season, and the media were sitting up and taking notice. He wanted to see how it would affect my lifestyle and that of the entire team. Attending a practice seemed a logical thing to do.

Visitors cannot just walk into the gym and watch. There is a special section of the upper section of seats reserved for observers. One of the managers will arrive with a clipboard and a list containing the names of those whose presence has been approved by either the basketball office or the coaching staff. Anyone who is not included on this list will be asked to leave and informed as to the proper procedure needed to attend a practice in the future. On this day, some high school coaches from Missouri, Kansas and Oklahoma are present, along with a few friends of TJ's and CB's, plus three members of the local media. The group is keenly watching the action on the floor, with pens and clipboards ready to take notes.

A typical practice day commands four hours of our time. Not all of that will be spent on the floor, and the routine will never be exactly the same, but the time frame is generally consistent. It's prescheduled, so the guys will know when practice will be held, and on what days, almost a month in advance. We are given the equivalent of a syllabus for basketball practice, and this allows us to budget our time accordingly.

Most often, I begin my practice day with a trip to the trainer's room to get taped and treated for whatever ails me. As much time as I spend literally on the floor, there are always some bumps, bruises or floor burns to treat. When this is complete, it is off to the gym floor to begin shooting. A few minutes later, the team will do a few laps around the court to loosen up, stretch a bit, and then begin the practice for the day.

Some of the drills are rudimentary, the same type that any 9th grade team does. There are some parts of basketball, such as ballhandling, that can never be worked on enough, and repetition does help. Some of the drills are fast-paced and complicated, the type that could not be performed with most high school teams. This is a different level of competition, and the players here should be able to grasp the more intricate patterns and faster motion involved.

Watching a Kansas practice, a few things strike the observer immediately. One is the general atmosphere of the team. We come out as a group and don't divide up into any noticeable grouping, such as starters, mid-level players and seldom seen walk-ons. We are what we advertise, a team in every sense of the word. There is no berating anyone when a play is flubbed or a pass is dropped in a drill. Instead there are generally words of encouragement and occasional hand-clapping. It's a supportive, rather than brutally competitive, atmosphere.

Everyone knows his role. There is hard work going on here, and the common goal to become the best team is obvious to anyone watching. We are usually sweating after only a few moments. We dive after any loose ball as if the gym were full and the game was on the line. We realize that if we all work hard, we all will succeed. It's an attitude that has not magically been created, but rather has been passed down from the seniors and accepted by the others. Some people have given me a large part of the credit for this. I don't think it's true, but I'm grateful for the thought.

Scot Pollard has told national magazines that "Jerod's work ethic is amazing. You can't be at a practice and just take it easy when he is going full steam. He makes you work harder because you'll look bad if you don't. It helps everyone push themselves."

Another notable part of a Kansas practice is the quiet tone of practice. Sitting in the section of balcony reserved for observers, it is almost impossible to hear the comments on the floor. Coach Williams and his staff have us in the center court area and outline what they want done, and we carry out their instructions. If there is a show of temper displayed, it is tolerated only if self directed. But there is no shouting at other teammates for a player's own mistake, and any profanity is dealt with immediately. At this practice, one player swears at a non-call of a perceived foul. The practice is stopped, the team assembled and Coach quietly explained why he won't put up with this behavior. Player and coach shake hands, smile, and continue with the session.

No yelling. No screaming. No berating of players. Simply an atmosphere of instruction and support. Everyone has his own style of coaching and running a program. At KU, we have gone this route to become No.1.

SATURDAY, DECEMBER 21
North Carolina State would pose an interesting test for us tonight. This was a team that liked to hold the ball. They had one of the stingiest defenses in the nation, and no team had scored more than 53 points against them thus far, including second-ranked Wake Forest. I was concerned and so was CB.

"J, can these guys actually keep us from running?" CB asked.

"I don't know but I hope I don't find out," I responded.

We were both were silent for a good part of the afternoon. CB was playing around with the computer, sending e-mail messages to

Fans line the hallways after home games, trying to get an autograph or a picture. Photo by Earl Richardson.

his girlfriend Kris in New Jersey, and watching basketball games on TV. He was worried more than he had been about any other opponent except Cincinnati. "They just are so different," he mentioned once to Mark that afternoon. "And Wake Forest had a lot of trouble beating them. What does that mean about our chances?"

CB was voicing a suspicion many had about the Jayhawks. We could outrun almost anyone. But could we play the controlled game? Nobody had yet tried to use that style of play against us, and all the comments about how amazing it would be if we went undefeated up to Christmas were colliding with the concerns about the ball-control offense and tough defense of NC State.

Mark and I went on a last-minute Christmas shopping trip to downtown Lawrence. It was 1 o'clock and there were still two hours until pre-game mealtime, so I decided to hit a local boutique specializing in candles. Unique gifts for the family and friends were something I wanted this year, and time away from basketball was what I sought. I drove with my mind somewhat on the gifts but never far from the game.

"I can't wait to get home for Christmas," I said, trying to steer conversation away from the game. "Maybe it's because we played at Santa Clara last month, I don't know, it just seems like it's been such a long time since I've been home."

"Doesn't this feeling usually hit at Christmas?" Mark asked

"Yeah, but this year it seems more important to get home. Maybe it's because I know I'll have more time to spend there than any of my other three years here. Last year the team went to France over the break and I only had one day at home. I'm looking forward to a week this time," he said.

After driving up and down the main street containing the downtown shops, I finally found a place to park about two blocks away. "Even Lawrence has parking problems this time of year," I joked. We walked to the shopping area but my mind kept going back to the game. I headed straight for the candle shop, which was bustling with customers, and said," I'm getting most of my shopping done right here," as I opened the door and went inside.

After sauntering around the store for a half hour, I found all the candles I wanted and stepped into a typical long holiday checkout line. "It figures," I thought to myself. "The slowdown already has begun. Might as well learn how to deal with it." The guy at the register recognized me and wished the team good luck in tonight's game. I mechanically thanked him, took my bag full of presents and left the store. My mind had gone back to the game and I was starting to focus solely on that. We gave up any plans of getting any other gifts and headed back to the apartment.

When pregame dinner was over, I returned home and tried to take the usual hour-long nap, but I could not fall asleep. Between thinking about the game and the anticipation of going home for six days, I could not fully relax. Giving up, I wandered back into the living room and plopped down onto a chair to watch the end of another college game. Michigan had just defeated Arizona in overtime by two points. Number 4 defeats number 6. It was almost 5 p.m. Time to get over to Allen and get ready. CB grabbed his coat, checked the e-mail one last time, and the two of us left.

It was a large crowd, but not the typical one, for this game. The fall semester had just ended and the Fieldhouse was full of families and residents from all over the area. Most of the student body had left for home. So while the crowd would be loud, it would not be as rowdy as usual. As it turned out, crowd rowdiness would not be a problem.

NC State opened the game by running the entire 35 seconds off the clock before taking a shot. They continued to be as patient as they could, as we pressured them into turnovers and led 15-9. I had only two free throws to show for the first seven minutes, and really had not made much of an impact on the game. After a time-out, the Wolfpack climbed back into the game and closed the gap to 20-19 halfway through the period.

I had landed on my shoulder earlier in the game and it began to tighten up. I had been taken out after playing only about 6 minutes and had yet to return. As I saw the lead dwindle, I began to fidget on the bench. "I've got to get back in there," I thought to myself. "Time to make something happen." Just then time-out was called and Coach Williams inserted a few substitutions into the game. Raef and I were among them.

The team took off on an 8-0 run. After two free throws by NC State, we really went on another tear, outscoring the Wolfpack 11-4. I hit the final shot of the half, an off-balance 18-foot jumper from the corner that swished through the net as the gun went off ending the half. Kansas had again taken the offensive, and the team was in high gear.

The second half was a complete rout. I went 5-7 from the field and the line, finishing with 15 points, but the night's best individual performance belonged to Paul Pierce, who led the team with 21, and had 7 of the first 12 points in the half to set an early tone. As usual, it was a complete team effort, with nine Jayhawks contributing to the point total. North Carolina State's defensive stats were destroyed, as KU hit the 53 total early in the second half, and went on to win 84 - 56. It gave us a perfect 10-0 record before Christmas, a goal we had set and had now achieved.

The locker room was full of laughter and happy faces. Everyone felt good about the game, and about the season. As I sat and surveyed the scene I thought about the coming break. It sure is better to leave like this than if we had lost. Nothing hanging over us for the next week. Just get home and relax. But relaxing would have to wait for a little while. It was time to greet the fans.

After every Kansas home game, fans line the exit from the locker room to the old indoor track. It is an amazing thing to see. As each Jayhawk comes through the door to the lobby, cheers and a rush of fans greet them. Tonight, CB McGrath was the first to come out. followed by TJ Pugh. Kids pressed for an autograph, and the players obliged, soon finding themselves trapped against the white walls of Allen Fieldhouse. Moments later I entered and heard the screams erupting from the crowd. Little kids and adults rushed towards me, and I could only grin as I began to have objects thrust in my face. Taking pens offered by the fans, I signed autograph after autograph.

It continued for an hour. I would move to my left, and more fans would appear with programs, shirts, pictures and shirts. Some high school-aged girls asked to have their pictures taken with me. I obliged. A little boy, about 9, wanted his photo taken with his favorite Jayhawk. A middle-aged man just wanted to shake hands and tell me how much of a positive influence I had been on the man's son. And so it went. I stood against the wall, moving from right to left, signing and smiling. Ryan Robertson and Raef LaFrentz had also joined in the frenzy, and finally all three of us were about done. Nobody but family members and close friends were left when the last objects were signed and the last hand shaken. The game ended at 9:00. The night at Allen Fieldhouse was over at 10:50. It was a long but happy night for everyone. The team had won and the fans were pleased.

I enjoy signing autographs. I know that some people think that this is a real pain, the signing and the pictures after a tough game. But I look at it this way: How many people get this chance? How long will this continue? Someday nobody will want to talk to me or even notice me. When I was young, I used to dream about people wanting my autograph. I can't believe it's now happening. It's a dream come true, and I think it makes people feel good. Looking into their faces as I sign those shirts and hats, I can see it.

CHRISTMAS BREAK - SUNDAY, DECEMBER 22

The game was over and it was time to head home. Coach Williams had given us a six day break, and considering the difficult schedule we had endured, it was welcome. Many of the guys who lived in the area left with their families immediately after the game. Ryan Robertson went back to his dorm room, grabbed a few things and was off with his grandparents. CB left for Topeka with his parents. Jacque Vaughn and Paul Pierce were headed to the airport and a flight back home to Southern California that night. I went back to my room and finished packing.

My flight was the next morning out of Kansas City, with a brief layover in Minneapolis, and then the final leg of the trip to Reno. There I would be met by my mother and the two of us would make the hour drive to South Lake Tahoe. I could hardly wait. Since the end of October I had wanted to see my mom, and the feeling of going home had grown stronger since the trip to Santa Clara. Seeing all the family and friends there had made me more anxious.

The phone rang. It was my mother, telling me about the snow that was falling in the Lake Tahoe region. Deep snow, about four feet at that time. "The Reno airport may be closed, Jerod, "Mom said, sounding concerned. "You'd better check with the airlines and see if your flight is still going through as scheduled."

I didn't need this right now. I had played a tough game and just wanted to get on a place, relax, and get home. I hung up the phone

***The Kansas Jayhawks visit France during the Christmas season in
1995-96.*** *Photo by KU Sports Information.*

and began to search for the phone book behind the couch. Finding
an agent for the airline, I reconfirmed the flight for Sunday. "Yes sir,"
the representative stated, "that flight is still scheduled to go to Minneapolis, have an hour and ten minute layover, and then proceed
on to Reno. As long as the weather holds current, there should be
no problem."

I felt relieved. At least there would be no problem getting to
Reno. The only possible problem I could foresee would be how my
mother would fare driving over the mountains in all that snow
already on the ground. "Maybe Karin & Chris (my sister and broth-
er-in -law) will come with her," I thought. I then turned the television to the Weather Channel and saw pictures of the snow for the
first time. It left me stunned.

The forecaster was predicting a possible two feet additional
snow! The scenes were out of some Alaskan blizzard, and the roads
being called impassible were all those leading into and out of Tahoe.
There was a chance that this additional snow would miss the region,
and so the announcer was saying to keep tuned for the latest
updates on the situation. But the California Highway Patrol was
advising that nobody travel in the area.

Around 11:30 p.m., I received a call from one of my friends who
wanted to go out for awhile, just hanging out kind of stuff. I

thought about the fact that my flight wasn't leaving until 6:45 the next morning. and I wasn't really tired. Probably too excited about going home. I needed to keep busy and forget about the snow, so I agreed and left the apartment.

The next morning, Mark took me to the airport. We arrived at 5:30 and were greeted by a familiar scene to holiday travelers: a long line to check in luggage. There were only two people working at the counters and at least 50 people in line waiting ahead of him. "Geez, I can't catch a break," I thought to myself. I had only been able to get about a half hour's worth of sleep during the entire night, still being too wound up. I stood in line, waiting patiently, and started to feel tired for the first time.

As the line slowly progressed, I felt the exhaustion creeping up on me My eyes were beginning to get sore, and I put my baggage down on the floor and just pushed it as the line inched forward. I didn't want to read. That would only make things worse. I left the bags and took a short walk down the concourse, just to keep active. I returned and saw that some additional attendants had arrived, and now people were being booked rapidly for the flight. An hour had passed and I was just now checking my luggage. I said goodbye to Mark, who had to catch his own flight back home, and went to the waiting area for boarding the plane. Finally I was going home.

The flight to Minneapolis arrived on time. As I got off the plane, I thought immediately about finding a television set and seeing if there were any more pictures about the blizzard out west. It was as bad as I had imagined. The weather had changed again, and now the storm was dumping three additional feet of snow on the Tahoe area! It was reaching record levels, and the situation looked hopeless. The airlines announced that the flight would be delayed for two hours.

As the plane finally took off for Reno, I felt anxious. I had managed to get a brief nap during the short flight from Kansas City my plans for the break, how I might not get to see my grandparents due to the road closings and deep snow. I worried about my mother driving to get me at the airport. I recalled Christmas break last year. Then, the team had played a game in New Jersey on December 23 and was going to leave for Paris on the 26th. I had flown home to be with my family for the holiday, but by the time I reached the airport, waited for a slight delay and flown home I was drained. Kansas had just played a tough game against Temple and lost, so the feeling of exhaustion was even more acute. I slept most of Christmas Eve. That left me with half of Christmas Day to visit, because I had to be back in New York that night for the flight to Europe. It was almost not worth the effort, but I needed to see my family. It was my only visit since August and one of only two that year.

The flight from Minneapolis to Reno had been in the air nearly an hour when the pilot came on the intercom with the bad news. The flight would have to be rerouted to Las Vegas. The weather in the Reno area was simply too bad for any attempted landing. Passengers would be told what would happen next when the flight neared the airport.

I sank back in my seat with a feeling of despair. I was already dead tired from the experiences of the past 36 hours, and now I would have to deal with this. It was not something I was looking forward to. Would I have to wait long? Would it be an overnight stay in the airport? Was there any chance of getting to Tahoe by Christmas? Being tired made it all the more difficult to deal with. At the moment, I just wanted to get off this plane.

The plane landed and we were informed that the airline would be sending us to a motel for the night. I called home and told Mom about the arrangements. It would be five hours later that a flight for Reno would take off, weather permitting. I would land in Reno an hour after that I'd wait until someone could come and get me.

I spent a fitful night in the motel. I couldn't seem to get to sleep, and after a few hours of dozing, I went to the casino in the motel and played a few games on the slots. After losing $20, I thought to myself, "With the luck I've been having, why would I ever think I'd win at this?" I went back to the room, picked up my things and headed back to the airport to wait there.

About three hours later, the announcement came over the airport public address system. the flight to Reno would be taking off within the hour. At last, I was finally going home. I boarded the plane, sank back into my seat, and thought about all the things I wanted to do during this now shortened visit. But the journey still wasn't over.

When the plane landed, I was confronted with the reality that there still were no open roads back to South Lake Tahoe. Nobody had arrived to greet me at the airport, so I had no way to get from Reno back to my home. However, fate was about to turn my way.

The back roads had been clear, and Mom had finally made it through. As I looked down the length of the terminal walkway, I thought I saw familiar figures running towards me. Standing up, I realized that I was right. A broad smile crossed my face and with outstretched arms, I moved forward and hugged my mother, all the while being myself surrounded by my nephew, niece and the rest of the family.

It probably looked like any other holiday embrace to the casual airport observer. But to me it was the happy end to what had been a very trying two days. The ride home, usually an hour, was extended to six, due to the dangerous road conditions and the roundabout route they were forced to take. The kids were happily talking away, Karin and Chris were asking questions and Mom was also talking about events that had been occurring in their lives. I should have been thoroughly exhausted.

But I wasn't. I was just so glad to be with the people I loved, back home at the best time of the year. I walked into the comfortable living room, gazed at the tree, the hardwood floor, the snow covered trees at the side of the house and in the yard out back, and felt overwhelmed by my feelings. I dropped the bags and just sat in the rocking chair by the fireplace.

"I love it here," I told Mom. The look in my eyes probably said more than that..

"And I love you," my mother replied, emotion filling her voice. She moved towards me and gave me a hug. It was good to finally be home for Christmas.

CHRISTMAS WEEK
I spent my day and a half of vacation as many others do when free time is short. I visited my friends Scott Gilliland, Christi and Heidi Hosman, my high school coach, Tom Orlich, and others. But the weather had reduced my time at home, and the plans I had made to see my grandparents and other family members were ruined, since most of the roads were still impassible even two days later. All too soon, it was time to head back to Kansas.

The next week was filled with activity. CB and I went to the Missouri River riverboats one evening, and I visited with my former roommate, Mike Sykes, who was in town for a few days. We took in a basketball game in Kansas City, where Sykes' team from Colorado was playing, and by then it was time to get back to the routine.

Practice resumed on the 27th. A few days later, we played Washburn, a division II school about three hours away. The main reason for this game was that Scot Pollard's brother plays for this school, and Coach Williams tries to get games like this for the benefit of his senior players. It was an easy win for us, 90-65 ,but there was one unexpected event during this game.

Right before game time, I noticed that Jacque was about to suit up and join the téam. Since his injury, JV had sat in street clothes on the bench, supporting the team while dying on the inside. He had practiced two days before the NC State game, took the week off, and started to play again after Christmas. He was healed and ready to return. Tonight was the night.

The gym erupted with a thunderous ovation when Jacque took the floor. He was back. The team had just added depth most other programs could only dream about. I know how much he has hated sitting and just watching us. I've been out with an injury and know lousy you can feel. But for Ryan, it's a test of character. He always knew this day would come, and now he has to take his old spot on the bench and realize that while he may still play, his time to star is still in the future. He helped us tremendously. We could never have done so well this season without him stepping up to the challenge. He's become a veteran overnight. But sitting down was still rough for him after starting all those games.

It was a good game for everyone, and I had one of those nights that anyone dreams about. Playing only 18 minutes, I went 3-3 from the field, 1-1 from 3 point range and 2-2 from the free throw line. If I'd known I was going to be perfect tonight, I would've shot every time I got the ball. Considering some of my past games, this was a good way to end 1996.

SATURDAY, DECEMBER 28

Since we were about to start conference play, I decided to break in a pair of new shoes. I asked Jill Johansen, our head manager, for a new pair. She handed them to me and I proceeded to try them on and go through my ritual of getting new shoes ready.

We are provided with 10 pair of shoes a season. This may sound like a lot, but consider how many hours we are in them, constantly moving, cutting and wearing down the sole. We need to be able to stop without sliding and be able to turn and run down the floor quickly. The shoes must be in excellent shape for this to happen.

The team signs a contract with a shoe manufacturer, and that company will provide the shoes for the entire season. This year Nike won the contract to provide athletic footwear for the team. Shoes have become a fashion statement in sports, but I'm not concerned with whose name is on the shoe. I want to be able to play to the best of my ability, and if a shoe can help me reach that goal, that's the one I want to wear.

Socks are also provided by the basketball program. There is not a limit on these. I don't abuse the privilege and try to avoid getting too many pairs. Sometimes, however, I can't avoid it.

All our athletic laundry is done by the managers. When I'm working out, I can leave those clothes with the managers and when I open my locker the next time I'm in the gym, the clothes will be there, completely clean. Most of the guys say they really notice the increase in laundry back at their homes when the season is over. We never have to wash any athletic wear during the season. I admit we're a bit spoiled.

I'm checking my locker now to see what needs replacing with new items from either home or the department. I don't need a T-shirt, since I don't wear one when I play. Some guys, like Paul, always wear a T-shirt under their jersey. I can't stand that. I feel very restricted on the floor if I have a shirt on. My own feelings are that wearing a T-or cut-off T-shirt is mainly a fashion statement. I prefer to not have something on under the jersey.

My own fashion statement of sorts is the length of my shorts. The trend in recent years has been to have baggy knee-length shorts, and some teams have even gone below the knee for their own distinctive look. The guys at KU have also opted for the longer length, stopping about an inch above the knee. I wore these the past few seasons, but this year wanted to go back to what makes me more comfortable. With that in mind, I asked if my game and practice shorts could be shortened about two more inches, back to the length that was popular in the early and mid-80's.

I hadn't told the other guys about this and when the uniforms were issued last month, they were all very "sympathetic". Many expressed how bad they felt for me to have to wear those "ugly" shorts for the first home game of my senior year. Then I told everyone that this was what I really wanted. The look on their faces was priceless!

Suddenly, the atmosphere changed. Immediately, everyone began to tease me, to make comments about my legs or living in a different era. At practice, when I swiped a bad pass and took off down the floor, JV began yelling "Havlicek steals the ball, Havlicek steals the ball!" (after the Boston Celtic great John Havlicek, who wore possibly the shortest shorts ever seen in pro ball.). All the guys broke up at that, as did I.

The shorts became my trademark this year. The school athletic paper, the student newspaper and other publications wrote little blurbs about them. People have asked me why I chose to do this. It seemed as if I were some kind of rebel, challenging the accepted fashion norm. Jerod Haase, stylistic innovator.

The only reason this occurred was so I would feel more comfortable. I feel as though I am moving faster and, as with the T-shirts, am less restricted in my movements. I did it to make my game more effective. That's it. The attention was extra.

TUESDAY, DECEMBER 31

It's New Years' Eve, but during the day, I decided to get around to answering some of the fan mail that has piled up on my desk. Besides, most of my plans are for tonight.

College players do get fan mail. It may surprise some people, because we are, after all, just young men in our late teens and early twenties. But people regard college athletes as something different from the average person of that age. And when they get the urge, people write .

Most of the letters are simply addressed to "Jerod Haase, University of Kansas." Some are sent to the basketball office. Some are sent to the coach. And once in a while, someone really takes great pains and succeeds in finding out the actual address of my apartment. The letters come in all types of envelopes, from colored and scented to crayon scribbled and slightly torn or folded. They usually have a return address, but sometimes it's not legible. But one thing is clear from all of the mail: this is someone who wants to come into contact with me, and the reason is enclosed.

Today's assortment of mail is not atypical of what I receive in a given week. There are probably about 30 letters, and they are from all over the country. Granted, about one-third are from the states of Kansas or Missouri, but others are from upstate New York, Tennessee, Indiana and New Hampshire.

The letters are almost evenly split by gender, and the most common request is for a signed photo or an autograph on a sheet of paper. The bulk of the younger writers, especially those under 13, want both. I will spend time reading each letter and then deciding which ones I should answer immediately, and which can be put off for another day. But I will answer nearly all the letters I receive, no matter how long it takes me to respond.

Here is a sampling of the letters received today:

A young man from New Jersey writes:

"Dear Jerod, You are my favorite basketball player, not only for your tenacious defense, your all-around hustle and your picture-perfect shot, but I admire you for the fact that you have managed a 3.6 GPA.

He continues in this vein, and then concludes with:

"I have one very big problem being a fan of yours in New Jersey. I cannot find a number 35 jersey at any sports store. Can you believe that? Can you help me find a place to buy one? Can you sell me one of your old ones? I'll be happy to pay for it, 'cause I know college players can get in all kinds of trouble doing this."

Another letter, an older fan, reads:

"When I was a freshman in high school, you were at Cal, and I saw you play at Oregon. I thought it was cool that you could put up big numbers on offense, but still go so hard on defense. I've followed you since you transferred to KU. I've looked up to a few college players, like Damon Stoudamire, but you are the last one I can really admire. I just wanted to write and tell you good luck, win a lot of games, and individually have a good year too."

There are letters from the female fans:

Dear Jerod, "Can we meet after the game? I'll wait off to one side and be wearing a red and blue KU hat with a number 35 on it."

Dear Jerod, "Can I get a picture taken with you sometime? It would be soooo cool just to meet you and have something to remember "

Dear Jerod, "I've written to you a few times already. Now I'd like to meet with you and maybe go out to eat or something. How about after a home game sometime?

Inevitably, there will be one letter that stands out as unique or poignant. It's the kind of thing that people will write from the heart, and it is truly special.

Dear Jerod, "I've been a basketball coach for many years, went to camps at KU and have been a fan of the Jayhawks for years. My son is an even bigger fan of yours, but I only recently learned how big.

He was feeling down because we had moved to a new state, California. I wanted to cheer him up a suggested a vacation. He said Lake Tahoe. I thought it was a natural choice. When we arrived, he got all excited. He wanted to see the high school, and then said 'Dad, Jerod played here.' It was then that I realized why we had come to Tahoe.

We went all over town the next few days. He kept saying, 'Jerod ate here' or 'Jerod shopped here'. He started to ask people if they knew you, and if one said they did it just made him smile, as if he now knew you too. It was a special vacation for him.

I save nearly all of my fan mail. It's something that I will never forget. Some of the guys wonder why I would save or even respond to all this. I look at it this way. These people took the time to write. I should at least try and get something back to them, even if it's only a signed picture or schedule card. As far as saving the mail, when I read this, it makes me feel fortunate. How could I ever stay depressed, knowing that all these people out there are supporting me? It's a special feeling, and one that I don't ever think I'll forget.

THURSDAY, JANUARY 2, 1997
This is a slow stretch for basketball players. The student body is gone, home for the long break between the end of the semester on December 20 and the start of the second semester, beginning on January 14. Everyone is trying to find some way to keep occupied or have fun.

I had gone a few days without shaving and decided to have some fun with my appearance. Scot Pollard had attracted attention with his unique lamb chop sideburns and goatee. I decided to shave my face the same way, and when I appeared at practice, there were stares, laughs and comments from everyone. The coaching staff broke up at the sight of me, the normally clean-cut Jerod, looking like the most colorful character on the team.

Three days later, Brown University came to Lawrence and again, it was a case of too much talent versus an overmatched opponent. I noticed the difference in our approach to this game. Because there was not much videotape about this team, we tended to focus more on what need to do ourselves rather than what they do. There is a more relaxed atmosphere before a game like this. Not to sound cocky, but we realize we are more talented and if we play our game, we'll win.

The game went according to plan. We were never threatened, and won handily. After the game, there is a happy feeling, but it's more matter of fact than winning a game like UCLA. Still, we'll always take a win.

FRIDAY, JANUARY 3
Playing far away from my home in Tahoe has its drawbacks. The biggest is the fact that people from home cannot come to see me play very often. I realize that all college students who leave their

home state have the same adjustment problems. It's part of life. We all leave one set of surroundings and adopt another.

People sometimes make a big deal of the fact that Kansas has five players from California. They make it seem as though because we are from the same state, we somehow all have known one another our entire lives. They tend to forget that we met for the first time at Kansas, just as most of the other students did. We are not in some magical world where we know all basketball players from all over the nation. We have gotten to know one another through our time as teammates, and have become friends as a result.

The people I've met in my life fall into two categories. There are the those who know me as Jerod, the basketball player. Many of these people are the ones I know here at KU. They are nice and have been friendly, and they generally want to talk about basketball, or somehow get around to the topic of sports. There is nothing wrong with this, because I know they think that is my favorite subject. They are what I would call friends and acquaintances. They don't generally try to get to know me other than as an athlete.

The other group of people are those who know me as Jerod the person. These are the friends I've had for years, those who take me as I am, and don't talk about only basketball with me. They will accept me whether I am playing for Kansas or am just sitting in the bleachers. These people are my closest friends, and I am grateful for having them in my life.

The guys on the team are pretty much the same. We have gotten close to one another due to the life we lead. Of course, we have made friends outside the team, but none of us is a campus party animal. A few of the guys are in a fraternity, but most of us from outside the area have a small group of friends and that's it. With our schedule, it's not really possible to hang out with large groups of people.

This week, three of my friends from home have flown out to see me. Scott and Brett were teammates of mine from high school, and Lon, who is a few years younger, is also a good friend. It's great to them around for a few days. It makes it seem as if I'm back in Tahoe again.

It's funny to listen to some of the things my friends say about me playing basketball for the number one team in the country. Scott has always maintained that it is really strange seeing his best friend on television, and listening to the remarks of the commentators, who act as if they know me personally and then say something that is completely incorrect about me. I would guess that anyone who knows a member of the team probably feels that way. I'm not saying we are famous celebrities, but we are in the public eye, our pictures are in national magazines, and our names become well-known in the sports world. It's the same way I felt when I saw my brother Steven playing for the Air Force Academy, while I was in high school. It was a strange mixture of pride and yet a weird feeling that I personally knew the guy performing on television. Better yet, he was my older brother. It's a feeling I'll never forget.

Others have said that they get angry when I am criticized by commentators. They want to tell everyone about what I'm like, how hard I work, how I give a full effort. Still others say it bothers them when fans yell my name and act as though they know me, when they have never met me. That's part of being an athlete. Fans do feel as though they can call you by your first name, and I think we all have become the property of these loyal supporters. They want us to win, and at times want to identify with us. Using our names is part of that identification. It's a sign of support, and I'll take that over being ignored anytime.

Since Brett and Lon have never been to Kansas before, I took them around campus today. Scott has been here before, but he still gets a kick out of seeing the gym, locker room and everything else associated with KU basketball. For the other guys, it's all new and they seem to enjoy it.

Knowing how much the guys like basketball, I thought I would give them a unique experience today. I took them over to the fieldhouse and turned on the lights over the main floor. Then we played a few games of two on two, horse, and had 3-point shooting contests. It was fun to fool around like the old days, playing without any pressure or any goal except to have fun. Then we decided to make the night complete.

I took Scott's camera and knelt below the basket. Each of the guys took turns trying to dunk the ball, and I got a picture of them from an angle that made it appear they were leaping high above the rim. Scott wanted one final shot, but it turned out to be the funniest moment of the night. As he went up to dunk the ball, his knee gave out, and when I snapped the shot all I took was a picture of air. Scott ended up on the floor, the ball went in another direction, and we all had a good laugh. Scott's big moment at Allen Fieldhouse. Nothing but air.

We went back to the apartment, rented a few movies, and sat around talking late into the night. It was really a good time for me, like reliving the old days back home. Sometimes the best nights are just simple times like this.

A New Era

THE BIG 12 SEASON

The conference season is the major part of any schedule. Our goal has always been to win both the conference and the post-season tournament. Then comes the ultimate goal: the National Championship.

As we enter this phase of the season, we are the top-ranked team in America for the fourth week in a row. It's becoming apparent to many that we have all the necessary ingredients for success. We have talent, depth and balanced scoring. We've been able to win tough games on the road and maintain the nation's longest home-court winning streak. Things are looking good.

The first poll of the New Year finds Wake Forest ranked right behind us at No. 2. The rest of the Top Ten has continually changed but our conference is represented well, with four other teams in the Top 25. Iowa State is ranked 8th, Texas 18th, Texas Tech 22nd and Colorado 25th. We play all of these teams in January. It's the toughest part of the season.

Some of the ranked teams we defeated in December have fallen on tough times. George Washington has dropped out of the Top 25, UCLA fell to 23rd and Cincinnati lost another game and dropped out of the Top 10.

The conference is never easy. No matter what people say, any conference is difficult. The coaches don't change their styles drastically, the players remain from previous years and everyone tends to know what the other guy's going to do.

It means that execution is what separates good teams from the rest of the league. If you play your game well, the other teams can't stop you. There are no real surprises when it comes to conference play.

The arenas are also familiar ground. You learn after one trip which crowds are the rowdiest, the meanest, and the loudest. You discover which floors are better for shooting, seeing the basket and simply dribbling the ball. You know what trips are going to be the easiest, most difficult and most boring.

It's the central part of the schedule, the section filled with the great rivalries which make college basketball exciting. Kansas vs. Missouri, Oklahoma vs. Oklahoma State, Kansas vs. Kansas State. These are intense games, where more than just a victory is important. Schools carry the hopes of a state along with them, and bragging rights for the next year are at stake. To fans, there is nothing more important than saying your team beat the other guys. To players, there is nothing quite as exciting as playing these conference games in front of a gym full of rowdy, enthusiastic fans.

SATURDAY, JANUARY 4

I was ready to get the conference season going. After the games this week against opponents that were competitive, but not seriously challenging, I wanted to get back to the intensity I knew Kansas State would bring to the game. K-State is only a 90-minute drive across the state, and the fierce rivalry is legendary. This year would be no exception.

We were all aware that Kansas State could beat anyone in the league. Although they had not played well this year, we knew they would be up for us. We had heard that this was going to be their biggest crowd in years, and we knew that our fans would be in a distinct minority. It would not be an easy game tonight.

The game opened as if we were going to blow our opponents off the floor. Scot scored an quick inside hoop, and Jacque hit a three the next trip down. After four free throws, Jacque hit Paul with a lob for a dunk, and the score was 11-1, Kansas. And a minute later, I dove for a loose ball, drove the baseline and fed Scot with a bounce pass for another close-in basket. We had increased the lead to 13-3.

After K-State closed the gap to 15-10, I was leveled going in on a 3-on-1 break. I hit both free throws, and when Scot dunked a moment later, it was 19-10. It looked as if we had regained the momentum.

But something happened, and Kansas State fought its way back. Down 29-19, they put together a 7-0 run, and held close while we went ice-cold. Kansas went 1-12 from the field during this period, and at the half, the score was 33-29.

Our play on offense left something to be desired. But our defense was pretty solid. Kansas State was trying too hard to get a shot, and we would block or steal the ball at critical moments. I recall that I retrieved two consecutive blocks by the big men, in the middle of three K-State players who were simply looking at the ball. I was trying to make up for my lousy shooting night by diving for loose balls more than any game this year. I also was trying to get as many rebounds as possible, as if to take out my aggression and anger on the boards.

The second half saw our shooting miseries continue. There seemed to be a lid on the basket. No matter who shot the ball, it seemed as if there was a hand over the cylinder. I went 0-7 from the field before finally connecting on a baseline drive, well into the second half. It would be a milestone basket, since it put me over the

1,000-point mark for my career at Kansas, the 34th player to reach this goal. Some small consolation.

We committed a lot of aggressive fouls. At one point, Paul was whistled for three fouls in a 28-second stretch. He ended up fouling out of the game on a reach-in attempt with about three minutes left in the game. Scot and Raef also had four fouls apiece.

In the end, we won because of our hustle on defense and our experience. Our shooting from the field was abysmal, ending up at 29% for the night. But it was defense which won this game. Final score, 62-59.

After the game, I thought about what had happened. I was extremely frustrated with myself and my performance. I felt that I had let the team down, that I had not contributed what was expected of me. I was disappointed in what I felt was a lack of leadership on my part. The team had not played with the intensity needed to win, we had slacked off, and it had almost cost us this game. Much of the blame for that rested with me.

I decided to call a quick team meeting immediately after the game. The coaches were not in the locker room. I faced my teammates directly. "I want you guys to know how disappointed I am with my own performance tonight," I told them. "You guys know how much I want to win. I didn't contribute much tonight. But that'll change."

There was muttering from the group. "C'mon Jerod," someone said. "We all know you try. Don't take it so hard. We won."

"But that's my point, "I continued. "We need to learn from this. Some teams learn from a loss. We need to learn to never take anyone lightly again. I need to learn to concentrate in these games. We all can improve from a game like this."

It was over that quickly. The team filed out and boarded the bus for the ride back to Lawrence. All the way, I felt sick about my performance. I couldn't enjoy the fact that we had won. I started to worry again about my poor shooting performance. It was all too reminiscent of that terrible day last March, the 0-9 game in the NCAA tournament.

I came home, threw my bags in the center of the room, and plopped down on the sofa. I laid on my back and stared at the ceiling. Nothing any of my friends could say or do would shake my moodiness tonight. I began to think how much I stunk up the place. What if this continues? This is just when it started last year. Right after Christmas break. What if it continues? And those free throws! Damn, I really played lousy.

I wasn't the best of hosts tonight, but then my friend Scott and the others were used to my moods after games. Having been my teammates in high school, they knew how much of a perfectionist I could be when evaluating myself after a game. They tried to be understanding and kept the conversation off the game, talking about the flight home and other non-basketball subjects. But it wasn't working. Finally, I excused myself, and went back into my bedroom.

I finally drifted off to sleep, but it was not a night of comfortable sleep. I kept waking up and tossing, thinking about the game, about the missed opportunities. Somehow, I must have fallen asleep, because the next thing I knew the sun had come up again.

MONDAY, JANUARY 6

When a player has a game as frustrating as my last performance against Kansas State, he wants to get over it quickly. The best thing for me is to go out and play another game. That way, I can work out the problems right away, rather than dwell on them. Texas would provide this opportunity.

Texas was currently ranked 22nd in the polls. The Longhorns were new to our schedule. With the addition of four teams from the old Southwest Conference, the new Big 12 featured some new match-ups, and tonight was one of the better ones, a meeting between two programs that had been successful in recent years. It was another televised game, another late start, another challenge to our winning streak.

The start of the game featured a new twist, a slowdown offense from Texas, a team which had the reputation of run-and-gun. It took us awhile to adjust to what they were doing. The score after eleven minutes of play was 9-7, Texas. With only six minutes left in the half, we were shooting 3-18 from the field. Our poor shooting from the Kansas State game was still haunting us.

I was almost invisible in the early going of this game. I wasn't doing anything productive offensively. Right before the half, I faked a defender, drove to the free throw line, and sank a 15-foot jumper. "It's about time," I thought to myself. I played sound defense, but was a non-factor in the game, something that annoyed me at the half. I like to think that I can get the team moving, that I am always able to contribute, but this game, the first half was really frustrating. I was worried because I could not get focused during the pre-game warm-ups. My legs were very sore and I just couldn't seem to get in sync.

Nothing out of the ordinary occurred at the half. Sometimes Coach adopts a matter-of-fact attitude and goes over the ordinary normal details. He's not one always to come in with some fiery speech, getting us to leap into the air with cries of aggression. I appreciate his style. We are not a bunch of high school freshmen learning how to play the game. We have a lot to learn about the game, but one thing I think we have been taught by Coach and his staff is to play with our heads and not let our emotions run wild. That's an important distinction, because when the game gets close and there is pressure building in the final seconds, we still can look at the situation and think about what needs to be done. We don't panic and throw up wild shots. We try to cause the other team to do that.

Emotional outbursts have their place, but too often I think some coaches use them in place of calm analysis. We already have the fire within ourselves. When I think of our practices, and the intensity I experience on the floor between 4 and 7 most afternoons, I know that we will try our best and want to win our games. It's the mental aspect of the game where we always need reinforcement. At our halftime talks, Coach tries to remind us of that.

The second half of this game saw us go on a terrific run to break the game open. During this stretch, I had gone inside for a rebound and was called for a foul. The Texas player and I ended up on the ground, and as I got up to return to the huddle, the Texas player began to talk trash. I didn't hear what he said, so I left the huddle and asked him to repeat it.

"You are one crazy mother........,"said the Longhorn

"Why thank you, I guess you're right," I responded, laughing.

The Texas player walked off, shaking his head as though he had spoken to a nut case.

Jacque and I each had six assists, and the big men had responded well. We believed we had answered the critics who said that a running team like Texas would pose a problem for Kansas. Coach Williams even said that the "running Horns were walking tonight."

Everyone felt good after this game. It was time to make sure the freshmen remembered their duties. There are only two freshman this year, Nick Bradford and walk-on Terry Nooner. They were about to be re-educated.

"Freshmen! Get everything ready," Scot called out in his booming voice.

"You freshmen better take care of things now," Paul warned.

After each game, a freshman has to turn on the showers for the rest of the team. They make sure the water is just the right temperature,and arrange the towels for the upperclassmen. When we go on the road, they carry any food, such as brownies, and bring it to any team member who requests something. It's not much in the way of hazing, in fact it's relatively minor. But after all, they are freshmen.

Nick has a great sense of humor and one of those infectious smiles. On Coach Williams' TV show, before Christmas, Nick told the audience that his wish for my present was that I'd get a girl-friend and get away from my computer. He jokes easily and fits in with the personalities on this team.

Terry, as a walk-on, is in a little different situation, but he also is a great guy. He is not as outspoken as Nick, but also likes to joke around. Paul drew a picture of Terry with his goatee and noted how he looked like Jacque, who also is currently wearing facial hair. He has started calling him JV's little brother. Paul's picture is so bad it's funny, and Terry seems to like the razzing he gets.

The game has loosened up everyone, the freshmen do their jobs and the post- game autograph session is relaxed and not as long as after some recent games. This is what it's all about.

FRIDAY, JANUARY 10

"It's ready," I called to CB, who was in his bedroom getting dressed.

"This better be good," CB warned, as he headed down the hall-way towards the kitchen. "I'm starving."

A new bread machine graced the kitchen counter in our apart-ment, and I had been experimenting with all sorts of new breads for the past few weeks. I had become reasonably adept, I felt, at setting the machine so that we would always have fresh bread ready when the evening rolled around. But now I was expanding into morning sweet rolls, and today it was going to be cinnamon rolls. The aroma drifted through the apartment, and we both were anticipating breakfast.

"Umm, pretty good," said CB, his mouth full of dough. "Give me another."

I grabbed for the cinnamon roll, but CB was too quick and raced down the hall to his room, laughing and eating at the same time. "Too slow for the ultra quick McGrath," he teased.

"At least he's eating it," I thought to myself, taking a bite out of what remained in the pan.

Food is always an issue with any college student, and at Kansas, the basketball team is encouraged to eat well. We eat at a training table meal in the Burge Union building four days a week. The time of the meal varies, and it could be with athletes from other sports such as football. One night a week, the team eats at a specified restaurant in Lawrence as a group. The eating establishments rotate, and the time of day is usually dinner, but the idea is to make sure that the players are eating right. The rest of the time, we are on our own.

College basketball players can get a meal allowance. In the past, actual money was not used and the system at Kansas involved a sort of debit card for meals, which were presented at the time the athlete would pay for the meal. This year, with a veteran team, the players are given monthly meal money allowance checks of $280. This money comes from the Athletic Department's NCAA compliance office, and the players are free to spend it on whatever food we wish. The checks are issued for the entire school year, not only during the season. The coaching staff trusts us to eat right and knows that we are mature enough to that. There are a lot of choices for meals, and many varying tastes on our team.

Fast-food is always the most convenient option. CB is a self-confessed junk food addict, eating at least once each day at some local chain. Ryan is another of the continual patrons. I am more likely to try to make something at home or hit a deli-style restaurant, and often I can get Raef to go along. Mexican food is another favorite of mine. I think I'm well known to the employees of all three of Lawrence's Mexican restaurants.

We eat best at the pre-game meals, where steak and chicken are the predominant meats, but there is always an array of fruits and vegetables, pasta and other "energy" foods. This is the time when any coach wants to make certain his players are eating their best, and not ingesting something that will inhibit their performance. We all look forward to this meal, especially when it is before a night game.

I was pleased with the results of my experiment today. "Hey C, how about if I try pizza dough next?" I asked.

MONDAY, JANUARY 13
Iowa State was coming to town. It was billed as the biggest test thus far. This was the team that had their entire starting five returning, a team that had beaten us last February in the Big 8 tournament final, a team that had stated it believed it could continue defeating Kansas. If ever there was an opponent to be respected, it was Iowa State's Cyclones.

I had gone through a busy day. It was the first day of classes for the new semester. I had spent the morning meeting with my academic adviser, planning courses and my future after graduation. By this point, I had already accumulated enough credits to graduate and so it was time to think about life after KU. Go to grad school? Look for a job? Wait until the NBA draft? All of these were options to consider, and we spent the time discussing these topics. It took a

Dick Vitale, ESPN basketball color analyst, gets Jacque Vaughn to smile during a post-game interview. Photo by KU Sports Information.

good part of the morning.

Matt Doherty, an assistant coach and former star at North Carolina, also wanted some of my time this morning. He wanted to discuss how the season had progressed and how I had been performing. Our conversation went well, and soon it was already mid-afternoon.   I returned to the apartment and took care of some more school-related matters and then headed out for the pregame meal. Game time was getting close.

The crowd for this game was enormous. The lobbies were full and the crowd spilled outside. Students were lining up three hours before the game, oblivious to the fact that the temperature was 4 degrees above zero. It was frigid, but the mood of the crowd was hot. People were chanting "Rock Chalk", others were yelling impromptu cheers, and most were happily waiting the chance to see this game. Scalpers were everywhere, trying their best to make a buck selling what appeared to be the hottest ticket in town. (It should be noted that ticket scalping is legal in the state of Kansas.) Also as prevalent were the people begging for seats at any price, stopping those on their way to Allen Fieldhouse and pleading for a ticket, any seat just to get inside and see this game firsthand. It was an event.

ESPN had arrived earlier that day. My friends told me that television announcer Dick Vitale came in to the lobby of the Lawrence Holiday Inn Holidome and encountered people sitting in the lobby, waiting for a chance to get his autograph and speak their mind about the Jayhawks. Vitale would smile, sign the paper, and nod in agreement about the success of the team. Happy fans would then leave, excitedly telling one another of their good fortune at getting the signature and the sense that someone else realized how good our team was.

Vitale worked the crowd at Allen Fieldhouse like a warm-up man at a TV game show. He shot free throws with students, played a brief game of horse with another student, and gestured happily at the student cheering section. Responding in kind, the KU student body cheered and chanted and helped create the atmosphere desired by any television producer. Vitale had done his job well. The crowd would certainly be cooking when the cameras started rolling at 8:30.

And when Iowa State took the floor for the pregame warm-up, they were greeted with a standing ovation by a crowd wearing red and blue, chanting "Over-rated (clap, clap, clap-clap-clap)." The students greeted us with a thunderous roar, standing, pounding their feet and clapping in unison. By the time the school song had been sung and the Rock Chalk Chant delivered, the crowd was on its feet, impatient to get the game under way.

There was a sense of importance to this game that had been missing from any played at Allen Fieldhouse this season. I could sense this as I walked onto the floor. Even the GW game a month earlier had lacked this atmosphere. I realized what it was one minute into the game. The conference. The familiarity between the two schools. The rivalry that Iowa State had built up with KU. Over the past three seasons, we had gone 3-3 against each other. We knew what one another were going to do. This would raise the level of difficulty and make each player work harder to be successful, on offense or defense.

The crowd reflected this tension. The noise level in the old gym was deafening, and as we started to pull away, the crowd became more frenzied. When I drove to the free throw line to sink a short jumper, I could feel the crowd scream encouragement all the more. At the midway point of the half, Iowa State had climbed back into the lead, taking a 23-19 margin.

It would increase to 26-23 and we had to take a time-out. It was then that the momentum of the game would change. It was now that KU would put on one of our now-famous runs.

It began with Jacque Vaughn throwing a lob pass to Scot, who back-cut for an easy dunk. The next trip down, Paul Pierce fed Pollard for another dunk. Iowa State took a time-out, but it didn't stop our momentum. BJ Williams hit off a rebound, then I faked my man into the air, drove inside for a short 10-foot jumper. The run was well under way.

When the horn sounded three minutes later, ending the half, we had taken a 17-4 run, and led 40-30 at the half. We were never seriously challenged the rest of the night.

Iowa State fell behind by as much as 15 in the second half, and then with about seven minutes left, tried one last time to make a game of it. After they got to within seven, we closed strong, winning by a final of 80-67.

As the teams shook hands and left the floor, Iowa State's coach Tim Floyd, came up to me for a few words. "Just wanted to say that I respect the way you play and wish you the best this year," Floyd said. Feeling a bit surprised at this, I responded, "Thanks, coach, I appreciate that." We shook hands and Floyd said again," You're a real credit to your team." They left the floor, and I thought to myself, "That was a really nice gesture on his part."

After the game, I dressed quickly and faced the reporters. The obligatory autograph session was next, and it was shorter that those from a few weeks earlier, a sure sign that the student body had returned. Driving back to the apartment, I suddenly realized how tired I was.

In the first half, I had felt weird, as though something was wrong with my stomach. I felt sluggish and couldn't really get myself going into high gear. It wasn't until the final five minutes of the half that I got over that feeling, and then all my energy returned. In the second half, I felt better, but never really comfortable all night.

I opened the door to the apartment, went into the living room, took the cordless phone off the receiver and called my sister Karin. This was my habit after every game. This time the talk was short, and I was falling asleep within a few minutes.

TUESDAY, JANUARY 14

Morning came early the next day. Even though I had played a tough game the night before, and went to bed around midnight, I was up at 6 the next morning. The Optimist Club of Lawrence wanted me as a guest speaker for the monthly breakfast meeting and I had agreed. The request had come a few weeks earlier, and I had not checked to see if there was a game the night before. I wished that I had. This was not an easy assignment, since the game the night before had taken so much out of me. But as usual, I couldn't say no.

Driving to the Holiday Inn at the edge of town, I was wondering why I had agreed to do this. Not that I was against speaking to groups of business and civic leaders rather than the schools and students I usually visited. Rather, it was simply the hour, the 7 a.m. breakfast session that seemed difficult today. Maybe it was the cold, since the temperature was at 4 degrees . Or it could be the fact that it was a cloudy day, which always makes waking up a chore.

Despite my doldrums, the meeting went well. I was treated as the guest of honor, so I spoke at the end of the meeting, after the food had been served and the business of the club had been conducted. There was the usual assortment of questions afterwards, and the whole thing ended about 8:15. Shaking the last few hands, I climbed back into my car and headed back to the room.

But there would be no chance to get into bed again. I had to sign up for the semester classes I had selected and go out to lunch with Mark and his son, Andy, who were still in town from the game last night. It was about 2 in the afternoon when I finally got time to just sit and unwind.

Something made me start to think about my situation in life. Not the success but the future. Here I was, almost 23 years old, and what was I going to do next? Students in their senior year of college all have this moment, when they realize that the world they have known is coming to an end and the future is uncertain. I knew that. This was my time of uncertainty.

"In some ways, I wish it could continue forever," I told CB, "because it's a year I'll never forget and never experience again."

"Yeah, I guess I'd feel the same way, if I were a senior," he answered

"You know, I wish I could make it last, "I continued, "but at the same time I want it to end so I can get on with my life. College is over for me, and I want to know what is ahead. What will I do, get a job, go to grad school, wait for the NBA?"

"Those are some tough choices," CB sympathized. "But at least they are good choices, know what I mean?"

"Yeah, I sure do have it rough," I laughed. "Some guys are just hoping to graduate. I guess I should quit worrying."

"Why stop doing what you do best?" CB teased.

But I couldn't get it out of my head, even though CB had succeeded in cheering me up for the moment. I went for a walk and thought about it some more. This was one of those life decisions that I knew would come someday. People would tell me to wait because the NBA was sure to draft me. But who really knew that? Certainly, I felt I could play at the next level, I knew my game had improved, I remembered those sessions with Rex Walters in the fall. I saw the people in the pros and knew I could compete with them.

Yet, I didn't want to think ahead. This was the season of my dreams. Five months ago I had been unpacking my bags in the heat, and thinking of what the best scenario could be for this team. Now, here I was in January, helping an undefeated team become No. 1, living a season that was on a record pace. My game had improved, as I had hoped all the summer work would ensure. I was more relaxed, more confident that I had been since high school. I was enjoying this year of my life as I had no other, and I didn't want the feeling to end. Things were going so well. God, let it go on forever.

At the same time, I had to progress, because I wanted to see how the year ended. If I stayed in this spot, I'd never know if I was going to relive the feeling of high school, the feeling of being a true champion. We all had worked so hard. It was all coming true. It was destiny.

And after it was over, if the NBA didn't come calling, I would be able to make a choice. I could continue to play basketball overseas. My grades were good enough that I could most likely get a job anywhere I chose to apply. I also could enter grad school for a masters' degree, and that also should not be a problem. Where I would go to school was a decision my advisor had been discussing with me the previous day, whether to choose a school on the West Coast like Cal, or an Eastern school of prominence like Duke. But all those decisions seemed so far off right now.

I also was thinking of what to do when the season ended. Should I go visit my brothers and sisters when the school year ended? I hadn't seen them much the past four years. How long would I spend at home this summer? What to do for a job if I went home?

"Geez, this is too much ," I said aloud. And with that, I headed back to the apartment, simply deciding to go with the flow, to savor the moment. Coach is right. I should just enjoy the ride.

THURSDAY, JANUARY 16
Looking at the calendar, I realized that it was almost the halfway point of the season. Not only that, but it was also the halfway point of the school year, and the halfway point of this book. Considering that, I felt it was a time of self evaluation and the thoughts that came to mind were all pleasant.

I am happiest about all the winning we have done. That is the bottom line. Our best performances as a team have been, in my mind, NC State, UCLA and three or four other games. The best feelings I've had personally after a win were after the Cincinnati, UCLA and Maui Classic games. Beating Iowa State and Texas also left me feeling pumped.

Individually, I felt great after the Hawaii trip and after GW. I thought that I had played as well as I could, but I am nowhere satisfied with where I am right now. I feel I can really improve on handling the ball. I also want to remain confident on offense and keep attacking. I can't afford to become passive out there.

Defensively, I've been pretty good all year, but I want to become even better. I want to take each opponent as an individual challenge, and shut him down.

As far as school is concerned, I got a straight-A, 4.0 average this semester, so I can't improve that. I killed myself the last two years with as many hours as I took, and the grades came because of a lot of work. Now I can reap the rewards of that schedule, and this final semester will be the easiest I've ever had.

Continuing my reflective mood, I considered at the team's personnel and one thing stood out in my mind. I can't say enough about the contributions that Ryan has made to our success. Without his steady play at the start of the year, who knows where we'd be today? I look at him and think that his attitude is remarkable, considering what he's been through. I have a ton of respect for him.

SUNDAY, JANUARY 19

This is the second appearance for KU on CBS. It's a nationally televised game, a Sunday afternoon game, the marquee matchup for the start of the college basketball season in the world of winter sports television . I can feel the excitement in the air as we enter the court of the Hartford Civic Center to play the University of Connecticut (UConn).

It's the first long trip in a month. We flew to Philadelphia, then on to Hartford, Connecticut. We went directly to the University of Hartford and got ready for practice. Some of the guys needed treatment for a variety of minor injuries, and between that and the usual taping, the start of practice was delayed. This led to a rumor about possible injured Kansas players that hit the air before the broadcast.

Jacque Vaughn was the only guy still in the trainers room when practice was about to begin. Paul, Ryan and some of the others started to ask "Where's Jacque?" or "We can't start without JV." It was all in jest, and when Jacque arrived 10 minutes later, I started to clap. The guys joined in and soon we had an ovation greeting Jacque, who smiled sheepishly. Someone screamed, then everyone began cheering and hollering, making JV laugh all the more. We broke up and began the practice, really enjoying ourselves this day.

The day would get better. After practice, the coaching staff had a surprise for the team. We headed out for a tour of the ESPN studios, which are headquartered in Hartford. I walked around the sets of SportsCenter and ESPN News and thought to myself, "It's like a dream. Every kid wants to be on TV and now I've been in front and in back of the camera."

We met the hosts of the various programs. The team went on the air as a group for a live interview. Jacque and I were interviewed for a few minutes. Individual players were given lines to recite as on-air promos for various ESPN segments. We viewed the sets for NBA and NHL sports segments. I felt like a kid in a candy store, looking in wonder at the things I had seen for years on television. I loved it. That night, I went back to my hotel room and watched myself on television.

This game against UConn would be a big test and the team was ready. We have come to the realization that we are now marked men, a team that everyone gets up to play. Being No. 1 for five weeks, we are now being compared to dynasties, and everywhere we go the winning streak is advertised. When will we lose? Will we lose at all? Who will topple the Jayhawks? The questions are becoming more insistent, and the pressure is starting to build.

But we don't feel the pressure the way some people might think. If anything, this Kansas team savors the attention we are receiving. I look at this as a direct result of our winning games and reaching our potential. The ranking is a reward for our hard work. We are not only trying to beat teams but instead trying to reach our full potential. The victories flow from effort.

UConn is a program that has almost as much success as we have, with one notable exception: they have never been to the Final Four. In the 90's, Connecticut has a better winning percentage than all but four other programs, (KU being one of those) but the big prize has eluded them. This year, they have a young but successful team, and they would like nothing better than to defeat us, the top-ranked team, on national TV.

The game began and UConn was on fire. They came out with intensity and hustle, making the tempo of the game as fast as any we have encountered all season. They nearly swept us off the floor. The score was 20-4 before four minutes have elapsed, and the crowd is going wild, disbelieving at what has happened. The television announcers were remarking on the over-confidence they feel we have shown, and how it might catch up to us. To them and the partisan crowd, the Jayhawks were in trouble.

But there is one trait about this Kansas team that makes us unique. We are confident in our ability. Even though this is a deep hole to climb out of, we don't panic. We believe in ourselves and feel that if we play our best, it's good enough to beat anyone. That poise carries us through bad moments like the start of this game.

I give full credit for that composure in tight spots to Coach Williams. All during the first half of this game, Coach kept telling us to just play Kansas basketball and over the course of the game we'd be all right. The message was that if we played hard defense, no team could shoot like this for 40 minutes.

I brought the ball up the court, passed it around the circle, and finally launched a three from the top of the key. Swish! At last, an outside hoop for Kansas. But it was answered the next trip down the floor by UConn. Jacque Vaughn hit another three and the score was 23-10. After a TV time-out, we put together one of the runs that have characterized all of our games this season. With four different players contributing, the score narrowed to 23-19, then 27-23, and finally at the half, 34-31, UConn. While it was only the second time all year that we have trailed at the half, we have crawled back into the game, thanks to the 9-0 run after the time-out.

At the half, the theme of remaining calm was reinforced. The coaches stressed to us that while we have worked ourselves back into the game, we couldn't let UConn 'outwork' us on the boards or defensively in the second half. Again, we were reminded to just "play Kansas basketball".

The second half began and we took charge of the game. The time for motivating through actions was right now, and I could feel that old energy flowing once again. I fed Paul Pierce for an easy layup, and the margin was cut to one. The next trip down the floor, UConn threw a wild pass, and I raced for the loose ball, gathering it in and driving to the hoop. But as I took off for the basket, someone hit me from behind and I fell to the floor. I hit the two free throws, putting Kansas ahead for the first time in the game, 35-34. Then after another missed UConn attempt, I took a great pass from JV, drove the baseline and dished off to Raef for an easy two points. We were starting another of our runs.

It continued. LaFrentz was fouled and hit two free throws, I dove and grabbed a loose ball causing a possession arrow turnover. UConn missed the shot, Paul rebounded, fed Jacque, who in turn found me driving the right baseline for another layup. Suddenly, we had a 10-0 run, and the lead was now 41-34.

A time-out didn't help them much. UConn finally scored, but the next time down, Pollard blocked a shot, grabbed the ball and fed me as I was racing down the court for another layup. It was 43-36, and in five minutes the momentum of the game had swung back to KU. UConn sank a three to narrow the gap to four, but Scot hit a close shot, and the lead was back to six. It would stay secure until the final four minutes.

But this was a tough stretch for me. I suddenly went cold from the field, missing my next four attempts and eventually UConn tied the game. Coach Williams turned to the only guard to hit today from the outside with consistency. Billy Thomas came in from the bench.

As I took my place on the bench, I thought to myself, "Why did coach take me out? I can still help get us this win." But as I sat for a moment, I realized something. "Coach Williams knows this team. If he thinks Billy can help us, he can. I have been out of sync today. Maybe this is what we really need." The strategy worked, as Billy hit two consecutive three-point shots and the team pulled away to win a hard-fought contest, 73-65.

After the game, I thought about this team and my own performance. This was a game we won, which is the main goal, but I didn't feel that I played my best. I had my moments, such as at the start of the second half, but basically I stunk it up today. Sure, I had 5 assists and 3 steals, but 3-9 from the field is lousy. I could've had a great game but didn't.

And I never question Coach. He made a great decision, and it won the game for us. Billy was incredible today. I have no problem with what coach did, and hopefully I'll give him reason to leave me in the next time. We won, I did contribute, and I'll take that any day.

TUESDAY, JANUARY 21
The light on the answering machine was blinking when I walked into my apartment. CB moved over towards the machine and flicked the playback button. The voice was that of an older female.

"Hello Jerod,"the woman said. "I'm Mrs. Brown (not her real name). My daughter is the one who has been writing you for the past month and wants to meet you. I'm calling to let you know that we are coming to the game tomorrow night and want you to meet her afterwards. You are going to be her birthday present. If she could just meet with you and go out for something to eat it would make her so happy. I can't think of a better present than you. Could you please call me back and let me know when and where you'll meet us? Thanks."

"Oh my God!" CB exclaimed. "That's the second time that woman has been on the machine."

"How'd she get our number?" I wondered.

"Maybe she found it in the campus directory," CB suggested.

"Wherever, I hope she stops calling. I'm not going to meet her or her daughter. This is too strange. I don't need something like this right now."

"You don't need something like this ever," CB replied.

The phone call illustrates something that players in college basketball live with all the time. Fans want to become our friends, and it can get to be an annoyance. It never bothers me to sign autographs, and I will make small talk with those who are waiting in line for me after games. But when the phone calls and letters start to become a constant part of my life, and invade my time at home, it can get annoying.

Some of the other guys also have to deal with phone calls. JV and Scot just let their answering machine pick up every call. They could be sitting right there, but they will never answer the phone until they hear and recognize the voice on the other end. When I call them, I usually start by saying "If you're there, pick up the phone." They have spent time in past years talking to someone they don't know, and have decided this is a better method.

CB is great at screening calls for me. He knows most of my friends and who I would rather not talk with on any given day. Even so, there are times when I've spent 15 minutes talking with someone who is just a passing acquaintance. They won't hang up and I guess I'm not adept or rude enough to get off the phone.

The girls who write letters are looking for a boyfriend, and I'm flattered that they think of me."You seem to be so nice,"many of the letters state, or "you are someone who I think I can talk to very easily" is another common phrase. The writers feel that if they can convince me of their good intentions, I will respond to their requests for a date.

The number and frequency of the letters vary. In November, one young girl wrote seven letters in a nine-day stretch. She included photos of herself in her home, sent thoughts for the day, suggestions for positive performances and finally requests to meet after the games. She was a high school senior and wanted to meet the college player she thought would be most receptive and understanding towards someone her age. After the Maui trip, the letters came less frequently and finally stopped after Christmas.

The girl whose mother was on the machine was another regular correspondent. She had written six letters since the start of the season, and her mother had also added to the volume of mail. They both seemed to want nothing more than to meet, sit down and spend a few hours with Jerod Haase. But I am a bit wary of anyone who is this persistent. When I was presented with a stocking full of homemade food, from an admiring fan in the autograph line after one game, I looked carefully at the items. Thinking that it would be better to be cautious, and on the advice of others, I discarded the items. I'd really hate to think that someone would go out of their way to harm me, but how can you really tell anymore? I want to trust these fans, but yet, knowing that I had more or less rejected their offers to meet, it seems I'd be better off being too careful than too trusting.

Occasionally, a female fan will make the bold move of walking up to and talking with me. After one home game, a girl followed Raef LaFrentz and me as we walked back from the fieldhouse. She stayed about forty feet behind us, walking with a few friends and thus not really being noticed by the two of us as we made our way home. But when Raef went his way, and I was now alone, she quickly ran up and called out to me.

Turning around, I noticed that she was probably only a freshman, and seemed very shy and nervous about this meeting. But she spoke up and told me that we had met once before, a few days earlier at a track meet. I vaguely recalled the meeting, as it had only been for a moment. Feeling relaxed, the girl started to talk about seeing me play, wanting to meet me, and waiting for a chance like this to just talk alone. It was cold, and I wanted to get away, so I let her continue for a few minutes and then excused myself, saying that after a game and a shower, I didn't like to stand in the cold for very long. I don't, and that part is true. But it was a convenient excuse to leave and yet not be rude. When I got back into the apartment, I thought about the encounter.

I know most guys would just say hi and keep on walking, but I guess I can't be that way to someone like her. It's part of being a basketball player at Kansas. Everyone feels they are part of the program, and the students and fans want to get involved with us. It's fun and for the most part, I don't mind. The phone calls are probably the only part I could do without.

WEDNESDAY, JANUARY 22

There is something about playing basketball at this level that gives people strange ideas. Today, I was thinking about friendships. Not with my teammates, but guys from other schools in the conference. Apparently some folks think that we strike up friendships during the course of a game.

I don't talk much during games. It's something I just can't do. I concentrate on the game and get myself completely focused. Because of that, I'm not one for making small talk at the free throw line or anywhere else on the court. I'm out there to play ball.

It's really difficult to become friends with guys from the other conference schools if you have no personal history with them. When could we get together ? If we met in the summer or knew each other before college, sure it's possible. Rivalries aren't that intense. For example, I roomed with Tim Duncan and Brian Evans when I was on the World University Games team in the summer of 1995. We were together for three weeks in Japan and I got to know and like them. We may meet Wake Forest this season in the NCAA tourney and if that happens, I'd enjoy getting to talk with Tim for a few minutes. I'd try to find a few minutes for him because I remember the time we spent together as fun.

I'd say we were acquaintances. We spent part of a month together two years ago. That was a special trip and he and Brian were part of it. But there is a difference between that and being good friends. Friendships take time to develop. There's a mutual interest factor, not to mention trust. It can't be accomplished between players at our level, at schools in different states. The distance, the time spent at practice and school, traveling and numerous other factors make it nearly impossible to keep up with someone.

Acquaintances are always possible. I can say a few words to someone after a game or at early warm-up shoot-arounds. But I wouldn't stop my pregame preparation for any length of time just to talk with someone from another team. If I really wanted to talk, it would be on the phone. But when would that happen? I already have explained the time involved in practicing, studying, travel and there isn't much left after that. The players at other schools lead similar lives, I'd guess. Unless we were high school buddies or summer league teammates and friends, I don't know what we'd find to talk about.

I'm not trying to sound as though I don't want to make friends. It just isn't as simple as talking at a free throw lane and having a new buddy. Just because we all play in the Big 12 doesn't mean we have common interests.

THURSDAY, JANUARY 23

The date will forever be etched in my mind. It's the fourth anniversary of the death of my father. And it comes this year on a day that follows a pretty decisive win for the Kansas team. However, a series of events will once again put a strain on my emotions.

The night before, I had experienced a multitude of feelings. The day had gone pretty well, and I entered Allen Fieldhouse feeling excited to play this game. I sensed that it was going to be a good night, and I wanted to get it underway. But then, as I opened the outer doors, I started to get a sense of deja vu. For some reason, I started thinking about the Syracuse game a year ago. The poor shooting, the feeling of utter despair afterwards, the total frustration and anger with my performance. I didn't know why it had entered my mind, and I quickly tried to think of how to get this awful memory out of my mind.

I walked into the locker room, hoping to find someone who could help me think about another something else. But as I moved through to the training room I discovered that everyone was in a somber mood. It was then that I found out that a KU swimmer had died that afternoon of an apparent heart attack. The swimmer was 21 years old.

I played a fairly strong game that night, going 7-11 from the field and totalling 17 points in a 20 minute appearance. The game was over early, and Kansas had won 89-60. But the incident in the training room had brought back memories of 1993, and although it wasn't weighing on my mind continually, thoughts about my father's death must have been swirling about in my subconscious.

This afternoon I dressed and made my way to the floor with the rest of the team. Practice would last from 4 until 7, and it would be a tough day. Colorado was coming up on Sunday, and the Buffalos were playing well this year. Coach Williams wasn't about to lighten up at this stage of the season.

The team went through a few of the usual drills, doing some three-on-two breaks and some ballhandling drills. After a few more breakdown sessions, groups of five were assembled and we did some full-court work. It was after a few bad plays that I would suddenly realize how this day was affecting me.

The next time down the court, I took a particularly aggressive dive into another teammate, taking the player down while going for the ball. While I am known to do this in games, I had not usually gone this wild at practice. My teammates stared at me, surprised and confused.

It continued. When the coaching staff blew their whistles to give advice, I took it personally. I was setting illegal screens, diving on the floor and acting as if I were challenging anyone to come forward and say something directly to me. It was completely out of character.

Practice finally ended and the team left the floor. All but me. I sat in the bleachers and felt mad at the world. I looked at the field-house walls and let the anger sweep over me. Coach Joe Holladay came up to me and sat down.

"Want to talk about it?" he asked.

"I guess," I replied. I waited a moment and then continued. "Coach, it's just that this is the day my father died. And I think about how it happened, and try and figure out why it happened, and it makes me feel terrible. I guess I'm just really down today."

Holladay nodded in silent agreement. He was at a loss for words for a moment. He tried to be sympathetic, and told me about a similar experience he had gone through. I listened and appreciated the concern shown by Coach, but didn't feel any better. Finally, Holladay left.

I was feeling sad and mournful. It hurt to think of Dad, and all the good times we had. But it hurt even more to think of all the good times we were missing. I knew that Dad was watching, but still wished he could be here just to talk.

Coach Williams had talked to Joe Holladay about me and he must have decided to try to say a few words. Approaching me, still sitting in the bleachers, he said, "Jerod, I want to tell you a few things." I looked in his direction, then moved and sat beside Coach.

Williams continued, "Jerod, you probably didn't know this but my mother passed away a few years ago. I can tell you that I do know what you are going through. The year doesn't pass when I don't think about her, and I get the same feelings of sadness that you are probably feeling. It's understandable. We love them and then they're gone."

"I just miss him so much. I wish he could be here to see what all of us in the family have been doing and how are lives have turned out," I said, with what I'm sure was sadness in my voice.

Coach replied, "I can tell you one thing for certain. Your father would be proud that he had raised a good son and a fine man."

I looked at Coach and felt appreciative. I thanked him for the understanding and left. It was nice that the coaches cared, and I really did feel grateful for their attention, but this was a time when words alone did not help. I had to work this out for myself.

Arriving back at the apartment, I fixed something to eat and called my mother. We talked about things in general, but never discussed the significance of the date. I sensed that my mother knew why I'd called, but I didn't want to bring up the subject. Shortly after we hung up, Jacque came down for a visit. Talking about what was wrong, JV said he was concerned because he knew I was upset about my father.

I was struck by the concern. I told JV that I never realized that so many people would be so affected by how I act.

Jacque replied, "Try this. Your dad is probably up there smiling down right now. Try smiling back. It'll work. You'll feel better."

The idea made me laugh, but I realized the meaning behind it. As Jacque left, I felt more relaxed. I watched television for about another hour and felt more at ease. The mood of the day was finally gone.

FRIDAY, JANUARY 24
It was official and it was bad. News had been circulating that Scot Pollard, KU's leading shot blocker and rebounder had injured his foot and would be out of action for some time. I could tell that he was hurting, but Scot is one tough guy, and he'd play through any pain to help the team.

We had finally put all the pieces in place, and with Jacque getting back to the form of last year, we seemed ready to dominate. We had depth at every position and experience in key areas. An injury to Scot right now was not going to help the team solidify itself.

Coach came in with the news. Scot would be out for about 4-6 weeks. He had broken a bone in his foot and could not ignore it any longer. It would affect the way he ran, it limited his rebounding, and the sooner we had him healed and back to normal, the better our chances in the post-season would look.

The team handled the news much as we had with JV. We knew we had to expect some barriers on our road to success and this was one of them. Personally, I thought it was lousy. Two of the seniors now had lost part of their season due to injuries. It's the worst feeling in the world to sit and watch. Especially when you know that these games are never going to be replaced.

Scot would handle it in his own way, and I was sure that it would be with some crazy remark or unique stunt. He'd try to get our minds off his injury and onto something that would make us smile. He'd be back in time for the most important games of all. And we would need him then.

SUNDAY, JANUARY 26
I had gone to bed early last night, wanting to have a good performance in this game. My thoughts ran to the last trip to Denver, the NCAA regional final last March. I had played a lousy game. There was no way this would be a repeat of that game.

I was also worried about Colorado. Were they as good on their homecourt as advertised, and were they as confident as they appeared? That would be a tough combination to beat. It was also the first game without Scot, and that would be a big hole to fill. Could we beat them on the boards without half of our Twin Towers? This was going to be a big test for BJ and TJ. They had been working hard all season, and we always knew we could count on them for some quality minutes. Now, they would have to split the entire game time between themselves. I knew they had improved, as we all had, from last season. Ryan had done the job filling in for Jacque. It was time for these guys step up and help the team. I was sure they'd handle the challenge well.

Another concern was the effect the altitude might have on the team. I had grown up in the high altitude of the Sierra Nevada mountains, but had played a few years away from that atmosphere. Would the rest of the team adjust? It's not easy if you haven't ever played an intense game in the thinner air of high altitudes. It catches you by surprise.

Before I could worry any more, I realized what I was doing.

"There's no point to this," I thought. "We are a great team, I am playing well.....what am I worrying about?" Comforted by these thoughts, I boarded the bus with the rest of the team and headed for Coors Arena.

Colorado would prove to be a very tough opponent today. It was the first time in 28 years they were ranked in the top 20, coming in at number 18. Their gym was filled to capacity, the crowd was energized, and it was a nationally televised game.

I felt good as the game began. It seemed as though everything was working and the team was motivated by the challenge directed at us by the Colorado team and their fans. They wanted to prove they were our equals, and defeating us on national television would do just that. We were determined to show that we could survive the loss of one of our starters and still win because we had depth and heart. It would be a serious test for both teams.

We scored the first 13 points of the game. I was on the floor immediately, getting a loose ball and feeding it to Jacque who hit Raef for another basket. I stole the next pass, drove to the basket for a layup and was fouled, hitting the free throw. We were up 10-0, and Colorado called a time-out.

I was glad we started out the game with a run, because it really helps to quiet a crowd like that. The home team starts to feel as if they have let everyone down, and I really enjoy hearing the silence fall over people who moments earlier were yelling at us, hoping we would fail. It motivates me tremendously, and I inject more energy into my game.

We went into the locker room happy to be up by 12 points at the half. We knew that our defense had been excellent, but all of us were displeased with our offensive showing the first half. We knew it was only a matter of time before Colorado started hitting from the outside. We would have to get going before it became a close game.

The second half opened and Colorado came out shooting. Chauncey Billups, their star guard, finally got hot, and the lead dwindled to seven. I answered with a three and then another steal. We kept our composure but they kept coming at us and with eight minutes left, Colorado took the lead at 64-63. Then Raef came alive. The big guy scored the next six points and was a force inside. JV and I fed him, he pounded the boards, and we built the lead back up to nine. They never came within seven the rest of the way. It was a hard fought, 77-68 Kansas win, one that was well deserved.

It seemed as though I wound up in one of those zones players find themselves in every so often. I went 4-5 from behind the three-point arc and 6-8 for the day. Both JV and I were able to get a lot of assists. Everything was working. I was able to anticipate correctly and get some steals that got the rest of the guys fired up. We ran the floor well and the rebounding was really strong. BJ and TJ played tough, and Raef really stepped it up a notch. He did exactly what I expected him to do, asserting himself as one of the premier players in America.

Coach Doherty told the press I had an excellent game, my best of the season. But I felt that all of us played our hearts out today. We needed to show everyone in the conference that we are a strong team and that our depth is one of out strengths. I think we did that today. It was a great win, a huge win, and the plane ride back to Lawrence was full of laughter and smiling faces. We had passed another test.

MONDAY, JANUARY 27

We're still ranked No. 1. It's been almost two months for us at the top of the polls. Now the reporters are asking what it's like and if we feel any pressure for every team we play.

Almost all the guys feel the same as I do. We enjoy being the top-ranked team in America. Why wouldn't we? It's what we always wanted, to be the best team possible. There's a lot of pride and happiness in reaching this point.

It's not the end of the road, however. This is something we have worked hard to achieve. The recognition is nice. It means that others see that our hard work has paid off. We always felt we could be the best. We believed in ourselves as a team. We wanted to be No. 1. At this time, halfway through the year, that's where we are. It's a very satisfying feeling.

There's a unique attitude that goes with this position. People around Lawrence are starting to come up, wanting to talk for a few moments. They are more friendly than ever. Sometimes it's an introduction or a wave, and many times it's accompanied by a greeting that involves calling me by my first name.

This throws me a bit. I'll often think that someone I know or have met before is talking to me when they call out "Hey, Jerod!" I'll look closer and realize that it's nobody I've ever met before. It's a fan who wants to be more personal. If I thought about it, I don't know how I'd react to being called "Mr. Haase." That might seem odd.

On campus it's hard to tell what the average student thinks. I'd say there's a sense of pride because the basketball team is ranked No. 1. We aren't held up as gods or some type of royalty. When I think about it, how could anyone seriously idolize someone who's their own age? Someone who lives down the floor and passes them in the hall every day? Would anyone revere the guy who's at the next computer pounding the keyboard, or the guy ahead of them in the checkout line at a video store?

Probably not. And that's who we are. We live average lives, and do the same things everyone else does. Except for those few nights a week, and an occasional Saturday or Sunday afternoon, when our actions are televised to thousands of people across the country. Our faces and bodies are shown in close-up and slow motion to viewers who develop feelings about us, attitudes that turn them into fans or enemies. They become people who talk about us and think they know what we're like because they watch us on television.

Thinking about this makes me feel special. I used to do the same thing watching basketball players when I was a kid. Now I'm the guy that other kids observe. It's awesome when you think about it.

WEDNESDAY, JANUARY 29
Texas Tech was another of the ranked teams in our conference (22nd in the polls), and this was our first trip to their campus. To say the least, it was one I'd rather forget.

Tech has an unusual gym. It seems almost too dark, and they never seemed to turn on the lights in the upper half of the arena. We were told it was their biggest crowd in many years, a sign that we were a good draw as the top-ranked team. Their fans seemed to sense an upset was possible, and I got the feeling they would not have called it an upset at all.

Their big men were really tough, Tony Battie in particular. Their big guys played most of the game and I think that's what helped us pull this out. Tech took a big lead in the first half, and we had to put on what I'd call our best comeback of the year to win this one. Raef again played a spectacular game, but I wasn't much help to him tonight. I played a lousy game. I had too many turnovers and I couldn't hit a shot tonight. I played some solid defense, but even there I could have done better. It was a great win, and a terrific comeback by the team. I wish I had been more helpful in the effort.

On the way back home, I noticed it was a beautiful moonlit night. The sky was clear and stars were really bright. JV came over and we played a game of golf on the computer. I think he can sense I'm a bit down and he knows golf cheers me up.

I also know that the guys are getting into playing this computer game. JV likes to challenge me to games like this, and I've got BJ Williams hooked on it as well. The golf game is fun and it allows us to compete in a different way. I guess competition is in our blood, but it's never serious. Just a way to pass the travel time on the road.

The game is getting addictive however. When we get home, I know that sometime in the next 24 hours, someone will drop in and want to play a game. Probably BJ, but I'll play it with anyone. Hey, it's golf.

SATURDAY, FEBRUARY 1

I woke up and thought about the game against Nebraska. This was the day that an old record could be shattered. It had been almost 60 years since a Kansas basketball team had opened the season with a 21-0 start. Today, the 1997 Jayhawks would go for 22 victories. It could be historic.

This was only the second Saturday game we had played all year. The crowd would again be another full house, but as before would contain more families than usual. And they were ready to see the record fall.

I was glad that it was an afternoon contest, since that meant I got to sleep in a little longer. It also was better for my energy level. The day games, especially those with mid-afternoon starts, were easier to play, since my eating patterns were closer to normal. The pregame meal would be at 11 a.m., I'd be back in the apartment by noon, catch an extra hour of sleep, get up and still get to the gym at 1:30. With a 3 o'clock start, I'd be well-rested and ready to go.

But I had encountered a problem that had never really surfaced before. For some reason, this game was not getting me "psyched"up. I had never really experienced a lack of emotion for basketball games. Usually game day was an event for me, and I was motivated and excited from the time I awoke until tip-off. Then the intensity would kick in, and that would last until the final horn had sounded.

Mark was in town for this game, and he noticed my mood today was different from usual. He asked me why I seemed so unemotional I couldn't put my finger on it, but I just wasn't up for this game. It certainly wasn't over-confidence. Long ago I had learned not to take any opponent lightly. Nebraska was our opponent for this game. Coming into the contest, the Cornhuskers were an enigmatic team, having won games against some formidable teams but losing other games to squads most people thought they could beat. No, it wasn't the fact that we're playing Nebraska.

So what was wrong with me? I wondered. It's the final third of the season. I could end up like Scot, missing the whole month. I'd hate that. I know this is one of my last games in this gym. But in spite of all this, I just can't get fired up. I was puzzled, but got ready and left for the game.

Walking over to Allen, I noticed how nice the weather had become. It was almost 50 degrees, unusually warm for February. Most of the snow which had fallen early in the week had melted off , and a hint of spring was in the air. Maybe it's just the length of the season. I was still dwelling on the lack of involvement I was feeling. I rationalized that it had been almost four months since we began. It's hard to get totally pumped for every single game before they even start. People don't realize that nobody can get that high every night. You do once the game starts, but beforehand it's not always that easy. I entered the locker room, began to get taped, and was ready to get in some early shooting before the full warmups began.

The game was not artistic. Nebraska scored the first basket on a dunk, but then we took off. Paul scored on a drive to the basket, then Jacque fed me as I cut in from the right baseline for a reverse layup. After trading turnovers, I hit a 15-foot jumper and B.J.picked up a loose ball and scored . The team was on fire, the score was 8-2 and it looked as if we would have our way in this game.

But Nebraska came back quickly. And two injuries changed the course of this game. About five minutes into the game, Paul began to hold his index finger. He left the game and returned four minutes later with the first two fingers taped together. It didn't appear serious, but would affect his shot for the remainder of the game. He would snare rebounds with his left arm extended first, tried to block shots with the left hand, and in general tried to avoid contact with the right hand.

I also suffered an injury. Mid-way through the first half, I dove for a loose ball and jammed my right wrist again, the same one that had been injured at Santa Clara in the first game. It began to throb immediately, and I held it any chance I got, whether in time-outs or standing at the free throw line. I missed a free throw, and was taken out moments later. The wrist was killing me.

When I re-entered the game five minutes later, I caught a pass and felt the pain again. I dribbled with my left hand, and found that to be more effective. For the rest of the half, I tried to have as little contact as possible with the ball on offense, preferring to play hard defensively and simply pass to others who might be more effective.

In the second half, for the first time all season, we could not muster a run. As the game moved to the final minute, we committed two turnovers and the Cornhuskers tied the game at 63. Amazingly, the longest home court winning streak in the nation was in jeopardy. And with 23 seconds left in the game, Nebraska controlled the ball and the last shot. But our defense rose to the occasion. Paul

This tape on the wrist became essential as the season progressed. The size also began to increase. Photo by KU Sports Information.

and Jacque pressured guard Tyronn Lue into another turnover and time ran out. Overtime!

Off the tip, I took the ball to the corner, fed Raef in the lane, who hit a turnaround shot. A quick lead. Another LaFrentz basket moments later put us up by four, and we would never relinquish the lead again. Nebraska hung tough, hitting two amazing three-point shots, but Raef and JV sank clutch shots from the free throw line in the closing minute. The final was a hard fought 83-77 win.

Afterwards, reaction varied among the players. Coach Williams was angrier than he had been all season and also puzzled at our attitude. He pointedly asked us, "Are you guys getting tired of the ride? Would you like it to end?" There was complete silence in the room.

Then Raef spoke up. "We played like crap except for the overtime. Other than that, we stunk." Jacque couldn't deal with his performance. He dressed hurriedly, put on a stocking cap, pulling it down over his ears, grabbed a coat and left. He spoke to no one.

I was glad for the win, but felt as if it were a loss. A reporter sarcastically asked me if we were sad about losing in regulation time. The question stuck in my mind. "That's probably the way we should be looking at this," I answered. "Maybe that would shake us up a bit, if we thought of what things would be like if we had lost this one at home."

We never seemed to wake-up today and it almost cost us the one record we prized the most: the home court winning streak. It's our gym, we seniors have not lost here since our freshman year, my redshirt year, and we certainly don't want to lose now, in our most successful season of all.

Landing on my wrist put a different spin on the game for me. I didn't want to let anyone know about it, because I have learned to ignore these incidents. When you fall as often as I do, you expect to have aches and pains. But I am worried about how much it affected my ability to control the ball at times. And I've rarely had that pain when I catch a ball. But at least it all came in the context of a winning effort. That makes the pain go away for awhile.

As usual, the crowds were lined up afterwards. It seemed they were more insistent and had some unusual requests. Some of the guys signed autographs, but now we were moving towards the exits as we signed, rather than standing and waiting for the crowd to come to us.

As I moved along the rope separating the throng of autograph seekers from the players, a young girl in a wheelchair near the door caught my eye. I passed a few fans and went up to the girl, who was about 10 years old. She smiled shyly and handed me a program, but spoke so softly I could hardly hear her. Standing behind her, the girl's father told me that she really wanted a picture of me standing beside her. Smiling at the girl, I knelt down beside her and told her father, "Take as many as you want." The man snapped the shutter a few times, and the girl beamed with delight. As I stood up and prepared to leave, the father took my hand, looked me in the eye and said, "Thank you. You'll never know how much this meant." It really made me stop and think about what he said. I was humbled by the sincerity in his voice. I looked down at the girl one last time and answered, "Oh, I think I do." Then I smiled and moved away.

A woman in her mid-40's came running up as I headed towards the door and asked me to sign her hand. I was quite startled and asked her, "Are you sure you wouldn't rather have me use a piece of paper?" She replied, "No, use this permanent marker. The women I work with won't believe it was you unless I do it this way." Shaking my head, I obliged and wrote on the hand.

Again, thinking it was time to finally leave, I took a few more steps towards the door, but was intercepted by three more women holding dollar bills. "Sign these," they shouted. "Sign them, please!" I started to comply, but jokingly asked one of the women, "Could I trade you an autographed piece of paper for this dollar bill?" She giggled and answered, "You can give me anything you want, honey!" That caught me by surprise. I quickly signed the last bill and left the fieldhouse, with Raef close behind. We caught up with Mark in the parking lot.

"There were some real strange people here today," Mark commented.

"You said it. I was asked to sign things I've never touched before," Raef replied.

"I'm starved. I'm just glad to get out and get some food," I said.

"Yeah, I've got to get home too. I wasn't hungry before, but now..." Raef let his voice drift off, leaving the end of the sentence unspoken. We all quickly made our way across the parking lot back to the Towers, discussing the game as we went. Everyone agreed that it was an ugly win, but still better than a loss.

Mark and I went to dinner at a local Mexican restaurant. The autograph hounds were still hot on my trail. No sooner had we sat down than a man came to the table, offering congratulations on the game. Another man and his son wanted to shake hands and say what a good game they thought it had been.

We were going to discuss the game, but found ourselves talking about the fans. As we started to munch the nachos set before us, a woman came to the table. She asked me for an autograph, and then told me that her expectant friend was going to name her newborn child 'Jerod '. As she left, I turned to Mark and said, "Now that was really a first. I've never had that said to me. I don't believe this."

"How often does this go on?" Mark inquired.

"It's getting so I can't go out to eat anywhere without at least a few requests," I told him. "But that 's one of the strangest comments yet."

"At least it's better than being ignored," he pointed out.

"Yeah, that's true. "

I don't mind when people talk to me while I'm eating. It's part of the experience of playing at Kansas, and it is something that I'll always remember. Besides, as I've suggested before, who knows how long it will last?

We finished our dinner, the hostess and waitress both offered their praise, and it was time to leave. People waiting in line for a table all smiled or just stared as we walked out. Some of them were turning completely around to gaze at us, and a few parents were holding up their kids to get a better look. Mark laughed at the sight of this as we got in the car to head home.

On the way we stopped to rent a video. The manager came out from behind the counter to offer congratulations for the game and said he hoped it would continue. Customers looked our way the entire time we walked the aisles looking for a video. I was positive they wanted to see what kind of movies I watched. Everyone on the team was probably going through this. It was the price of success, becoming a celebrity, and we would have to learn to live with it for the rest of the year.

As we got home and began to watch the movie, (for the record, it was Clint Eastwood in "In the Line of Fire"), I was icing my wrist, and the throbbing was constant. Mark asked to see the wrist, but as he touched the area, I pulled back quickly and yelped "Take it easy!" He had barely touched it.

Mark looked at me and said, "You better get that looked at right away. That's not an ordinary sprain and you know it."

I responded, dejectedly, "I'm afraid to find out I'm right, but I think it's broken this time." I walked out of the room and went into my bedroom. The look on my face was not anger, but dread. Mark could tell I was worried about the rest of the season. I was.

MONDAY, FEBRUARY 3
The pain in my wrist wouldn't go away. Sunday had been a busy day. I had gone to church that morning, then along with the rest of the team, had been host and guest coach at the Special Olympics

Working with kids at Camp Jayhawk at the Special Olympics is something the team does every year. Photo by KU Sports Information.

session held in Allen Fieldhouse that afternoon. We put on this program every year and Coach Williams thinks it's a good idea that players get involved. The kids are always thrilled and the guys sometimes need to see something separate from basketball.

We all were getting involved in games with the kids. I was moving around a young man who was in a wheelchair. Acting as a referee, the young man would call fouls and violations as I pushed him up and down the court. Seeing a chance to liven up the proceedings, I told the boy he could call technical fouls if he thought the attitude of the players was disrespectful.

That was all the encouragement he needed. He started blowing his whistle, pointing to Lester Earl and shouting, "Yer outta here!" As Lester looked in mock anguish, the boy turned to Ryan Robertson and again yelled, "Technical! Yer outta here." Ryan pretended to protest, I laughed, and the kid beamed. He was into it.

Although I was having a good time, my mind couldn't get away from the fact that this time the pain in the wrist wasn't going away. I had iced it again that afternoon, taped it tightly, but it still throbbed. I realized that there was only one way to find out what had happened. It was time to visit the doctor.

On Monday, I went to classes as usual, but in the afternoon, went to a local doctor and had X-rays taken of the wrist. It was not long after that I learned the results: the wrist was broken. I had go to the apartment and get packed. The team bus was leaving for Columbia, Missouri late that afternoon. The team was headed for a major conference battle with our arch-rivals, the University of Missouri, and the two-hour ride would bring us to the motel just in time to unpack and get ready for bed.

I spent most of the trip thinking. What if this turns out like Jacque's injury? I can't believe that my season would come to an end right now. I brooded for a while, but then started to write notes on the laptop, and another idea shifted my mood.

If this is really my season of destiny, then this won't be a serious setback. I've worked so hard, and overcome so much, that I can't believe that it would end this way. I know it's going to be okay. These thoughts made me feel more optimistic, like my brother Steven. He can always see the bright side of things, and never seems to get down for more than a few moments. Maybe I was developing this trait, instead of being the worrier I have been in the past.

I put away the computer and relaxed. Sure, the throbbing in my wrist was still there, but then it had felt like this at Maui, and look how well that turned out. It would be all right. "No wonder Steven's always so positive," I thought. "It makes every bad situation seem so minor."

TUESDAY, FEBRUARY 4

Walking into the gym at the University of Missouri, the first thing you notice is the Tiger Paw at center court. The colors, the gym lighting and the nature of the crowd are unique to this school. It all combines to create an atmosphere that is characterizes college basketball.

We know this is going to be a rough game, and we're undermanned. Losing a front-line player like Scot Pollard always makes for a difficult adjustment, but having to alter things against our arch rival makes it even tougher. Derek Grimm, Missouri's big man, is an outside shooting threat, and now it meant that if Raef went out to guard him, there would be one less big man under the boards. The biggest concern was that with the physical style that Missouri employs, the loss of five fouls under the basket could prove crucial. Either way, we would have our hands full.

The game started as expected. It was tight all the way, both teams came out shooting, and after 10 minutes the margin would never vary more than 7 points in either direction. In fact. after the 10 minute mark in the second half, the margin never was more than three in either direction. It remained a tight game.

As I feared, fouls played a crucial role in this game. We went deep into foul trouble, and eventually TJ Pugh, BJ Williams and Paul Pierce all fouled out. I ended up playing the four spot normally played by Raef, and both of us had four fouls by the end of the game.

Missouri took the lead into the final seconds of regulation, but after Grimm missed two of his four free throws, Jacque was fouled while driving and stepped to the line for two shots. We were down by three and we needed to a break. We got one when JV missed his second shot after sinking the first, and Raef got the rebound. He banked it home, sending the game into overtime.

I had played pretty well so far, in spite of my broken wrist. Raef had been a tower of strength under the boards, scoring 26 points. I had 20, and Jacque returned to his old self, hitting for 19 points and handing out 9 assists.

In the first overtime, we tried to put the game away but Missouri hung tough, hitting everything from the free throw line. And as the game entered the second overtime, Missouri took advantage of the foul situation that now was crippling us underneath.

The game wore down to a nail-biting finish. With seven seconds left, Missouri guard Tyron Lee drove the lane for what he hoped was the shot that would put Missouri ahead to stay. Jacque converged upon him, and using his quick hands, stripped the ball loose. But

Missouri senior Corey Tate picked up the loose ball at the free throw line and heaved up a 15-foot shot. It rattled in.

After a time-out, Ryan inbounded the ball, I drove the sideline but was cut off near the extended free throw line, behind the arc. Rather than heave up a 30-foot prayer, I passed to Raef who was about 18 feet out at the free throw line. But time had virtually elapsed and all Raef could do was fire the ball at the rim without even getting set. The ball hit the right side of the rim and bounced off. Missouri had broken our winning streak a game after we had set a new record. We were now 22-1.

The streak did not have to end sometime. I hate when people say that. We are a good team, a veteran team, and we have overcome adversity all year. The injury to Jacque tested our will to win, Ryan responded with terrific performances, and we grew as a team. The loss of Scot would test us the same way.

We knew Missouri was going to be tough. Throughout my career, there was always a special feeling surrounding these games. This was one team we always knew would never take the game lightly, would always come after us with everything they had. There is so much bad blood between our two schools.

Since Ryan chose to come here after being Missouri Player of the Year in high school, he gets the most abuse of all. The crowd boos every time he walks on the floor and really gets on him when he is about to shoot. If he misses, they cheer, and he just smiles and keeps on going. He wants to beat them at least as much as we seniors do.

I never noticed my wrist at all during this game. This was an amazing college basketball game. Every time we challenged them, they came back. Although I felt they hit some shots that can only be called lucky, I have to give Missouri credit. They responded every time they needed to, hung in throughout the game, and made big plays down the stretch. When you do that, and are playing at home, good things happen. Tonight it was their turn.

We played with a lot of foul problems, and they are a good free throw shooting team. That only helped their effort. I was nervous when it went into overtime. Relieved, but nervous. We were in a tough spot with the foul trouble. Raef had hit a tremendous shot to put it into overtime, but what would happen next?

It was an incredible finish. Every time we hit a clutch basket, they came down, we would foul, and they would hit their free throws. In the second overtime, they hit some mind-boggling shots. It was their night. We gave our best effort, so I can't feel too let down.

The streak was over. Now it was time to move on and continue the overall success of the season. The mood in the locker room was dejection, but not nearly as bad as most people would think. We knew that we had a great team and were having a great season. This was a test of what kind of team we are. Our response will demonstrate we are a special kind of team.

THURSDAY, FEBRUARY 5

The game against Missouri had been disappointing, but today was going to test my character as no other day had this year. We had returned early this morning from Missouri and gone straight to bed. When I awoke, I drove to Kansas City to see a specialist about the wrist.

I had discussed the injury with Coach before the Missouri game. "We want you to go see a specialist in Kansas City," he had said. "Find out for certain what's at stake. Then make your decision. I want you to do what's best for you. And I'll support whatever you decide. Call your mother when you get the results. Talk it over with her."

The diagnosis from this doctor was bleak. I would be out at least two to three weeks if I had surgery now. It was not what I wanted to hear. I'd be in the same boat as Scot Pollard. Two seniors sitting on the bench in street clothes as our final season at Kansas came to a close. The thought made me shudder, and I left the office and drove back to Lawrence listening to the radio, trying to take my mind off the depressing prospect.

Back home, I plopped down on the couch and picked up the phone. After trying to reach my mother and sister unsuccessfully , I called the one other person I would trust for advice on a matter of this seriousness. Coach Tom Orlich was free to talk that afternoon, and I told him what was happening.

Tom Orlich has always been a person I turn to for advice in troubling times. For the past eight years, Orlich has been a major influence on me as a basketball player. What many don't know is his impact upon Jerod Haase the person. As I matured in the Tahoe program, Orlich began to treat me as an adult, a player who could be relied on to set the tone a coach wanted for his team. He gave me responsibility, and I tried to come through for him.

As the time came to choose a college,for example, Orlich had waded through the numerous letters and phone calls I had received from universities and basketball programs around the nation. He contacted friends who could assist him with my questions about the quality of the programs and people in those schools with whom Orlich was not familiar. He laid out the choices for my parents and me with facts and information we would need to select the correct environment. He knew me well. He knew what kind of level of basketball I could play, but also knew the kind of people I would be comfortable with, and the type of coach who could get the most out of me, both as a person and as a player.

Now, almost 23, I considered my old coach as a friend and adviser. Coach Orlich was someone I could have fun with as an equal, but still look to for sound advice. And when he talked about my injury, I listened.

Orlich asked me to spell out the situation, complete with the options. I told him that if the wrist were operated on now, I would miss about 2 to 3 weeks. It would mean returning in time for the final home game of my career against Kansas State, at the earliest. The worst-case scenario would mean missing all remaining home games.

Orlich asked if there would be any long term damage if I continued to play with the wrist in its current condition. I said I hadn't been told of any problems. "In that case," said Tom Orlich, "I'd say you have to make the decision based upon how you'll feel."

The response was typical of Coach Orlich. I had always liked the fact that Coach never told me what to do, but rather would summarize all the options and then tell me to consider them before making a decision. But it would always be my decision, not the one he would prefer.

I thanked him and hung up the phone. I decided to try my mother again, but she was still not home. (I later discovered that she had been at a state program involving her school.) It was time to head over to the locker room for a team meeting. I'd have to call later.

On the way over to the gym, I thought of the parallel between this season and my senior year in high school. Once again, there was an eerie similarity. I had broken the same bone in my left wrist that year, in August, before the start of the state championship season. Of course, I had continued to play and the end result was what I had dreamed: a trophy and a title. Another positive angle to take, I thought, as I walked across the parking lot.

The meeting went fairly well, with team members talking about various things that seemed to be changing our focus. Chemistry was not a problem. The team all agreed that each person in the room was a welcomed part of the team, someone in whom each player had complete faith. I was glad about that because I had never seen any signs of dissension, and would have been shocked if someone had actually spoken negatively about another. After all the experiences we had been through, from August to LateNight to Maui, if there had been anyone who was an irritant, it would have been apparent by now. No, this team still enjoyed one anothers' company.

I spoke out and said, "You know, one thing I've noticed is that we don't chest butt anymore. When a guy makes a great play, we used to run up to him and get in his face. Now we just let the good plays go unrecognized." A few others in the room voiced agreement that this was missing from their past few games, and nobody could seem to say exactly when or why it had happened. But we all agreed that it certainly wouldn't hurt to make the effort to encourage one another during the game.

Jacque Vaughn mentioned that the team needed to quit talking about having fun and actually go out and do something that was fun. After a few suggestions, some of which are better left in the locker room, we decided that bowling would be the chosen activity. This elicited howls of laughter from Ryan, who remembered his past bowling excursions, and we agreed to hit the lanes. *(Later that week, when asked what Kansas was doing to cope with the loss, Jacque would tell reporters that we had a plan in mind, but it would remain within the team. Speculation was rampant, running from an open blow-off steam session to extra time shooting free throws. Not one member of the press corps guessed bowling.)

I left the meeting and went right into another with Coach Williams and the team trainer, Mark Cairns. By this time, the doctors' report on the X-rays had been received at the university, and the diagnosis was much worse than I had initially thought. The period involved would be much longer than originally predicted. Instead of two weeks out of action, it would be as long as three months!

I had not merely fractured the bone, but actually had been playing with a broken wrist for most of the season. Probably since Santa Clara. Now I knew why I had days when the wrist hurt and other times when it had been just fine. It had been partially broken, but the fall against Nebraska had completed the break. Considering this, it was somewhat amazing that I had been shooting as well as I had been this year. And when I thought of the steals and the dives, it was remarkable that the wrist had not been injured more seriously. "Once again, it's proof of the destiny of the season," I thought.

It was time to consider the options facing me. The first was to have immediate surgery and place the wrist in a cast. That would effectively end my season, since that would mean a period of three months recuperation. My future prospects for the NBA would be secure, and I would head for the showcase camps completely healed. But basketball at Kansas would be over. I wanted to finish the season, I wanted to play the remaining four home games at Allen Fieldhouse and participate in every moment of this year. I had worked too hard and come too far to see it end so suddenly. There had to be another choice. "What else could I consider?" I asked the trainer.

Cairns and Williams looked at one another. Then, looking me straight in the eye, Cairns said, matter of factly, "You could continue to tape the wrist tightly and play with the pain." Nobody spoke for a moment.

I asked," And what about long-term damage?"

Cairns answered, "As far as I can tell, there would be nothing worse that you have right now."

"And how would I know for sure?" I continued.

"We wouldn't ever know for sure," Cairns stated.

The second option was to wait until after the season to take any action. Since I had played with the condition all season, and could possibly take cortisone shots if the pain became really severe, this would mean basically doing what I had been doing.

I didn't need to think about it. I decided that if there was any chance of continuing to play, I would take it. I had been able to withstand the pain thus far, and against Missouri I obviously had played with a broken wrist. It didn't affect my performance that game. I was not going to lose this chance. I'd talk to my mom, but I knew what she would say. And my decision was going to be to continue to play.

SUNDAY, FEBRUARY 9 - IOWA STATE

Snow covered the ground as the plane landed and the Kansas commuter bus drove into Ames, Iowa for the anxiously awaited rematch with Iowa State. Since the victory a month earlier, some in the media had pointed to this contest as the true test of which team was superior. A writer for the Kansas City Star had commented that with all the "home cooking" given Kansas by the officials, this game in Ames would prove whether the Jayhawks were better than the Cyclones.

We were coming off our first loss of the season. My wrist was still sore, and the diagnosis that indicated I would have to play in pain the rest of the year did nothing to make everyone feel any more confident. Iowa State was looking to climb into the Top Five nationally and take co-leadership of the conference with a win in this game.

Tim Floyd, Iowa State's coach, had praised me again this past week in Sports Illustrated, saying that any coach would love to have someone "who played as hard as Haase." After the game a month ago, Floyd had told me personally that he admired the way I played and wished me success. Now he was telling the media his thoughts.

The game began with both teams playing with a great deal of emotion. Raef dunked off the opening tip, but Iowa State answered with 5 points. I came off a screen and hit a three from the top of the key. We traded baskets for a few minutes and then on a fast break, I drove the baseline and laid off a no-look pass to a trailing LaFrentz, who jammed it home. Moments later, I rebounded an errant shot, fed JV, who fed it back for an easy lay-up. Kansas was suddenly up 13-7.

It wouldn't last. Iowa State cut the margin to one at 17-16, and it stayed close for the rest of the half. We were playing a suffocating defense, and most of the Cyclone offense was stymied. There was one notable exception: Dedric Willoughby. The senior guard was having a career day, hitting three-point shots with uncanny regularity. He was running off screens continually, sometimes as many as five or six per possession, and the entire offense seemed to consist of the four other Iowa State players setting screens to keep me away from Willoughby. It was working, and Willoughby hit 5 of 6 from three-point range, including a 28-foot shot right before the end of the half, to give Iowa State a four point margin, 32-28.

As the team filed into the locker room, ahead of the coaches, all was quiet. I was thinking, "What's wrong with us? We just don't seem to have the fire anymore." As I looked around the room, I could see the same expression on the faces of my teammates. I thought about speaking, but Scot Pollard beat me to it.

"What happened, did somebody die?" Scot asked, half-jokingly. "You guys need to hear something. Let me tell you a story." He then proceeded to tell us a joke about their mothers. It broke everyone up, and laughter filled the room. Scot had done his job. The team was loose once again.

I realized at that moment what had been missing. The team was talking about having fun, but we weren't doing that. We hadn't laughed at something stupid in a while, and needed to loosen up and play basketball for fun. When the coaches came in and talked to us, it was a more relaxed group that listened to their strategy.

And the second half saw us come from behind and take control. Slowly plugging away at the lead, we forced Iowa State to take bad shots and capitalized on those errors. Paul came alive and scored 11 points. The defense smothered Iowa State, and they only managed six field goals the entire half. More importantly, I was able to get some help and stuck to Willoughby tightly. He finished with 36 points, a career high, but scored many of those after we had taken a secure lead.

Iowa State guard Jacy Holloway and I had a minor confrontation in the second half. Holloway was face-guarding me and getting frustrated. He had been knocked down going for a loose ball midway through the half. Moments later, he returned the favor, knocking me down from the side, and then straddling me as I lay on the floor. I leapt to my feet, but the officials seemed to think I had provoked the confrontation. The next time down the floor, at a break in the action, one of the officials told me that if Holloway and I didn't stop this, he would throw both of us out of the game.

We kept the lead, built it up to 8, and finished with a 69-62 victory. KU would remain No. 1, but more importantly, we had rebounded from a loss with a convincing road win. This put us in great position to win the Big 12. It was an important win in so many ways.

After the game, I wondered if I were getting an undeserved reputation. I play hard. I don't back down from guys who play overly aggressive and sometimes dirty. I get knocked down, I get up and go back hard, don't back down, and now am getting into trouble. Am I getting a bad reputation when guys come at me?

Whatever, we needed to win a game like this. Playing on their home floor, coming from behind when they had one of the largest crowds in their history, meant that we could take the pressure and ignore it. It's the kind of thing we have to get used to from now on. We are No. 1. People like to cheer for the underdog. Everywhere we go, the crowds will be hoping we fall. We have to expect that and use it to motivate ourselves.

The other positive from this game was the fact that it came after our first loss of the year. It was a test of our character to overcome a loss and rebound quickly. We did it, and did it on the road. That means a lot for our confidence, plus it shows the younger guys how to deal with these situations. When we seniors are gone, they'll have to teach the guys who follow them. It's one thing to talk about it. It's entirely another to go out and get it done.

Scot deserves credit for helping us win this game, even though he didn't set foot on the floor. His attitude at the half helped break the tension when we needed help. That's what so great about our team. Everyone contributes in his own way. We pick each other up, and in his own unique style, Scot picked us up today.

MONDAY, FEBRUARY 10
As the season has progressed, the media have placed us under more scrutiny. Coach tries to make our lives easier by restricting access to us, and I think it works. It would be very difficult for any outsider to

have much contact with us unless they were to camp by the front door of Jayhawker Towers.

This kind of treatment can work both ways. I feel as though my life is normal and I live what I call a routine existence. I go to class, practice, study, eat, visit with my friends and go to bed. It's certainly not what many people imagine my life to be like. Some of this regimen is my choice, and some is because Coach has prevented outside contact. It produces a stability I enjoy.

On the other hand, this distance could make us feel as though we are an elite group of guys. We could believe that we are better than the rest of the student body. Everywhere we go, people talk to and about us. They follow us, stare at us, wave and ask for autographs. At times, it seems like a form of hero worship. It's easy to see how guys could get a big head from all this attention.

When I go to class, for instance, I know that every student in that room knows my background. They know my hometown, my GPA, even my birthday and middle name. They look at me and know details about my life. I have no idea of who they are, and this can be disconcerting, especially to the freshmen. It creates the idea that we live in a separate world. The trick is to always be aware that this is temporary, a condition which owes its existence to basketball. It's not the same in September and it won't be the same in June.

TUESDAY, FEBRUARY 11
BJ Williams was sitting around the locker room, talking about food. "My wife's a pretty good cook. We have something different every night and she can really make some fine home cookin'," he said. "I don't know anyone who can match her."

"Hey, BJ, get Jerod to cook for you," CB suggested. "He thinks he's a great chef."

"Man, I don't think I could eat something cooked by Jerod," BJ laughed.

I overheard this conversation and came in from the other room, smiling as I spoke.

"BJ, you don't think I can cook? I'm the best chef in all of Tahoe. I'll make you a meal you'll never forget."

"That's what I'm afraid of," Williams said.

"No, really, bring the whole family over. I'll make you some Haase pizza."

I wanted to cook for BJ's family. I hadn't had anyone over for dinner since Christmas, and wanted to try my new bread machine pizza dough on someone besides CB. So, I went out to the store and did some quick shopping, getting everything I needed for the meal that night.

BJ Williams is the only Jayhawk who is married. He and his wife Jennifer have two children, Alex, age 3, and Jaiden, age 1. They live on campus in a section for married students, and the children are regulars at the KU games. Tonight, the Williams family arrived, ready for an eating adventure.

"Hey, come on in," I said, bending over to give Alex a slap on the hands.

"Where's the food?" Alex shouted, running into the room.

"J, he's ready to eat and so am I," BJ declared.

"BJ!," Jennifer scolded. "At least let Jerod get everything ready." She paused and then said teasingly, "Then we can make fun of him!"

The pizza was served and everyone plunged in. It must have been good, because it was gone in about 15 minutes. Afterwards, we sat around, telling stories, reminiscing about the four years at KU, while the kids played with a soccer ball and a nerf basketball. Finally, I decided to tell the kids some of my best childrens' stories. These are the tales that I use on my own nieces and nephews, and they are guaranteed to work. At least I think so. Except for one problem: it has been a while since I've told these particular stories, and some of the details have become jumbled together. Jaiden is too young to notice, but Alex gave me some puzzled looks as he listened and finally said, "That don't make sense." BJ, Jennifer and I laughed and went back to talking among ourselves.

Four hours go by and it seemed like only minutes since they sat down to eat, but it's time to get the kids home. BJ and I wanted to go see an intramural basketball league game taking place tonight, featuring some of the KU team managers. We headed over to watch and ended up spending another hour cheering on the managers, talking to other friends watching the game, and having a great evening relaxing and not worrying about anything.

"This was fun," I said to BJ as we started to leave.

"Yeah, thanks for having us. We need a few nights like this," BJ responded.

"We'll do it again," I replied. "I told you...I'm the pizza king."

WEDNESDAY, FEBRUARY 12 - SATURDAY, FEBRUARY 15

As the week began, it dawned on me that this was it. The last home stand of my career. Four games in a row and then my time on the floor of Allen Fieldhouse would be over. I would become another of the hundreds of alumni who could come back and point with pride to the floor, telling my kids that I had played on that special surface.

But I would never again be able to dress in the locker room beforehand, never be able to run out to the cheers of the 16,300 fans who give us such fantastic support. It would never be the same.

I wanted to be sure and savor every moment of these next two weeks. Each practice seemed to take on a special significance, and I found myself paying more attention to details. It's not easy coming to the end of anything you love, and I certainly have loved my time here. I never want to forget any part of this experience.

The game against Oklahoma State was a laugher. Everyone played and the margin of victory reflected the surprising ease with which we handled the Cowboys. The highlight was a half court bounce pass I made to a streaking Paul Pierce. I had 13 points in the first half, and between the fast break, the rebounding, and 64 % shooting from the floor, we won 104-72. It was the biggest margin of victory ever in this long series.

The games brought with them an added incentive. Since they were the final moments, I promised myself to give extra effort at all times. Not that I had ever slacked off, because I hadn't, but I wanted to pour my heart and soul out onto that floor. We'd win these games by playing the best we possibly could, and I was going to try and lead by example. I'd hold nothing back.

Jacque, Raef and I enjoy a break during the game against Oklahoma State. Photo by Earl Richardson.

Colorado came in on Saturday and the result was the same. We raced out to a huge lead and never looked back. This was the team that had been promoted as our top challengers this season, especially after their fast start. At the time of this game, the Buffalos were still ranked 15 th in the nation. But on this day, Kansas was simply too much.

I went 7-11 from the field and had 20 points overall. In one stretch during the first half, I launched three successful bombs from behind the arc in a span of 56 seconds. Raef snared five rebounds in the first two and a half minutes and was on his way to a team leading 23 points. Jacque had an amazing day, dishing out 11 assists and hodling Colorado sharpshooter Chauncey Billups to 3 for 14 shooting from the floor. Paul, B.J. Williams and Billy all hit double figures. Even walk-on Terry Nooner had a big day, hitting two three-point shots and a total of 8 points in just three minutes of floor time.

The final was 114-74. It marked the first time Kansas had ever recorded back to back conference wins where the team had scored over 100 points.

We had two victories and I felt that I had fulfilled the vow I had made to myself. Anyone who had seen the games knew that the team seemed to be reborn, and our scoring was at the highest level it had been all season. At the other end, our defense had even pleased our demanding coaches.

I was feeling good about my shooting and the five steals I had, all of which led to KU buckets. It felt good to play well at home, especially knowing that this was the last home stand. These past two games were fun. We are really playing well, winning and enjoying it. This is why you spend all those hours, summer and winter, preparing yourself. This is the payoff that makes it worthwhile.

MONDAY, FEBRUARY 17- MISSOURI -
THE REMATCH IN LAWRENCE

Today is the day we try to avenge the only loss of the season. I would never tell the press, but this day has been locked in my mind for two weeks. I hate to lose to Missouri. I want to win this game in the worst way.

It's been two weeks since the loss, and although we have played and defeated two ranked opponents in that time, the Missouri game stands out as a blemish on a perfect year. The seniors especially want to win, since it's the next-to-last home game. Closing out our careers with a perfect year at home is extremely important to all of us.

During the day, I tried to get some time alone. The past weekend has been a busy one, with visitors from home coming to see the game against Colorado. In addition, a friend from Chicago has flown in for a two-day visit, and longtime family friend John Downing is staying for a week, to see the conclusion of my Kansas career. My mother will be coming for the game on Saturday. All in all, it's something I deeply appreciate, and am happy about, but it does put a strain on my time.

Following my normal routine, I went to class and then took John on a quick tour of the area. Returning to my room, I wrote for a while, and then left for the pregame meal. When I came back, I found some messages on the answering machine. Deciding to grab the usual pregame nap, I tried to lie down, but the phone kept ringing. Well-wishers were calling, and the messages piled up. Finally realizing that sleep was not possible, I went to the phone and looked at the counter on the dial. Eleven messages. Everybody sure was excited about this game.

I paced around the room, arranging things and listening to music for a while. Finally, I gave up and walked over to the fieldhouse. I went through the normal shoot-around, but found my mind distracted by the thought of the game. Especially about Missouri. This is a game I really want to win, but I realized that emotion was replacing calm focus. I tried to get back to thinking about the game at hand, and not the individuals involved.

As the game began, I realized that this was not going to be a clean game. It would test my ability to deal with the questionable style of play from two Missouri players, Sutherland and Grimm.

Since my broken wrist was now common knowledge, having been covered extensively in the press, I knew that someone would try and take advantage of me, to test my ability to play at the same level with this injury. Even so, I never expected what happened.

During the first 10 minutes of the game, Sutherland was continually grabbing at my wrist. I was dismayed he would do that, to try to deliberately aggravate what he knew was a painful injury. I was disappointed that someone like him was playing at this level. Then came a real shock. I was in a crowd under the basket and was hit from two sides and knocked down. Both Sutherland and Grimm had sandwiched me and made sure that I fell. They had to know that I would try to break my fall, and probably hoped I'd use the broken wrist to do it.

It wasn't over. Once again, in a crowd inside the lane, Grimm threw an elbow in my direction and it caught me in the throat. I had trouble getting my wind, and found that I couldn't speak. I played about another minute and then motioned to Coach, who took me out of the game.

My voice wasn't coming back immediately. My breathing got better, and by the end of the half my voice was slowly returning, but for the remainder of the game, I noticed that I was winded and could not breathe normally. I played about 10 minutes in the second half, but had problems whenever we ran for a long stretch of time.

With a little over one minute remaining in the game, a near

brawl erupted as Raef, who had a career record-tying game scoring 31 points, was sandwiched between three Tiger defenders and thrown to the floor. As he fell, Derek Grimm hit him across the face with a forearm. I raced in and pulled Raef away from a possible fight as both benches emptied. Sutherland headed towards me and Raef, Missouri Coach Norm Stewart was yelling from the bench, and it looked as if a fight was coming. But the officials took control, ejecting Grimm and calling a foul on Sutherland. Raef shot a total of four free throws, sinking three of them, to effectively put the game out of reach.

The final score was 79-72. Both teams left the floor, barely shaking hands and not talking or looking at each other. The season series is a draw, and it means that nobody will have bragging rights this year.

It was great to win, but the near brawl in the last few seconds of the game was as close as I've ever come to fighting on the basketball court. The way Grimm just smacked Raef when he wasn't looking or expecting it set me off. I guess he and Sutherland think that style of play works, but to me they will always represent what is not right with sports today. I'm glad they will be leaving after this year. Maybe Missouri basketball can get back to a classier style.

I was still having trouble with my voice and throat. After looking at it, the trainers decided to send me to a throat specialist in Lawrence. Getting dressed, I left immediately through a side door and headed to the specialist's office. Driving there, I thought about the style of play that caused this. Those two guys are the antithesis of what I am. I play hard, but they feel you have to play dirty. I want to play well, but their desire is to see the other team play bad. I don't believe in trash-talking, but they never stop yapping. I hope that little kids watching see that my way is better. It's disappointing to see guys play the game that way.

By 11:30 that night, I was sitting in the doctor's office, having my throat examined. It wasn't pleasant. After gagging on the tools used by the physician who discovered nothing wrong, I was given another kind of exam. The doctor numbed my nose and then inserted a probe through it, reaching down into my throat. Finally able to get to the injured area, he said the results were inconclusive. A CAT scan was ordered for the next morning.

TUESDAY, FEBRUARY 18
I was given the CAT scan and the results weren't good. The test revealed swelling, but the doctors concluded that it may be broken in the Adam's apple area, with a possible cracked cartilage. It is asymmetric, and at times I can actually feel the area move when I

swallow. Now it's time for another decision.

The doctors told me that there was nothing they could do for this type of injury. It simply needs to heal by itself. There is always the risk that I could be hit there again, which could result in a far more serious injury. But the initial blow was somewhat freakish in nature, and although I am aggressive and do have my share of collisions with opponents, I have never been hit in the throat before. That helps me to make the decision.

I will continue to play. I can't stop now. I've come too far and played with the wrist and other assorted injuries and pain. I can go another six weeks. We're going to win it all. I've got to be here for the finish.

But this decision will not be made known to the public. Coach and I were concerned about my becoming a target for the cheap-shot artists out there, guys who would go after the injured area. I knew the style of play I encountered from the two Missouri players was not only case I'd run into. If the public knew about this, it could almost guarantee that someone could take a shot at my throat. It wasn't worth the risk.

The situation involving the injury, the negative style of play I endured involving my wrist and other things I have seen this year combined to put me in a serious mood. I spent time walking and thinking about basketball and people.

How can someone get enjoyment out of injuring someone ? Especially in a game. I've always believed that sports are good, but not totally good. I've thought that competition should be fierce and intense. But not dirty. Something's seriously wrong when dirty tactics are tolerated and encouraged. And I wonder if I want to be a part of sports if that's what it becomes.

I went back to the apartment but was still feeling upset and confused. It's not as if I have never encountered this kind of play. It's that they seem to enjoy doing this. It's depressing to see anyone play like that. It's not basketball. Deep down, I know the injuries have started to bum me out. Two near misses in the past two weeks. All the work of the summer, all the dreams for the year and for the future. To lose those chances, which come once in a lifetime, to a style of play that I would never condone really has me upset. Losing is one thing. Permanent injury or the loss of an opportunity is another.

Eventually, I realized it was not worth my time worrying about it any more. It's over and time to move ahead. I arrived back at the Towers and discovered a surprise. CB was rearranging things.

"Time for a new look," CB said with a smile, dragging the sofa across the room.

"I'm all for that," I replied. "I definitely need to change some things."

I grabbed one end of the sofa and helped CB move it to the other side of the room.

THURSDAY, FEBRUARY 20

Senior Day. A time to say goodbye to the players who have been part of the Jayhawk basketball program for the past four years. A time for the players to express their feelings to the fans for the last time. A tradition that I have witnessed for three years. The difference this year is obvious. I am one of those seniors saying goodbye.

The game Saturday against Kansas State will be the last time I take the floor in Allen Fieldhouse. It's two days away, but already I was thinking about it, and tides of emotion came rolling across me, changing my mood from moment to moment. I thought about the first time I set foot in the fieldhouse, on the trip I requested to decide if I wanted to make the switch from Cal. I recalled the redshirt year, when I practiced but could not play, feeling part of the team yet frustrated that I could not contribute in games. It seemed then that I'd never get to play, that the season lasted forever. I couldn't wait until my sophomore year. I wanted that redshirt year to go by as fast as possible.

Today, the local press was conducting interviews with the seniors. Each guy was reminiscing about the years that have gone by, and pictures were taken. When it's over, I changed out of my uniform and started to leave the room. Turning back towards the others I called out, "See you guys, it's been fun," and headed out the door. As I walked down the hall towards the exit, I suddenly stopped in my tracks with the realization of what I had just said.

"I wonder if they thought about what I said," I thought. "I meant it a little sarcastically, as though we would joke about the questions asked during the interviews. But it could be taken two ways. I guess I also want them to know how great this has been the past four years." As I went out the door, lifting up the collar on my jacket against the wind that was whipping around me, another thought entered my mind. "This will be a real tear-jerker on Saturday." I turned around for a moment and looked at the side of the fieldhouse. Then I slowly walked home.

FRIDAY, FEBRUARY 21

Today, I get to escort one of my favorite women around the campus : my mother. Mom has arrived for Senior Day, and will spend the entire day with me. She loves the campus, and wants to experience

My mother (Carol Haase) and I share a happy moment on Senior Day. Photo by Steve Puppe.

what it was like for me to be here.

Some people would be very self-conscious having their mothers around for a few moments, let alone the entire day, but not me. The unique bond between my mother and me is apparent in the way we treat each other, as very good friends not as parent-child. I walked around the campus using my mother as a crutch, and passers-by stared with bemused looks, realizing that the guard who dives for loose balls, knocking over those who are in his way, was now just another student teasing his mother. I liked that kind of attention. It gave me a kick to see people laughing at the way I drape my large frame over the smaller figure of my mother.

The day began with a visit to the doctor, checking the throat injury. Then, Mom and I attended a class and walked around the campus. That afternoon, I went to practice and Mom met old family friend John Downing, from Tahoe, who was in for the game. They strolled around, commenting on the architecture and style of the campus.

At practice, I looked at the seniors on the floor and suddenly was hit by the realization that there are six of us, and only five can start. So much attention has been paid to the starters that the two walk-on players, Steve Ransom and Joel Branstrom, are being overlooked. I thought about this for a while and came to a decision.

I've been here three years as a player, but those two guys came in as freshmen with Scot, BJ and JV. They should be the ones who start, since they were here for all four years. I was certain this was the right thing to do, so I went to discuss the idea with Coach Williams.

"Why would you think of that?" Coach asked.

"Coach, I just think it's the right thing to do," I declared. I elaborated on my thinking. "Steve and Joel have been here for two years, going through everything with the team, giving their hearts and bodies just as I have. The memory of starting their final game at KU will stay with them for the rest of their lives. They need the recognition. I'll get mine playing the rest of the game, and I would remember that more than just the start. But for them, it would mean everything, and I just think it's important for them to have this moment."

Coach Williams reflected for a few minutes. I sensed that he was not too thrilled with the idea, but when he spoke, the coach said it was a nice thought. He'd consider it. As I left the office, I decided that I would make one more attempt to change Coach's mind tomorrow. I like doing things for others, and this would make me feel good, about myself and for them. Besides, it will give me a chance to regain my composure after the opening greeting I know we're going to be getting from the crowd. The rumors were that each player and parent walking out onto the court before the game were going to be showered with flowers from the fans. I never liked public displays of emotion, but I felt that this was going to be a day where I might show some feelings myself.

I walked back to the dorm, changed clothes, and took my mother out to dinner. We spent the evening talking about family, friends and life in general. It was a great way to end the day, and I knew that my mother enjoyed herself.

Tomorrow is going to be another unforgettable day. I turned out the light in my bedroom, but it was a while before I fell asleep. My mind was working overtime, reminiscing.

SATURDAY, FEBRUARY 22- SENIOR DAY

The 1997 Kansas men's basketball team, a group that has broken records which had been untouched for 60 years, will take the floor for the last time today. It's the end of an era. The six seniors on this team have been involved with one of the most successful periods of basketball ever to be played at Kansas. The 16,300 fans who have jammed into Allen Fieldhouse are also aware of the significance of this day.

From the moment I awoke this morning, I was nostalgic. I was thinking about the fact that everything I was doing was for the last time. The time spent at Kansas has been among the best of my life, and I don't want to forget any of it. I tried to take extra notice of everything I was doing and made mental pictures I hoped I'd always recall. The pregame meal at the alumni center was a time not only to eat, but to look around the room. Sure, I'll be able to come here

Saying a few words to Jacque and Scot on Senior Day. Steve and Joel are stunned. Where did BJ go? Photo by Earl Richardson.

anytime, but it won't be with this group of guys and it won't be for a meal prior to a game. It won't ever be the same.

I drove back to the apartment and didn't even bother to try to take a nap. Generally, I wouldn't do this before day games, and today I certainly couldn't even if I were tired. Too many things to think about. The music blared as I was getting dressed, but even this was different, as I played some of my favorites rather than any assortment of discs. I paced back and forth, going from the sofa to the kitchen, moving down the hallway to the bedroom and back to the sofa. I surfed through television channels and turned off the set.

Putting on my coat, I walked over to the gym, spent time getting taped and hung out in the locker room. I kept coming back to the idea that this was the last home game of my career. I had been aware for some time that I had never lost a game in Allen Fieldhouse. The other seniors had played in 1994, but that was my redshirt year. Since I had been playing, the Jayhawks had begun what was now the nation's longest home court winning streak. It stood at 43 games. I had no intention of ending my home career with a loss. I knew the others felt the same.

My mind went back to some of the same things I had been thinking about a few days earlier. How fast time had flown. I had really wanted to get back to playing after the redshirt year. I thought that the games would go on forever. I knew, of course, that this day would come, but it had always seemed so far away in the future. The games came and the seasons passed, but the end never felt real. Today, it was all too real. I felt a surge of emotion coming on, and quickly moved around the room, talking to people and trying to put the melancholy out of my mind.

Finally, it was time for Coach Williams to tell the team who was starting. I hoped that my talk had persuaded him to start Joel and Steve. I listened and felt sad when he said I would be starting. I thought I had convinced him. I still thought they should be starting. Coach had to know what he was doing, I thought to myself. So, with that, the team raced out of the locker room and onto the floor for pregame warmups.

After returning to the locker room for the team prayer, we assembled by the door leading to the hallway. I took one look back at the guys I had known as teammates for these past four years. The other seniors seemed to have the same look in their eyes as I felt in my heart.

There was Jacque, looking straight ahead but behind his impassive expression I could sense he was trying to maintain his composure. But he'd never break down in the locker room. Scot was ready, finally back in uniform. I had helped him pick out the nail polish for his final home appearance. He wanted the colors to be just right, and the alternating red and blue nails seemed to satisfy his desire to be a Jayhawk to the end. BJ was always BJ, smiling that contented smile and in control of things, but I knew his insides were churning from the look in his eyes. Steve and Joel were more of a mystery to me, but I knew that they had enjoyed their time being a part of the team. The fact they earned this final tribute as walk-ons in pre-season tryouts made their pride all the more special.

It was all rushing to an end at KU. We'd continue to play, but never at this Fieldhouse. Before anybody could think anymore, I had one final comment to make to everyone. I usually said a few words each game before the team left the locker room, and today there was only one thing I could think of saying. I turned and looked at my assembled teammates. All I could say was "Thank you." They stood there for a moment. Then I turned and moved out the door. In a blurry red and blue line, they followed.

Out on the floor, the scene was incredible. The announcer introduced we seniors in a very emotional setting. Each of us was handed a rose and walked to the center circle on the court. We were met by our parent(s) and exchanged hugs and kisses as we presented the rose. I was the second one introduced. As I walked out I could feel a sadness and happiness swirling inside me. I was pleased my mother was there, smiling with pride. I wished my father could share in this special moment, but I knew that he was watching from above. The crowd was what moved me most. I hadn't expected the outpouring which cascaded from the seats. Listening to the cheers and feeling the warmth with which they were delivered, I realized that these fans were letting me and the others know how much they appreciated our efforts the past four years. The fans would miss watching this group of seniors perform, and they wanted to say goodbye with as much sincerity and noise as they could.

Then another incredible thing happened. From the stands on all sides of the court, flowers rained down on us, the seniors. The court was covered with flowers thrown by our fans. That did it. Our resolve to try to remain stoic crumbled. All six seniors and our teammates on the sidelines looked emotionally at the floor and the fans, feeling proud, sad and happy all at once. It was a ceremony and a tribute none of us in the fieldhouse that day will ever forget.

There was still one more event before tipoff. Looking at me as he spoke, Coach Williams announced the jump ball lineup. He was going to put seven men on the floor! The five starters would take our usual positions, but Joel and Steve would stand at the top of the key, the arc behind the free throw line. As each of us assumed our position, the crowd went even wilder. As the cheering reached deafening proportions, I looked over at Coach Williams. Coach was looking right at me and as we made eye contact, I mouthed the words "Thank you". He gave me a smile in return. That was so important to me. Steve and Joel got the recognition they deserved. Then the two players left the court, the ball was tossed for the opening tip, and the game was underway.

After trailing at the half, we went on one of our patented runs, outscoring K-State 24-4 in one stretch, and winning by a final score of 78-58. I scored 16 points, Raef led the team with 21, and every senior scored and contributed in our final home outing. It almost seemed as if the game were anticlimactic. The days' historic events were not over yet.

After the game, we assembled and cut down the nets. Everyone took a snip, since this game meant that Kansas was the first champion of the new Big 12 conference. "This feels great," I said to Jacque. "Sure does," JV agreed, with a wide smile on his face. It struck me at this time that I not only never experienced a loss at Kansas, but that at South Lake Tahoe High, I was also on a team that never lost a home game. The parallels between these two seasons continue. God, I hope they have the same ending.

Then, yet another highlights of Senior Day. Each senior went to the microphone to say a few words of farewell to the home crowd. Steve Ransom and Scot Pollard worked the crowd like stand-up comics with great timing and delivery. There were a lot of laughs when they spoke. BJ Williams and Joel Branstrom kept their remarks short, but full of meaning. Their sense of gratitude was evident and the crowd applauded warmly.

I was then introduced to the crowd. "Nobody has ever played harder for the Jayhawks than this young man," says Max Falkenstein, longtime announcer for Kansas sports events and Jayhawks basketball. I ran out to the applause of the crowd and took the mike with a smile. "There are so many things I wanted to say, but I can't put them all into words and I'm not going to try. I'm going to thank a few special people." I proceeded to thank the managers, who generally go unrecognized for all their hard work. I told my teammates "they are like brothers" and that I would always be there to help them if they need it. I thanked the coaching staff for everything, including non-basketball related issues.

Then came an emotional part for me. I told Coach Williams that although nobody could replace my father, he was like one to me. "I'm glad you're here," I said, my voice wavering. I looked squarely at Coach when I spoke. "Thank you," I said with as much conviction as I have ever used.

Then I addressed the most special person there. "Mom, thanks for everything. You raised the best family and you ought to write a book about how to do it. I'm so fortunate to have such a great family."

The fans were next. "You are a group that are loud, very knowledgeable and very loyal," I declared. "You make Kansas basketball what it is today. There are good crowds all over the nation, but you people are the best! Thank you." I walked off to the cheers of the crowd and gave Coach Williams a hug.

Jacque completed the day. He thanked the fans, the media, the coaches and his fellow players. He made Coach Williams come onto the floor, and with great emotion, his voice breaking, told Coach, "I hope our paths continue to cross." He embraced Coach Williams and the two of them left the floor to a wild round of cheers.

The fans gave us seniors a standing ovation as we left the floor for the last time. I took one long look up and around the stands, gazing at the banners, the signs and the fans. It was another of the mental pictures I was trying to take and keep in my memory. This was one I won't have any trouble remembering. It was unforgettable.

SUNDAY, FEBRUARY 23

Roy Williams was holding a net in his hand. I noticed it as soon as I walked into the gym, and wondered why coach was twirling it. He walked up to me and asked with a smile, "Want it?" I looked surprised and asked "To keep?" "Yes," answered Coach. "If you want it, it's yours."

I couldn't believe it. The net was special and it meant a lot to me that Coach was offering it to me. "I'd love to have it," I answered. "Then it's yours," Coach said. He handed it to me and looked me in the eye. I understood the meaning.

The net was cut from the other basket at yesterday's ceremonies. It was something the coach would be expected to keep, and giving it to me was as special an offering as Coach Williams could make. It was a way of making his feelings known, and the meaning was not lost on me. The original net had been given to Jacque, and it made clear something that Coach had said the day before. "I was the worst coach in America today," he had said. "I couldn't look at Jerod or Jacque. I couldn't even speak before the game." The emotional side of Coach had succumbed to his feelings then, and now he was expressing them in a way he knew that both JV and I, his two senior guards, would understand.

I felt a special bond I knew would not disappear. I had always felt that part of the experience at Kansas was not only basketball. As cliched as it sounds, I had learned another lesson in life from my coach. I appreciated it deeply.

MONDAY, FEBRUARY 24

Another Senior night, but this time it was on the road. Oklahoma was hosting the festivities, and there was a record crowd. They were all worked up, and not only due to Senior night. The opponent was Kansas, a big rival and current No.1 team in all of college basketball. The Oklahoma team had new warmups and was making a production out of this. There was a light show before the game, and a general party atmosphere. It would be a tough game.

One thing I noticed before the game was the music. The Sooner band blared and we huddled and swayed back and forth to their music. It was as though we were in our own little world, us against them.

Coach wanted this game bad. He mentioned a few times during the time outs that we would go in and sing the hymn,"Amen" after the game, if we won. When we asked why that hymn, Coach declined to say why, preferring to wait until the game was over.

The game was intense. Oklahoma started off running on adrenaline and used that emotion to fuel their early successful start. They rushed to a 16-9 lead and seemed to just draw strength from the roaring crowd. But then we fought back with one of our patented runs.

For the next 9 minutes, we could do no wrong. We outscored the Sooners 28-8 and took a 37-22 lead into halftime. Everyone contributed to this spurt, I had to play some tough defense on Nate Erdmann, the Sooners senior high scoring guard. Paul and Jacque were scoring easy baskets off the fast break, and right before the half Billy Thomas nailed a three to send the team off with momentum. Everything looked encouraging.

But Oklahoma fought back. They cut the lead to one with 8 minutes left. We then put another short burst together and built the lead back up to 9. With four and a half minutes left, that seemed to be comfortable. But again the Sooners fought back. They played some good defense of their own, and suddenly we were in trouble. Calling time-out with 16 seconds left, Oklahoma trailed by only two, 70 - 68. They had the ball and control of the game in their hands.

The ball came in to Erdmann, and Jerod raced towards him, sticking my hand up to distract him. His shot missed, however the rebound came down to Oklahoma's Eduardo Najera, who laid the ball of the glass and missed. Another rebound and another miss. Najera again came down with the rebound and I slapped the ball out of his hands. The final Oklahoma attempt came after the gun sounded and we had escaped with a victory.

The team gathered in the locker room and Coach Williams had us sing the hymn "Amen" as he had promised. Then he told us how the crowd at Maryland would sing that song when they beat North Carolina or anyone else. He remembered it from his days at Carolina, and with the OU crowd as boisterous as it was today, he felt it would be good to have his team sing the song. Forming our usual post game mosh pit, we all sang the song again, and danced in a circle.

It struck me while in the middle of the mosh pit that some of the guys had decent voices. Not me, but Raef was surprisingly good, and Paul hit some notes that I had only heard on records. There were a few pretty bad voices, but I'd rather not mention any names, because I think I'd be on a few lists if anyone else was keeping track. All in all, it was a cool way to put an exclamation mark after a "W!".

WEDNESDAY, FEBRUARY 26
The Red Team was ready to get things going. At practices all season, the team was divided into two groups for scrimmages. The Red Team was the second unit, comprised of walk-on players Steve Ransom, Joel Brandstrom and Terry Nooner, along with CB and other scholarship players.

CB was the leader of the bunch. Throughout the year he motivated them and pushed them to defeat the Blue Team, usually through jibes and sarcastic remarks. He called himself the general manager of the team, responsible for personnel moves to improve the squad. CB was quite proud of the fact that, as he said to the others, "I obtained Lester Earl (a transfer from LSU) without giving up a player. That helped make us stronger up front." He felt it was a better move when Scot Pollard went down and the Red Team lost TJ Pugh to the Blues. "Depth is something any good GM tries to have on his squad," CB said jokingly. He was always trying to get the red team pumped.

Today, they were possessed. They worked us hard, and took great pride in making the overall team better. They wanted to beat us at every practice, and we knew how important they were to the team's success. Without them challenging us all the time, we wouldn't be where we are today. They deserve so much credit.

Steve and CB played well this game. They pushed us to the limit and barely lost a close contest. As the horn sounded and practice moved on to the stretching phase, CB was pontificating on the success of the Reds.

"If you guys are No.1 in the polls, we've gotta be No.2," he said.

"Who ever heard of you?" said Ryan.

"You sure knew us last week, when we kicked your butts," answered CB.

"Yeah, CB's right," added Steve. "Go Red!"

"You got lucky one time," said Raef, jokingly. "We'll make sure that doesn't happen again."

SUNDAY, MARCH 2
I was anxious to get on the court and get started. In my own mind, I had played three poor games in a row, and wanted to redeem myself. Not by shooting the ball more often. Instead I would go back to what I'd been doing most of the season, being more selective in my shot selection. It's time to play smart, time to let the game come to me and get in the flow. Then good things will happen. I also had set a goal of limiting my turnovers, feeling that this would allow my game to get back to

it's former balanced self.

We embarked on a three hour bus ride to Lincoln and on the way I did some reading. Many of the others were doing class work, since the impending start of the tournament season meant they would miss a great deal of class time. The bus was fairly quiet for much of the ride.

I did some soul searching. I realized that my shot was not falling and it bothered me. I didn't want a repeat of last season, and felt it simply wasn't possible. Yet, I knew I had been playing poorly , or rather shooting poorly, since the Missouri game. I decided that what I needed was more practice time, and I vowed to do some extra shooting beginning tomorrow. For now, I would concentrate on the game.

Nebraska was feeling confident. Some of their starters had made comments to the press stating their belief they could beat the us. They had taken Kansas into overtime just a month earlier, and that was a tour place. Now it was on their home court, and in this final game of the regular season, the Huskers were ready to do some damage. They wanted to get into the NCAA tournament, and beating Kansas would send a message that they deserved an invitation.

Most of our team wanted the same thing. Closing out the season with a convincing win on the road would alert everyone that we were for real. Scot was returning to the playing style he demonstrated in January, and with the realization that his shortened season was ending, was more intent that ever on putting forth a great effort.

The game was never really in doubt. We moved ahead early, on the strength of our superior rebounding and 50% shooting from the floor. Nebraska cut the margin from 14 to 6, but then we worked hard and took it back up to 14. Our front line was murdering the Huskers, accounting for two thirds of the KU points. At the half, the margin stood at 41-28.

After a brief talk about keeping focused, Coach and his staff left the team to ourselves. Nothing really needed to be said. We were playing a good solid game, and we knew we had to put this team away . As I returned to the floor, I felt that I still was not shooting as I wanted, but would continue to pound the ball inside. That's what coach always said he wanted this year, and it's working. With Scot back, we are just that more effective.

I played set up man the rest of the way, garnering six assists and not committing one turnover. It was the front line's turn to shine, as they totalled 55 of the 85 points between the big three. Raef led the way with 23, and was virtually unstoppable late in the game.

Paul came alive for 18 and Scot finished with 14. Afterwards, Raef commented that "Scot played like the Pollard of old." and Coach Williams added that "it was good to have him back."

I couldn't help but think of how this team supported one another. On the ride back to Lawrence, I dwelt on this characteristic of my teammates. This is such a coachable team, and it's a tribute to Coach Williams. He recruits good people who are interested in improving and helping the team win. I came here because I knew that. When I was on the recruiting trip, I noticed that there weren't the egos that other programs have. This was a team then, and it is today.

Furthermore, coach has a great deal of respect for us and we have it for him. We respect the things he says. The basis for it all is that we are not individuals. We are a team with team goals. We want to win more than get our own personal glory. At least, that is my take on this.

I took a look around the bus. At Ryan reading a book, at Billy trying to sleep, at TJ, who also seemed deep in thought. They could have gone anywhere, but they chose Kansas. And they're a perfect fit. They're the future and they'll be successful.

I was still restless and bothered by my lack of offense. After the team unloaded from the bus, I went to the floor of the gym and shot for another half hour. It was ten o'clock, and I had just played my final regular season game, but I wanted to work. I asked one of the managers, Stephanie Temple, to help with the rebounding and worked up a good sweat. The shots were starting to fall as the time came to an end, and I realized that I had not noticed the wrist through most of the workout. The pain was constant, but not sharp.

I decided that I would start a daily shooting regimen, much as I had done in September. It would help me get back the touch. I should have never taken time off because of my wrist. It can't get any worse, so I might as well keep shooting.

THURSDAY, MARCH 6

The 45 minute drive to Kansas City gave me time to think. The past few days had been a time to get prepared for what was going to be a busy month. I answered mail, did some shopping, and spent a good deal of time catching up and trying to get ahead in my courses. This was the most difficult part for most of the team, since we had to get assignments in advance and try to complete the work while being part of a major conference tournament. As we had during the trip to Maui, the guys must budget their time and, in some cases, meet with the academic advisor during the breaks in the day.

Probing the defense against Iowa State. *Photo by Rich Clarkson.*

I thought about the past few days of practice. It hadn't been very inspired. The team was aware of the importance of performing well, but seemed flat at practice. Nothing Coach Williams had said seemed to register and at times it was just as routine as things had been in early November. We'd all been here before.

I had been upset with my own individual performances the past few games. Since the Colorado game, I didn't feel I had been very productive on offense. Against Kansas State I'd scored 16, but it was a sloppy game and I felt it wasn't a very good outing. While my defense had picked up, I needed to improve and start to score again. To remedy this, I began to take extra shooting practice, getting a manager to accompany him to the Fieldhouse and rebound any missed shots. I worked for about an hour on shooting each day. After all when I stopped shooting because of my wrist, my game suffered. But the pain hasn't gone away or even been less noticeable. So I might as well go back to shooting.

I also was concerned about how the team was entering the post season. We need to get off to a good start right here, and carry it over to the NCAA. Last year, we struggled in the conference tourney and lost the final game. We have to get momentum now. But I don't think we're all looking at it this way. And that could be a problem.

The team arrived at the Marriott and went to our rooms. For the next few days, we would be on a strict time schedule. From noon until 2 would be our games, showers and media sessions, followed by a team meal from 3 until 5. The next five hours were free time, where the players could either do homework, be with our families and friends, or watch the other teams play their games. At 10:30 until 11:30 each night, there would be a team meeting, when the coaches would go over the game plan for the next days' contest. Then it would be time for bed, since we would meet the following morning at 8:30 for pregame breakfast.

I really don't like getting up early, so I was not too pleased at the breakfast time we had each day, but I really did like the five hours of free time each night. This was going to be a family reunion weekend for the myself and my family. The entire Haase family, except for my brother David, would be flying in to see the four day tournament. It would be the first time in years that they had all assembled in one place, and everyone was looking forward to it. Especially me. I missed everyone, and the idea of seeing them all at once was very appealing.

It was a bit of a disappointment not to see David and his wife Julie. However, since David was a first time father, with a son only 8 days old, it was still nice to think of another little Haase running around the next reunion. For a moment, I flashed back to an incident between myself and my older brother as kids. I recalled a time when I had made David so mad that he chased me through the house and finally threw a plastic swimming fin at me in frustration. However, I ducked around the stairs and the fin went sailing through a picture window, landing on the front lawn. Needless to say, David was even angrier at me, since now he was in more trouble than before. I remembered laughing until I heard the crash of glass. It made me laugh now, thinking about the look on David's face.

The night was spent just talking as any family would at an occasion like this. The five hours seemed like a few minutes, and then it was time to get to the meeting. Oklahoma State was waiting, the first step into the postseason.

FRIDAY, MARCH 7

Oklahoma State was out for revenge. Just a few weeks earlier they had been embarrassed by us, losing by almost 40 points. The opening game of the tourney for Kansas was supposed to be a replay of the first encounter. At least, that was what was being stated in the papers.

I was going to be focused on defense. With my scoring output down the past few games, and with the need for improved defense in the tournament, it only seemed natural. With Scot returning to normal health, our team now had the line-up we had planned on using last November. Everything seemed in place for an excellent start to the tourney.

But Oklahoma State would not follow the script. They scrapped and fought and kept themselves in the game. I thought I was playing outstanding defense, but offensively I knew I was off form and couldn't seem to get the shots to fall. They were again on target, but just weren't going in.

The rest of the team seemed to be in the same shape. Emotions were flat, and by the half, the coaches were getting frustrated. It got so bad that in the second half, Coach Williams took out the entire starting five and benched us. He went with the second five for almost seven minutes, sending a message that was not misunderstood. Play with intensity, play smart or don't play at all.

The signal was received. When the starters returned to the floor, we took control of the game, and went on to a 74-59 victory. It was not pretty, and it wasn't one of our more memorable outings, but it was a win and we'd take it.

I was relieved, but not at all happy. I knew that we better not continue this, or someone is going to knock us off Every once in a while, we get a challenge like this. As long as we respond like we did tonight, we're okay. I dressed quickly, briefly met with the media and headed back to the hotel. After the team meal, I again went out with my family.

At the team meeting that night, nothing was mentioned about the benching. It was assumed that this was not going to happen again, and with the experienced nature of our team, that would not have to be spoken about. More important topics were discussed. Iowa State. The third meeting with the only other conference team to be ranked in the Top Ten all year. We went over tendencies, assignments and offensive schemes. It took about an hour, and then all of us went back to our rooms.

It was about 11:30 when the phone call came. "Open your door in one minute," said the mysterious voice. Then a click. Raef was my roommate on this trip, and he turned to me and delivered the message. Both of us smiled, raced to the door, and counted until we had reached one minute. Raef threw open the door and we looked out into the hall.

Every door of every room housing a Kansas basketball player was opening at about the same moment. And as the entire team looked out into the hall, we all witnessed the same sight. Coming down the hall, lifting his knees abnormally high and running like a total dork was a young man in his shorts. He was bounding from side to side, kicking his knees up and laughing hysterically. The faces from the rooms were laughing along with him. He raced up the hall to the end, and then back past all the rooms until he reached his room at the end of the hall. Then, with a flourish, he spun around and ran into the room.

Who was this, and what was it about? It was CB, and it had to do with a superstition. For the past three years, at the Big 12 tourney, CB had his trip roommate call everyone else and give the secretive message. Then he would race up and down the hall and go back to his room. He felt this was the inspiration needed to win the tourney.

Raef and I closed the door and got ready for bed. "You know, he's nuts," Raef said to me. "But it's hilarious to watch him go through the routine."

"He thinks it'll help us loosen up a bit. And he's right," I answered.

And maybe, this year it will work and we'll win this thing.

SATURDAY, MARCH 8
The pre-game breakfast was at 8 a.m., and I really hated getting up at 7:30. In the summer, working the basketball camps, it had not been as difficult to rise early, but after 6 months of living at school, I was used to sleeping in later. This was not fun. I sleepily dressed and headed downstairs to the dining room.

Iowa State, like anyone else in the conference, would be difficult to beat a third time. Playing teams that know your style, as conference teams do, makes it a tough task to try and continually dominate an opponent. After the game yesterday, we knew that we had to come out and play a solid game right from the start. To me, that meant playing defense against Dedric Willoughby, who had scored 36 points against us just one month ago. I would have to be at my best to stop Iowa State's sharpshooter.

Out team was ready and eager for this contest. Before the game, the coaching staff again stressed the importance of coming out and setting a tempo that let the opponent know who was in charge. I thought we did just that, taking control of the game immediately. And after finding our own offense misfiring, we turned to our defense for help. people have never really given us the credit we deserve for the way we can play tough defense. There have been many games this year where we would have had a much tougher time if we had not set the tone for the game with our defense. It's an area where we have great pride.

Early into the game, I took an elbow to the head from Kelvin Cato, the Cyclones 6'11" center. Dizzy, I left the game for about six minutes. The team kept playing hard, but still struggled on offense. After missing 8 three point tries, and still leading 27-23 at the break, we came out with a new fire to start the second half.

We had talked about the need to turn it up on defense. We knew that if we could get that part of our game going, it would carry over to the offense. I honestly felt that our defense was stifling today. Iowa State could not get a clear shot at the basket. Every screen that was set to free Willoughby, I tried to fight my way through. If I didn't make it, Jacque and Paul helped and shut down the guard. The big men intimidated all shots near the basket. They pressured ballhandlers into errors and held the Cyclones without a basket for the first 10 and a half minutes. It was an awesome display of defense.

Willoughby never scored a basket while being I guarded him. His only successful attempt came on a breakaway due to an errant pass. He was uncontested as he hit a layup. After the game, Scot told reporters jokingly, "Jerod was mad at me for that pass. If not for that, he would have had a perfect day defensively." I was really proud of this accomplishment.

Accolades abounded. Coach told the press, "I cannot remember a game where we were more alert to seeing the big picture defensively. I've never been more proud of a team defensively." I added to Coach's comments, telling the papers that "At all times, five guys were on the court hustling and playing defense." And Tim Floyd, Iowa State's coach, stated that, "I've never seen a defense that good since I've been in this conference."

I joined my family and ate dinner at the home of some friends now living in Kansas City. It was the final night to be with everyone and I wanted to savor the time. I also needed to unwind a bit. My mind would soon be occupied with only one thought: the final con-

Cutting down the nets after beating Missouri to win the first Big 12 conference tournament. Photo by Rich Clarkson.

test with Missouri. This time it was for the title.

SUNDAY, MARCH 9
The Big 12 title game was going to be more than just a battle. It would be a war. Four years of rivalry boiling down to one game. Mutual dislike and competition for the attention of the media had

driven out two teams. We had to defeat one another.

These were the guys that I had faced since my arrival at Kansas. My entire career has been spent dealing with the Missouri style of play and the simple fact is that this was the one school KU could truly call a rival. While it would seem natural that Kansas State would fit that title, the success of Missouri and the challenge they had presented made them the true roadblock. Today, it would be for the first Big 12 title. Today, it would be for the season series. Today, it would be brutal.

I had recovered from the injury of yesterday. My head was a little sore in the spot where the elbow hit, but it was okay and I could think of nothing else but this game. No matter what, I was going to play my best today. I would leave nothing behind. Whatever it took, I would be there when the game ended, celebrating the final victory over the most fierce rivals of my career. It would be vindication for the Kansas style of play.

There was an added incentive. No one on this team has ever won the tournament here and we want to go back to Lawrence with that feeling of victory. Scot added the comment that "I've never been in the NCAA tournament coming off a win. That's something I'd like to try." And Coach Williams reminded us, before the game, that "nobody in this room has ever won the conference tournament."

The game was a nationally televised contest. The pregame comments concentrated on the Missouri victory over KU a month earlier. Images of me passing the ball to Raef, who fired a shot too late, images of Sutherland dancing at mid-court amidst the celebration of the fans, were flashed across the country. This was the only blemish on a perfect season. This was the one thing we had to overcome, to prove to the nation that we could beat this team on a neutral site.

Kemper Arena in Kansas City was packed and the noise was deafening. Since it sits between the two campuses, almost directly at a mid-point distance wise, fans from both schools had flocked in to cheer their team. It took on the level of a mid-season game on a campus, instead of the generally sterile tone of most tournament games. This time, the fans were also students, who didn't have to travel around the country stretching their budgets beyond its limits. This was like a home game, for both schools.

I could sense the feeling, and it motivated me and my teammates. We came out alive and ready to play to our individual peaks. From the opening tip, we raced to the lead and never looked back. Missouri missed some early shots, while KU was on fire, hitting 66 percent of our shots at one point in the first half. We went on an 18-3 run late in the half, and led 51-26. We had effectively put the game out of reach early. Missouri shot 9-28 in the half, while we went 20-30. The fire was taken out of the Tigers, and it showed as they walked dejectedly off the court at halftime.

Paul was having his best game of the season. He was getting open, moving aggressively to the basket, and Jacque was hitting him time and again as he worked his way free for easy baskets. Raef and Scot were finally playing together against this team, Scot having missed both outings with his injury. The tandem proved unstoppable. I continued to concentrate on defense, keeping Sutherland off balance and unable to get a clear shot. Together, the team played what Coach Williams called "our best ten minutes of offense this year. It was an up and down game, and when we get into that, we're pretty good."

The second half was a repeat of the first. We took control early, and after Ryan hit a three pointer, led 72-41. The rest of the game was just played out about even, and the final score of 87-60 reflected the lopsided nature of the contest. Throughout the second half, I took a long look at the faces of these Missouri players who had been such rivals my entire career. They were still talking, still swaggering, but it was not with the same conviction as before. They knew they were being beaten, knew their careers were coming to an end, and they couldn't stop it. It was strange to see this, since there had always been the knowledge there would be another time when they would meet. Now it was finished, and Kansas was responsible. In my redshirt year, 1994, Missouri had taken both meetings, going perfect in the conference that season. We had been the team with that look. I was proud of my teammates, proud we had proven once and for all which was the better team. There could be no doubt after a win like this.

The cutting of the nets was a truly happy occasion. Coach Williams had never won this tourney since I had been at KU, and I was glad to be on the team that broke this unpleasant streak. Coach deserves this. As I watched my teammates cut down the nets, followed by the coaches, I felt the second part of the journey was complete. First came the conference, now the conference tourney. We've accomplished two of our goals. The biggest step is the only one left.

We all showered quickly, and dressed. Before we could meet with the media, however, Coach asked us to clean up the locker room. It was something none of the guys questioned although there were some surprised looks. It seemed an odd thing to do at a moment like this. But sometimes people do things without thinking . I'd had a similar moment during a game in my freshman year. I dove for a loose ball and landed on the scorers table, scattering all their material everywhere. Instead of returning to the game, I started to pick up the books and pencils, trying to arrange the microphones back to their original position. It took a few moments for me to realize that the game was on hold until I returned.

We met briefly with the media and boarded the bus back to Lawrence. There was celebrating, but not as much as one might think. We all knew that the real season was about to begin this coming week, the goal we had pursued since last March would soon be appearing on our television screens.

Coach took us all over to his house to have dessert and watch the selection show. To me, it really doesn't matter who we play. The only thing that matters is that we play our best. If we do that, things will take care of themselves, and we'll win the tournament. I smiled at the thought. The final phase of my repeat dream season would be complete.

My sister Mara, her husband Cameron and their family had returned to Lawrence for a brief visit. We went to dinner, I showed them a quick tour of campus, and said goodbye. The family reunion weekend was now over, and had enjoyed it as much as I'd anticipated. It was great to see everyone, great to have the family around again. I made a few phone calls to friends, and went to bed. This had been great, but the best was yet to come. I kept thinking about this as I fell asleep.

LAST DANCE,
LAST CHANCE

THE NCAA TOURNAMENT

This year Kansas was the heavy favorite to win the National Championship. Although there were other teams given a chance, most of the pundits added the phrase "if Kansas stumbles" before their names. We had finally arrived. We were the team to beat.

When the selection committee meets, they choose four No. 1 seeds for each of the regions of the country. This year the choices were Kansas, Kentucky, Minnesota and North Carolina. Other strong teams in this tournament were Utah, ranked in the Top 5 at the end of the season, UCLA, which had rebounded from its January slump to win their final 9 games, South Carolina, winners of 15 of their last 16 games and Wake Forest, still playing well as they had all season.

We had entered the tourney on a roll. Our strong conference tournament finish had been an exclamation point to the season. Our toughest rivals had been defeated handily and we seemed ready to take off in the tourney. Kentucky was also peaking and Minnesota had won the Big 10 conference for the first time. The field was set and although there was talk of the usual upsets, we were never mentioned. We had too much depth and too much experience to lose in the opening round. At least that's what everyone was saying.

Kentucky was the defending champion and was given the strongest chance to beat us. They had the same strong points as ours, with one notable exception: their bench was not as deep as ours. The same could be said for Minnesota, a team that had played well but was never given much respect. This was their chance to prove they deserved to be ranked No. 2, which is where they finished the season, right behind us. North Carolina had come on strong the second half of the season, and their coach, Dean Smith, was considered a legend. He had played at Kansas, and Coach Williams had worked for him as an assistant in the 1980's. There was a lot of sentiment possible, should we meet each other in the Final Four.

Two teams entered the tournament with losing records, Fairfield and Jackson State. The worst was Fairfield, at 11-18. We thought that was who we'd draw, since we had the best record. But instead we were paired with Jackson State while North Carolina drew Fairfield. It didn't matter. We had to win six more games and the title was ours.

TUESDAY, MARCH 11

The mail was piling into the basketball office. Well-wishers from all over the nation were writing to the Jayhawks, and I myself was getting a tremendous stack. People wanted to say good luck, offer their advice on what to do against this or that team, or as usual, ask for an autograph. It was getting hard to keep up with the flow of mail, and although I tried, I just had to stash some of it in the shoebox under my desk that held all the unanswered mail. I'd get to it when there was more time.

People were starting to get the fever known as "March Madness". Basketball- crazy fans from all over the state were gearing up for what they hoped would be a National Championship drive. It was infiltrating every facet of my life and it was exciting.

Not that there weren't moments when I wished it weren't so overwhelming. Going to the store became a time to smile, say thanks, and answer a few questions about the chances of the team or the health of myself and my teammates. Turning on the computer meant finding e-mail messages from friends but also from people who had stumbled on my address. There would be messages on the answering machine from those who learned our phone number. Our success was the dream of a lifetime, and I loved it. But sometimes it was such an overload. It had been building all year, and now reached the crest. If we make it to the Final Four, it will really get crazy.

Practice remained as controlled as ever. Coach Williams was masterful at trying to maintain the balance I had always liked. He would drive the team at times, and then lighten up and give us a loose moment or two. He didn't want to change what had been a successful practice regimen this season. He'd keep things the same.

The Red Team was riding high at practice. They were complaining that they should have received a No.2 seed in the tourney, since they had beaten the No.1 Jayhawks more than anyone else in the nation. "We have only three wins, but the highest RPI rating in the nation. We played the No.1 team every time," said GM CB. "If the NCAA reverses itself and invites us, we would be honored and excited." We Blues could only laugh.

Yesterday had been the only day off. We were still lifting weights twice a week, and I felt it had helped us tremendously this season. We were so much stronger than in the past. Now into spring we had kept up the lifting, probably doing 50 workouts this year during the season. We never did that before, nor the same type of workout.

I continued my extra shooting practice, and asked a manager to rebound for me each day. I wasn't panicky or depressed over my lack of scoring in the past few weeks. I was aware of the situation, but was handling it better than in the past. These things happen to any player. This year I knew that I was a better all- around player, so I can focus on other aspects of my game and still contribute to the team. We were winning as a team. My individual stats were not as important as us winning the title. I believe that with all my heart. I wanted to be on the team that becomes the NCAA champions. That was my goal and individual stuff took a backseat to that.

WEDNESDAY, MARCH 12
The team flew to Memphis, site of the first round of the NCAA tournament. We had been seeded No.1 in the Southeast Regional and would be playing the number 16 seed, Jackson State, a small college from Mississippi. We had to arrive a day early and deal with the formalities demanded by the NCAA and CBS, the network that was televising the tournament.

The tightness of the schedule was what first struck me upon our arrival. This team has traveled thousands of miles and gone through itineraries that included sightseeing and photo sessions, but nothing was quite like the NCAA tournament. Everything was planned down to the minute and they didn't give anyone any opportunity to alter it. It's pretty amazing.

Coach wanted us to have some time by ourselves, time that wasn't controlled by others. So he arranged for us to go to a local high school, where we lifted weights, had a shoot-around and walked through some patterns. It was an impressive school, plus it was nice to get off by ourselves. After that, we climbed back on the bus and headed over to the Pyramid, the arena where the tournament games were being played. Practice time on the floor of the Pyramid was restricted to one hour, and it was timed to the minute. Exactly one hour after we had begun, we were told our time was up and we were asked to leave the floor. We showered and then I went to a room where interviews are conducted with the media.

Throughout the season, Coach rotated players who were made available to the media for post-game sessions. Today, it was Jacque's and my turn to face the press, and we fielded a variety of questions, most of them standard. "How do you think you'll do?" or "Are you thinking at all of last year?" or "Is there any pressure being the No.1 team?" I wonder if anything new is ever asked, but then realize that most of these reporters have never covered Kansas before.

For about 10 minutes, questions deal with Scot Pollard, his quirks, his antics. Reporters are looking for color, and Scot obviously fills that criterion. After getting a few comments from Jacque(his roommate) the session is concluded.

We went back to the hotel for a meal and then were given about two hours free time in the hotel. I was ready to relax. It was my turn to get the single room, and since it was a suite, I enjoyed it even more. "Sort of like I was a traveling executive," I mused. "Laptop, speakerphone, and the entire suite to myself." I made a few phone calls, watched a bit of TV and then left for the team meeting to review our opponent.

Bedtime was 11:30 tonight. We will be getting up early for the game tomorrow and I want to be rested. "It's finally begun," I think, as I laid in bed. "The final leg of the journey is here." I closed my eyes and was asleep in minutes.

THURSDAY, MARCH 13

"Every oak tree begins with a tiny acorn." This was the thought for the day, something the coaches had done all season. We get a thought to consider and are asked by Coach Williams if we have grasped the meaning behind the phrase. It could be at practice, or before a game, but someone will be asked to explain the thought for the day. I pondered for just a few moments about today's thought and realized the coaches were right. We can't win the tournament if we lose the first game.

The trap for highly seeded teams in the NCAA tourney has always been that lower seeds have nothing to lose. They aren't expected to win, sportswriters talk about how long the odds are, and an atmosphere emerges which allows some teams to feel invincible. They start to look too far ahead and wind up watching the rest of the games at home.

I didn't want that to happen to us. Nor did I think it would. This team is too experienced to fall into that trap, and coach would never let us think that way. We know what we have to do and how hard we have worked to accomplish this goal. We aren't cocky, but we know what we can do if we play hard, smart and as a team.

Jackson State was seeded 16th, one of two teams to enter the tournament with a losing record. Their conference was not considered a strong one and although they had good athletes, they were not expected to give us much of a challenge after the first few minutes. At least, that's what the morning papers and sports talk radio stations were already concluding.

The game opened with the Jayhawks doing what we've done most of the season, playing even with our opponents for the first few minutes. I noticed immediately that my wrist was not allowing me to get control of the ball, and my shot was not there again. It was frustrating, but I was determined not to let it affect my play today. I'd work through it.

Jackson State stayed with us for the first 10 minutes, but eventually the Jayhawks pulled away and opened up a lead at the half of 10 points. By the mid point of the second half, the lead was safely at 17, and although it was cut to 9 late in the game, we were never threatened and won the game easily,

Highlights were few and far between. Paul had an exceptional offensive game, and Scot and Raef combined with Paul to control the boards and score 58 of the teams' 78 points. It was a game won under the boards and we grabbed most of the missed shots.

Nonetheless, there were a few things that bothered me. Mainly, we had come out flat. No emotion, no aggressive opening to the game, just a methodical approach and a workmanlike effort. We won, but it wasn't the type of victory that a veteran, top ranked team should be proud of accomplishing. We are missing something, but I can't place what it is. But I knew one thing. My game was not good at all. I have to pick it up, because I don't feel like I'm contributing anything right now.

That night, I went back to my room and laid down for a while before the team dinner. Outwardly I enjoyed the victory and joked and laughed with the rest of my teammates. But inside, the poor performances of the past two weeks were eating away at me. There has to be a way to shake this. This can't continue indefinitely.

FRIDAY, MARCH 14
The day off between games was interesting. Coach believes that we should get much more than a basketball education, so our trips never consist of only basketball-related themes. His reasoning: We're here, and we should see as much as possible, because we might never get to see these things again. Besides, if we sat in the hotel all day we'd get stale. Coach's tactic keeps us moving, keeps us involved in things. It also applies to our mental approach to the game. Today was an example of that philosophy.

After a 90-minute practice early that morning, we had breakfast. Then Coach arranged for a sightseeing tour of the Memphis area. It consisted of visiting two major landmarks. First, we went to the Lorain Hotel where the Rev. Martin Luther King was assassinated in 1968. It is a civil rights museum today, and we walked around the different exhibits, listened to an historical lecture and then walked around the site. We went into some of the rooms and eventually came to the balcony where Dr. King was shot. There are some thought provoking displays in this museum, and it was something that gave all of us pause to think.

We spent about an hour and a half there before driving on the bus and head to our next stop, a visit to the Graceland mansion of Elvis Presley, the King of Rock N' Roll. We walked around the estate, decorated in the best '70's style, participating in an audio guided tour. You wear headsets and listen to someone explaining what you are seeing.

Someone noticed that in a section where all of Elvis' awards were displayed, he was awarded keys to various cities. I spotted a police badge and saw that it was from Tahoe. Apparently he entertained at one of the casinos and was awarded the title of honorary policeman. It was a real surprise. The highlight of Graceland for me was the garage with all of Elvis' cars and the private planes he had on his estate. It was a break from the grind, and the first time we had been able to take this type of outing since the ESPN tour during the UConn trip back in January. I think everyone really enjoyed themselves, and the talk on the bus was lively.

By now it was late afternoon, and we were all starving, so Coach piled us on the bus and we headed to a restaurant for dinner, and then went back to the hotel for a little relaxation. It was brief because we had the pre-game meeting at 10:30. By 11:30 I was back in my room, falling asleep.

As I drifted off, I thought about the Purdue game tomorrow. We have to improve on our last performance. I think today will help us get focused again. Sometimes we need a break from the routine of basketball and experiencing the Memphis spectrum, from Martin Luther King Jr. to Elvis was certainly a break.

SATURDAY, MARCH 15

I awoke knowing that this would be a much different game than the first one, against a team that was from a tougher conference, a team that could beat us. I didn't know much about them, but I'd bet we won't be as flat as we were on Thursday. We know what we have to do today.

This game was also hyped much more than the first. CBS opened with a short segment about the kinds of players Coach Williams recruits, noting that nothing bad seems to happen at Kansas these days, and including the facts that the players get along with the coach and get good grades. Coach explained this in the interview, saying that by recruiting good people, he reduced the chance that something could go wrong.

I was assigned to stop Chad Austin, Purdue's top scorer, and it was a task I wanted. I seem to get the toughest defensive assignment each game, and have always liked the challenge. It's a way fir Coach to show that he believes in my defensive ability.

We pulled ahead and applied defensive pressure near the end of the half, holding Purdue without a field goal for five and a half minutes. Near the end of the half, after a KU basket, Jacque stole an inbounds pass and hit a shot as time expired. The lead was now 10, and we raced off the floor yelling and pumping our fists.

Once we got into the locker room, any wild celebration was replaced by calm talk about what has yet to be accomplished. It struck me again how laid back and quiet the team had become. We were still flat. We had to get ourselves motivated. But at the moment, I was also preoccupied with what had become for me a major distraction.

My wrist was affecting my play more than usual. Early in the game, as I tried to drive the baseline, I lost control of the ball after taking only a few steps. The first few times I shot the ball, I would release it and be uncertain of where it would land. I knew the wrist was getting worse, and after the pain I'd felt at yesterday's practice, I became convinced it was hurting my performance. I had known for some time that it was broken, and had been assured that it would not get worse, as far as the break was concerned. But there was never any guarantee about the pain. I was even having trouble catching a hard pass. It was constantly on my mind, and my usually upbeat mood was sinking downwards.

There was one other feeling gnawing in the back of my mind. It was something so abhorrent that I was trying to put it out of his mind, shoving the feeling aside by concentrating on the game. But now, with halftime here and no action to focus upon, I was forced to confront the feeling directly. And as I thought about it, I began to feel sick.

The last time I had this feeling was the Syracuse game last March. I don't know why, but I have a feeling that something is terribly wrong. I am playing like crap, doing nothing offensively out there. It was almost like last year. The biggest difference is that this time I am contributing on defense. But I'm not encouraged about my offense.

In addition to the pain in the wrist and the awful feeling in my mind, I had to cope with back spasms. Purdue center Brad Miller had fallen on top of me in the first half and I had landed squarely on the back of my head. It made a loud crack on the floor, and guys on the bench heard it and kept asking if I was all right. Surprisingly, it didn't hurt much at the time. And that fall didn't cause my back to go out. It was early in the second half, when I twisted under the basket going for a loose ball that the back was injured. It went out in the same spot where I had been hurt last spring. The same area where I had been getting treatment all summer and fall. Now this was added to my list of problems. It seemed like things could not get much worse for me, health-wise. It was frustrating and I tried to forget about it. I succeeded for a while, but I couldn't shove all the negative thoughts aside.

I intended to play the second half with the same intensity I had always demonstrated. But I simply could not contribute offensively, and didn't hit a shot until late in the game, when I took a pass from Raef under the basket and made a lay-up.

Meanwhile, Purdue had taken the lead at 53-52. We seemed to have lost our intensity, and with it, the lead. We needed to step up our effort. I sensed that the team knew this, but I was still haunted by the feeling of last year, and worried about whether we could climb back into control.

Then, the difference between last year and this current group of Jayhawks became clear: Poise. Determination. Defense. Confidence. We showed all of these, and with the defense that had carried us through many other tough outings this season, we regained control of the game. We held Purdue without a field goal the final six and a half minutes of the game, and we took some very smart shots. The combination clicked and the final score was 75-61.

At times I was lying down, trying to keep my back loose, but if I did that I couldn't see the action on the floor. Mark Cairns, KU trainer, was stretching my back, trying to keep me in shape to return to the game at regular intervals. I did return for a few short spells, but I left the floor with mixed feelings.

I was relieved that my teammates had risen to the occasion. We stepped up and overcame the poor start. That has been the difference all year. We've been flat for two straight games and yet we were able to advance. I don't think we'll be flat next week. We survived and won, that's the main thing.

But I am disgusted with myself and my performance. I was horrendous and was the only one who played crappy. I felt like I did nothing out there. I wasn't able to contribute a thing. I'm glad we advanced so I get another chance next week. I was in about as low a mood as I had been all season. The stress of the injuries and their effect on my performance were taking their toll.

We left Memphis immediately after the game and headed back home. For the tournament, we chartered a plane which operates from the airport in Topeka, about a 45-minute drive from Lawrence. When we arrived, there was an incredible reception.

Fans found out when the team plane was going to land and got to the airport to greet us. Topeka Forbes Field was a rather small terminal, and people jammed the place. It was total chaos. There were hundreds of people milling around, and when we got off the plane loud cheers erupted.

I noticed that my teammates seemed to be moving very quickly to get through the terminal. As is the case most of the time, I was the last one, especially since I was trying to sign as many things as possible for the fans.

Under normal circumstances, we would be very accommodating towards these requests, but it wasn't easy in this situation. Unlike after the home games, tonight we had a schedule to keep. There was a bus waiting to take us back to Lawrence, and the fans were delaying this leg of the journey. The KU supporters at this stop were more rabid than those after the games at Allen during the regular season.

When we left for Memphis, people literally surrounded us, pushing and shoving to get next to us. They pleaded and begged to get an autograph. It was crazy that day. I was knocked off balance three times, had marker lines all over my hands, and even had a huge mark on my face from another errant marker. I was given a rose and the crowd showered us with accolades. It was really wild. People went bonkers. It was great but a bit scary.

This time, the airport had a roped off lane that we could walk through and that seemed to control the crowd. Although they still lined up for autographs, they weren't nearly as frantic. They were screaming our names and yelling support, but at least they weren't knocking us down trying to greet us.

I'd still take this any day over being ignored. These fans are the most loyal, most enthusiastic people I've ever seen in a college setting. We are playing as a team, and we are carrying their hopes and good wishes along with our own. I want them to know it means a lot to see this kind of support. I think they can sense our gratitude.

SUNDAY, MARCH 16
Sunday morning meant sleeping later and trying to catch up on some much needed rest. I had been taking a physical beating the past month, and it was starting to have an effect on my mental state as well. Normally easy-going and happy, lately I've been much more serious and even moody. Mark called today and we talked about this.

"Physically I am a little beat up right now," I admitted. "In fact, later today I'll be going for treatment on my back. I twisted it, and it's the same thing that happened last summer, but today it's not hurting as bad as I thought it would."

"What about the wrist?" he asked.

"The wrist is up and down," I said dejectedly. "The practice between games last week was probably the worst it has felt in a long time. I think I'm becoming immune to the anti-inflammatories and there seems to be a little swelling in the wrist. I'm not in horrible pain all the time, but I sure do notice it."

"How is that affecting your shot?"

I thought for a moment. "On good days, it's easy to have good follow- through and I won't notice anything. On bad days, I have to adjust the shot, which causes a discrepancy and I feel terrible." I paused and added, "I wish it would just stay one way...good or bad, I don't care. I just don't feel comfortable handling the ball right now, especially on my shot."

I was frustrated with the obvious deterioration of the wrist. It was hampering my performance in the biggest event of my life, and it was getting me down. I was trying to find a solution to help myself feel better about my contributions to the team. I could tell I wasn't in the flow of a game and the physical adjustments I'm forced to make may have something to do with it. I think it would be good for me to start a game with a couple of lay-ups, and then I'd feel more comfortable. Maybe that's what I'll try to do next Friday.

As the day wore on, I could not shake the melancholy mood I was in. I told the newspapers who were calling for an interview that I had "played like crap." I was letting the injury get the better of me and I knew it. But the thought of how I was playing made me angry. I am a perfectionist when it comes to myself and basketball, and I grade myself by a much stricter standard than any applied even by the coaches.

I had to get over this last hurdle. I was determined that this would be the week when I finally put the pain of the wrist behind me.

MONDAY, MARCH 17

The pain was winning the battle. I could not shake it off anymore and I was reaching the point where I had to make a critical decision. I wanted to play and contribute. I wanted to get rid of the discomfort and take an injection without wondering how far up my arm the pain would travel and how sharp it would feel.

All along there had been one option that I had not considered. It struck me as extreme and I didn't think it would be necessary. I had long ago learned to play with nagging pain, and knew that in the heat of the battle I didn't notice small pains. This was the first time I could ever recall a pain affecting my concentration during the course of a game.

Now I was seriously considering a cortisone shot. The drug would numb the area and theoretically the feeling of pain would dissipate. Something that would work until the end of the tournament. Something that would bring me comfort and the ability to play as I normally had.

Sure, there was a risk that I would injure the wrist even more, but it was minimal. It was already broken. What else could you do to a broken wrist?

I trusted the trainers at Kansas. They had helped heal countless minor injuries, and had been open about what was wrong and how it would affect me. This year, with the wrist and throat injuries, Mark Cairns had been concerned and informative. My mother and I felt that the people in the athletic trainers office at Kansas would not risk any permanent injury to any player just to win a game. I was sure about that.

So, the decision was mine. I talked with Cairns and found out what was involved. A shot of cortisone would be injected in the wrist area. Swelling would follow, and when that receded, the pain would also be gone. Not permanently, of course, but for about two or three weeks. Long enough to play the final four games at my normal level of play. Nobody pressured me, nobody came around and offered their suggestions or encouragement in any direction. It was my call.

TUESDAY, MARCH 18

It didn't take long for me to make a decision. Another bad day of practice and another night of sleeping with pain made the choice easy. I'd go for the cortisone shot. There wasn't any point in fooling myself any longer. I couldn't shake off this injury the way I had so many others. The effect on my game was bothering me to the point where I felt that I had no choice.

I would never make excuses for my performance in any game. If I played badly, that's what happened and I'd have to work and improve. Nobody had any idea of how my wrist felt. I wrote these notes to myself and sent them to Mark, but even he had no idea of how the wrist felt. I couldn't even catch a pass unless I tried to do it one-handed, left-handed. The wrist hurt if it brushed against someone while on defense, and it was foolish to try to play when I would only be a liability on offense. I didn't want to be the one to take critical shot near the end of a game when I had no idea where that shot would end up.

The cortisone shot was administered in the training room. Almost 10cc of fluid was injected. The swelling was obvious, and my wrist felt numb instantly. I hoped this would be the end of the pain, the end of my problems. I couldn't wait to get out on the floor and help us win the title. It was as if a great weight had been lifted from my shoulders. I'd be okay.

WEDNESDAY, MARCH 19

I went to practice today and sat out. I wasn't sure about the wrist and wanted to make certain everything worked the way it was supposed to. It was difficult standing on the sidelines watching the team work out. I'd never been in this position before and it was mentally straining.

During my redshirt season I knew there was no chance of playing. Standing and observing was part of the deal. I participated as much as I was able to, but I had to learn the Kansas system. That was a completely different situation than this.

This was my last season of college ball. I'd never be here again. I didn't want to miss out on anything, and that included practice. Standing there, holding a ball with my left hand, I gazed out at the floor and kept hoping. Hoping that this would all work out as I'd dreamed, that I'd be out on the floor tomorrow in Birmingham, working up a sweat and helping us prepare for the next step in our journey.

I thought about how far I'd come through the years. How as a 12 year-old kid I'd watched my brother Steven and the other guys practice at South Tahoe High. I couldn't wait for the chance to get out on that floor and show Coach Orlich I could play basketball. Then I went to Cal and felt the same desire. I wanted to prove I belonged there, that I was the right choice to recruit for the guard spot.

Now I was feeling the same way once again. I wanted to know that I was healthy again, that I could once again perform at my normal level. I had to help the team win. It meant everything to me.

THURSDAY, MARCH 20

The wrist was killing me. The shot of cortisone wasn't working and the pain was more intense than ever. When it was first administered, I felt nothing. Within minutes, the entire area went numb, feeling like a large tree branch instead of my forearm. I was so glad the pain had stopped. But relief was temporary.

I had no mobility in my wrist, and the weird thing was how it seemed to feel twice its normal size. I was told that when that sensation wore off, I would be able to move the hand and wrist without pain. I couldn't wait to get back in action.

But as today wore on, I could feel the gnawing pain coming back. My spirits sank as the pain increased. The cortisone shot contained novocaine, which deadened the pain. However, that wears off after about 24 hours, and then what you feel is real. What I felt was the same sharp pain and now it was stronger. The increased fluid placed more pressure on the wrist, and it felt as if someone was squeezing my broken bone. It hurt.

I tried to play through it at practice, but it was obvious that I couldn't do anything with my right hand. After a few moments, I asked Mark Cairns to take me away and give me something for the pain. We tried electrical stimulation again, but it didn't help. The pain in the wrist was not going to be relieved this time.

I went to the team late-night dinner and kept my hand above my head, trying to reduce the swelling. I hated to seem as if I couldn't handle the pain, because I always had before. But this was different. I had never experienced anything like this. Coach asked Cairns to get me out of there and give me some treatment for the wrist. I can't ever recall someone leaving the late-night meal before. I went back to the room and kept the hand up in the air as long as I could, trying to reduce the swelling and relieve the pain. Mark Cairns had tried a few other treatments. Nothing worked.

I was getting depressed thinking about how unfair this was. I had worked since last May for this chance. All the hours in the gyms, all the shooting and ball handling, the quickness drills, the preparation... now an injury could keep me out of the final phase. I just had to find a way to gut it out, I told myself. I could overcome this. I had to.

The wrist appeared normal on the outside. It was swollen inside, fluid pressing on the broken section causing the pain. Sleep was going to be tough tonight. My mind was working overtime. I finally fell asleep, hoping that when I woke up it would all be a bad dream.

FRIDAY, MARCH 21
Morning came and I was apprehensive. I lay in bed for a minute, dreading what I had to do, fearful of the answer I thought was coming. Then I lifted my head off the pillow, moved my wrist from side to side and crashed back down onto the bed.

"Damn! Damn!" I yelled, pounding the pillow with my good fist. I knew that my prayers hadn't been answered. There wasn't any

Preparing for the Arizona game. *Photo by Rich Clarkson.*

improvement in the wrist and I had serious doubts whether I could play at all. My worst fears had come true.

Across the room, Ryan Robertson, my roommate for this trip, heard my anger. "You're not going to be ready," he asked. "The way it feels right now, I doubt it," I answered. "I really feel bad for you, J," he said. It was time to get up and go to the shoot around that morning. Ryan dressed but kept looking at me, keeping his thoughts to himself. I don't think he was quite sure what else to say.

Attempting to shoot the ball confirmed what I had already known. It was impossible to shoot a jumper, and a simple layup was extremely difficult and painful. I left the floor after only a few minutes, and went with the trainer's for various kinds of treatment. The anti-inflammatory drugs had long since ceased to have much effect, but I had continued to take them, feeling that they must be doing some good. But this time, with such an important game on the line, I was obsessed with a sense of urgency to find something to relieve the pain.

Mark Cairns suggested I try electrical stimulation again, and then heat treatment. Nothing worked. Another anti-inflammatory was prescribed and I even took a shot in my posterior to try and ease the pain. Neither had any effect. I went out to the pre-game warm-up, thinking that perhaps I could, through sheer will power, overcome the pain and play in this game. But it wasn't going to work this time.

I was able to get off some 10-foot jump shots, but the pain was shooting up my right arm. Any shot from farther out would never fall, and I was fearful I would become a liability rather than an asset to the team. I tried to fake my health, tried to play off the pain by saying it wasn't there due to adrenaline, but deep down I knew better. The pain was beyond description, but I still was going to find a way to play.

The game opened better than I could have imagined. I managed to steal the opening pass and race down the court for a lay-up. I ran back and flashed a wink at my teammates. "It's back," I thought. "I'm back to normal." The steal was reminiscent of the opening to the Cincinnati game, to those days in December when I was starting games with steals and fueling momentum for my teammates. I thought maybe God had finally answered my prayers and that I was in for a big night.

But moments later, the first signs surfaced of what the night would bring. The following possession, I again dribbled down the floor after a steal by Paul, but as I neared the free throw line, I lost control of the ball momentarily. I had to turn and try to pass the ball off to a teammate. A sharp pain raced up my arm. I felt myself wince and moved my feet. The whistle blew. Traveling.

After only three minutes, I was obviously using only my left hand. I could not grip the ball with any force. It simply hurt too much. From the bench, the coaching staff noticed this as well. They decided to take me out of the game and use me sparingly. I took a seat on the bench and kept my head down for a few moments. "It just isn't fair, not tonight, not in the NCAA's," I said to myself. Feeling dejected and depressed, I nonetheless knew that I couldn't let my teammates see this attitude. I was going to have to contribute from the bench, with vocal support and encouragement.

But this game was one where I thought my defense and desire would be needed. Arizona was playing an aggressive game, taking chances and gambling. It was the kind of game I felt I had played all year. I needed to get back in there.

Arizona opened up an early lead, but we stayed close. The biggest surprise came from the fact that their defense was keeping the ball out of the hands of our big men, forcing a change from our usual offensive style. Right before the half, Paul Pierce found the range, Jacque and Ryan got him the ball, and we were off on a short burst to take a brief lead. Arizona came back and at the half, Kansas was down by two.

The final huddle, after the loss to Arizona. Emotion filled the room as we gathered for the last time in a post-game setting. Photo by Rich Clarkson.

Halftime produced nothing out of the ordinary. We had been here before, many times this season, and had adjusted our game, focused ourselves on the task at hand, and fought our way to another win. Our team was not cocky, but confident in our own abilities.

I was still nervous about not being able to contribute. I had the gnawing feeling a time would come in the game when I would be needed and I would not be able to respond. It kept eating away at me, but I put it aside and hoped that I was wrong. I joined in the enthusiastic huddle as the team broke away to start the second half.

It didn't take long for problems to arise. Scot was whistled for his fourth foul and shortly thereafter, Jacque was called for his fourth. There were still 9 and a half minutes remaining in the game, and we were down by 7. Coach looked down the bench and signaled for me. As I entered the game, I hoped that by some miracle, my wrist would be sound. It wasn't.

I handled the ball during this time on the floor, passing by putting the most force from my left hand. I threw what I thought was one surprisingly crisp pass to Paul for an easy lay-up, and the next trip down I fed Paul again, leading to another short jumper which gently swished, cutting the margin to 5. But it was obvious that handling the ball brought back the pain and I was taken out shortly thereafter. I would never return to the floor.

It made me feel completely helpless. It was the most difficult time I had ever spent on a basketball court. I did what I felt were the only things I could do to support the team. Yell. Cheer. Encourage. It made me feel worse. This was not what I was used to doing when the team was down. I always regarded myself as the guy who dove on the floor, who fought with all his might to turn around a bad situation by playing as hard as he could. This wasn't the same.

I realized that one of my worst fears for this season was coming true, and it made me sick. All year long, the one thing I was afraid of seeing happen was not being there for this team. I didn't have a fear of getting hurt, or losing or anything like that. My fear was that they would not be able to count on me when they needed me. I never wanted to let them down. I wanted to be a cornerstone. Reliable. Dependable. Constant. Today, I couldn't do that, and it tore me up inside. I felt like I was letting down my teammates, my friends, and it hurt. Bad.

With a few minutes left in the game, and down by 11, Coach called a time-out. Only two and a half minutes remained in the game, and things looked bleak. It was about the worst situation KU had been in all year. I waited until after the coaches were done, and then, as the five players who were on the court were returning to the floor, quickly grabbed a few arms and pulled them into a huddle.

"Look, you know we're down 11, but you can do this," I said with as much intensity as I could put into my voice. "You are capable of it. You're the best team in the country. You ARE going to do it.!" I knew my voice rose a bit at the end, and they all looked at me and one another. It seemed to me that Billy Thomas was stronger afterwards, and Ryan, JV, Raef and TJ came out with a purpose. On the bench again, I kept telling myself," I know they can pull it off." Sitting next to me, BJ Williams began to sense something different and started to smile.

Kansas caught fire. Billy came out and hit two consecutive three-point shots. Jacque stole the ball and fed Ryan, who also connected and the lead was suddenly down to two! The arena was going wild, as this miraculous comeback was taking place. After Arizona hit a three pointer of their own, Billy again swished a shot from behind the arc and we trailed by only two with 40 seconds left to go. It was happening.

On the bench, nobody could sit still. Our entire group of was standing, jumping, yelling and pounding one another. I was ecstatic, Scot and BJ were smiling broadly, and it seemed as though we had control of our own fate at last. When Arizona hit a free throw with 14 seconds left to make the margin 85-82, I felt as though the game were going into overtime at least, and maybe we could still pull it out in regulation. We had the ball, the time and the shooters out there. It looked, as it had so many other times since 1995, as though the Jayhawks were going to pull out a hard fought win.

There are only so many times a team can make a comeback in any given year. Time runs out on everyone, and this time the magic of the 1997 season was about to evaporate. Jacque brought the ball down the floor and Billy set up in a spot behind the arc, to the right side of the basket. Billy took the pass, set his feet and fired. It hit the rim and bounced out.

The rebound ricocheted back to JV, who was at the top of the key. Nine seconds left. He passed to Ryan on the left side of the arc, who was covered by three men. Desperate, Ryan leaned into the defenders, hoping to draw a foul as he shot, but there was no call and the ball caromed off the rim. Raef snared the rebound as Arizona defenders desperately tried to slap the ball away. Spotting an open lane to the three point line, he drove to the corner and hurriedly turned and fired up the final shot with one second left on the clock. It headed straight for the cylinder, but then curved out, struck the front of the rim, and bounced off.

The final horn sounded. The arena was bedlam. Players were racing around the court, waving their arms high and the crowd was making the loudest noise heard yet in the NCAA tournament. But the only sound I could hear was silence. It was over.

We all walked out and shook a few hands but we were stunned into only the most mechanical of greetings. We filed out towards the locker room and looked straight ahead. I'm sure our faces were expressionless, as though the finality of it all had yet to sink in. Television cameras were focusing on the Arizona players exuberantly celebrating their moment of triumph. Mercifully, we were spared any questions regarding our feelings as we left the floor.

The locker room became a sanctuary. As the door closed behind us, and we were alone among ourselves, player after player began to break down. The loss was becoming real and the pain was beginning to show. It was a heart-rending scene.

I began to feel the emotion I had controlled all month come out. My body began to feel hot, my face flushed and my eyes began to water. I started to cry. It was not something I was embarrassed about or tried to hide. I couldn't and didn't even try. I just sat down on the stool by the locker and sobbed. There was nothing more anyone could do. The injury had kept me out of the final game of my college career. The realization that the dream was over was more than I could bear.

I heard the pain of everybody else in the room. I was tensed up, confused, burdened, scared and crushed. It was over. The ride of a lifetime had ended. My dream had not come true a second time.

There were very few words spoken at this time. I felt relieved, because words would only make the hurt worse. Words were not the answer. Nothing was going to make this feel better, not even time. This was one loss that time would only soothe someday, but never take away. Coach Williams, in tears himself, said that the team had to try and help one another and the coaches get through this. "It's said that life is not fair," he stated, emotion choking his voice. "You guys really are the best, but you won't have the title of national champions after your name." I felt myself getting sick as I listened, and the feeling of helplessness came back. I almost vomited. Catching myself in time, I sat back down and tried to regain my composure.

The media were starting to come in. Reporters were quietly going from player to player, trying to get statements to capture the feeling of the moment for their readers. Nobody was talking very much. I tried to maintain my outward calm but the normal cheeriness was painfully absent. I couldn't hide how I felt, and I didn't want to try. This was a nightmare that came true, and there was no way I would ever forget how it felt.

The team spent the night just hanging out with one another. Some of the guys had family in for the game, but others like me just wanted to be alone. I went back to my room and laid down, burying my face in the pillow. I kept thinking about the wrist and the game. Once again, I cried.

SATURDAY, MARCH 22
We had waited until the following morning to fly back to Topeka. It didn't seem urgent to get back right after the game, since the season was now over. After landing, we boarded a bus and headed back to Lawrence, the last time this group would make a trip as the Kansas Jayhawks.

I thought of this as I looked around the bus. I realized how much I would miss these guys. They had become my other family. We were guys from Shreveport to Monona, from St. Louis to Los Angeles. Some had money, others didn't. Some had great grades, another spear fishes, one wrote poetry, and another had blue fingernails. Some of us were tall, others short, some heavier and some skinny. One is married, others engaged and others without a date.

The unforgettable welcome home reception from our fans after the loss to Arizona. Photo by Earl Richardson.

We were so different, yet we were all Kansas basketball players. We were part of a family that brought us closer to one another than many blood families. We cared about the team, but even more than that we cared about one another. We have had huge wins, long practices and defeats that left us crying in each other's arms.

The guys on this team have been my security blanket for the past few years. They have given me anything I could ever ask for. We will not be called national champions, but what we have shared goes beyond wins and losses.

I was feeling melancholy and yet mysteriously happy. The thoughts of the years with these people, varied and yet similar, brought a warm feeling to my heart, and I started to relax in my seat. It dawned on me that this was one thing that can never be taken away from me. I was comforted by that idea. The games were over and my career at Kansas was complete, but I could carry the memories with me for the rest of my life.

More memories were still to be made as the bus arrived back at Allen Fieldhouse. A crowd of 6,000 was waiting to greet the team as we stepped off the bus. They lined the street and the walkways to the doors, wanting to show their appreciation to us. People were trying to shake hands, offer condolences, and offer thanks for various things.

I was surprised by how many people were telling me thanks for being such a good role model. I waited in the line the players had formed to get my chance to say a few words to the crowd, thinking about how awesome the fans were to stage a rally like this.

Suddenly, a little girl broke through the crowd and ran up to me. She was wearing a Kansas basketball jersey, number 35, and she was crying as she ran up to me. She handed me three balloons and I bent down and gave her a hug. "I still love you," she said softly. Then she went back and picked up her homemade sign. It read, "Jerod, will you marry me?"

I was struck again by the effect I seemed to have on these people. I guess my time here has been productive. I can't tell you how many people have said I've been an inspiration to them and that is what matters the most. People do care about people, and one of my greatest pleasures has always been to help others. I think I've helped people here. That made me feel a little bit better.

SUNDAY, MARCH 23
Ending the season means the end of a lifestyle, and that's one of the hardest facts I must face. It's bad enough to fall short of the goal I had set for myself one year ago this week. But the end of basketball will prove to be more difficult.

The people are what I will miss the most. These are the guys who have been the main part of my life anywhere from one to four years. It's impossible to spend as much time as we do and not have feelings about these people. We began conditioning in September and the time as a group grew from 90 minutes to 3 hours in October, to 4 hours a day during the season. There were meals as a group certain days of the week, the traveling to games, which meant entire days were spent with only these people. It's impossible not to have feelings and opinions about one's teammates.

It's Jacque that I first thought about. Earlier this season, I once said that we were friends but not extremely close. Now, looking at what we have gone through this year, the talks we've had and the times we've shared, I realize that I will miss JV more than I ever thought. We've become good friends. I look at him and see many of the same things I possess. We both work hard and have a passion to be the best at what we do. We were backcourt mates for three years and first team academic All-Americans, with the same GPA in the same major. We both have a need for competition. We have grown up together, and it's only now that I realize how much I will mis him. There is one other irony in this. He entered the year with a cast, and I'm leaving with one.

There are others I will miss as well, for a variety of reasons. Nick Bradford has a knack for telling stories and accenting them with multiple hand and facial gestures. It makes his story telling hilarious. Paul Pierce liked to predict where people would be in the future and also demonstrated his artistic ability to the team, drawing pictures of Terry Nooner and saying he was JV's little brother.

TJ Pugh had the ability to imitate any maid we encountered on the numerous road trips, and could mimic their wake-up calls perfectly. His antics had us laughing many times this year. And of course, I'd never forget Billy Thomas and his vocabulary.

Some of these guys are memorable for their inner selves. Joel Brandstrom is one of the nicest persons I've ever known. He will never put himself before anyone else, and is extremely considerate of others. Steve Ransom became a soul mate after helping me cope with a particularly poor shooting night after a loss at Temple my junior year. (We went to the Hard Rock Cafe in Philadelphia.) And BJ Williams' outward calm and relaxed smile was always reassuring, perhaps because of all the guys, he has the most to juggle in his personal life, being not only a student-athlete but also a family man.

Raef LaFrentz could always be counted on for a dinner and lots of conversation about the present and the future. Those were times I realized I looked forward to and now could not easily arrange. We would be going our separate ways. Then there was Scot Pollard. Who else would I ever know with painted fingernails and a car from the 60's, yet be such a down to earth person? He will never be duplicated and never replaced.

Of course I'll miss Ryan Robertson, a guy who gave up the limelight for the good of the team. Many lesser people would resent having to sit after leading a team to ten straight victories. Not Ryan. He accepted his role and never complained. I know I will always remember that quality.

Then there was CB. Roommates are always special. You are probably best known to them, since they live with you more than anyone. CB has kept up my spirits when I felt low and made life enjoyable. He was always up, ready to do something. In some ways, he might be the one I'll miss the most.

I realize that the uniform bonds the team together outwardly, but there is more than that holding us together. It is the shared lives, the shared experiences, the stories we exchanged at late night snacks held in someone's room that bonded us together. It was more than being teammates. It was being friends.

I feel very sad thinking about this. I wanted a way to thank them all one more time, making it as heartfelt as I can. This page will let them know. I will miss them.

MONDAY, MARCH 24
It was 2:45 in the morning and I couldn't sleep. The two nights since the Arizona game had been frustrating, and I haven't gotten much sleep. Every time I laid down, my mind would go back to the tournament, to the painful fact that my team, Kansas, had been eliminated. It made me feel so bad that I couldn't sleep. I'd get up and walk around, try to get my mind onto other things, but nothing worked.

There had been so much emphasis on going to the Final Four that I hadn't prepared for the possibility of not being in Indianapolis at the end of March. With the campus shut down due to spring break, there was nothing to keep me active, nothing to do that would take my mind off basketball. The only people I saw were those who would remind me of the game, and so I couldn't stop thinking about how bad it felt.

I decided to write an e-mail on the computer that had been the life blood of this project. Getting my ideas and feelings down has been a major focus of this book, and this seemed to be the perfect time to do that. After all, it's my feelings, ideas and emotions that had me sitting here at 3 in the morning, wide awake. And with that,

I proceeded to write the following thoughts.

"Dear Mark (the letter began), I'm sitting here unable to sleep, so I guess it's a good time to talk about dreams. This is something I'd like to get across to the kids out there.

When you dream and chase those dreams, you will often fail. That can be expected, but it is never a reason to stop chasing your dreams. This team fell short of one dream, our ultimate dream, but look what we managed to do in the meantime. We were the best team in the country this year."

"I'd like the kids to look at me and see that I am a dreamer, I failed at some things and then I bounced back and tried again. I never stopped. I also want them to know how hard I worked for everything I got. Hard work is the great equalizer. One with less talent can achieve as much as others by working hard.

I hope they watch and understand that you have to push yourself to experience the great things life has to offer. This may also bring greater heartache, but I believe that to really live you have to go for it. You have to go out on a limb to be the best.

But the most important thing I want them to see is that you can do things the right way and win. You don't have to drink and do drugs. Getting good grades is cool. Studying is cool. Scholarships to college are cool. Working hard is cool. Winning is cool. One thing leads to the next level. And dreams do come true.

EPILOGUE

I have come to the end of this diary. It began as a way to chronicle the year, a way for me to look back at the last year of my college career. I wanted this to be the perfect storybook ending, but things just didn't work out.

I haven't been sleeping well in the week since the last game. I even stopped shaving for a while and grew a beard. It actually looks pretty good, although it has raised some eyebrows and generated a few surprised looks. It's not meant to be a disguise, just a little change. I guess I'm not in the mood for shaving either.

It still is hard to reconcile what happened with what I had envisioned for this year. An injury is the one thing you can never plan around. The loss was bad, but not being able to contribute to the best of my ability in the game against Arizona is what I will never be able to forget. I know that I tried, and that I was able to get that first basket. But I'll always be troubled by the thought of, "What if?"

People assume I've been having a bad time. It's wonderful that they have sent me packages of food, cards and letters of support, showing that they care. I appreciate them taking the time to let me know how they feel. It has meant a lot.

But nothing will ever fully erase the disappointment.

This is not the same as the feeling after the loss in 1996. Last year I felt as though part of the loss was my fault. This time I don't feel as if I've let anyone down. I have worked hard to overcome that negative feeling and have emerged with a better attitude. I believe that this season, I matured as a player and more importantly as a person. I think that was evident in my play this year, and in my relationships with people on and off the court. The title just wasn't meant to be.

Earlier this year, I remember saying that if I was ever down, I would open up some of my mail and it would make me feel better. That's what I decided to do today.

The letter you are about to read is probably the best example of that positive reinforcement. It's a special letter, one that I will treasure along with all the others.

But today, reading it meant a lot:

Dear Jerod,
I am an old "has been" KU alumnus and have never written a fan letter to anyone.
As a Boy Scout usher (age 11) in Allen Field House when

Wilt played there, I have seen many many All-Americans on the Field House floor. Besides Wilt, Elvin Hayes, Oscar Robertson, Jo-Jo, Darnell and Danny are just a few that I have enjoyed.

I would like to believe that I am a knowledgeable fan and wanted to express my, as well as my 8th grade son's, "thanks" for what you do and how you conduct yourself on the court. The dedication, hustle, and sacrifice you demonstrate on both ends of the floor, I have never seen before in all my 40 years of watching Jayhawk basketball. It is really something special to behold and as much as I try, I cannot comprehend your level of effort for the team.

I believe I will see many more All-Americans in Allen Fieldhouse, but I don't think I will ever see another like Jerod Haase.

Thank you again —-from a basketball fan!

A letter like this is priceless. If I never get anywhere else in the world of basketball, I know that I have still achieved something special. I touched people's lives in a positive way. That thought is more than anything I would ever have dreamed when I was shooting on my backyard court in Tahoe.

I always wanted, like every kid, to sink the big basket, to have people cheer my name, to be on the winning team.

I guess you never realize until you grow up that there are more important things than those obvious rewards. Things that really matter. Being thought of as a role model is one of those. I hope I am up to that challenge. It's such a huge responsibility to have kids look up to you and want to be like you. It's humbling and exciting all at once.

There are only a few words I can think of to close this final chapter. It's something I'd like to say to everyone I have come in contact with, from Tahoe to Lawrence and everywhere else, to the letter writers and the people who have waited in lines to talk with me: Thank you. I'll never forget any of this. The floor burns—on and off the court—have only made me better.

About the Author

Mark Horvath has been teaching Economics and Government at Andrean High School in Merillville, Indiana, for 17 years. He has been a basketball coach at the freshman and junior varsity levels, as well as varsity cross country coach for 11 years. In 1988, Horvath was selected Teacher of the Year for Northwest Indiana by the Inland Steel Company. He is currently developing a new alternative education program, at the middle school level, for the Lake Ridge Schools.

Horvath, who also owns a painting contracting business, lives in Chicago Heights, Illinois, with his wife Nancy and two children, Alison and Andy. All are fans of KU basketball.

If copies of this book are unavailable from your local bookstore, copies may be ordered via mail by sending a check or money order in the amount of $14.95, plus $4.00 shipping and handling to:
H & H Enterprises
171 N. Pamela Dr.
Chicago Heights, IL 60411